The
American
Republic

The American Republic

to 1877

John A. Schutz

Richard S. Kirkendall

FORUM PRESS

Published simultaneously in Canada.

Printed in the United States of America.

Library of Congress Catalog Card Number: 77-093846

ISBN: 0-88273-250-1

Maps designed by: Daniel Irwin

Cover and text designed by: Jerry Moore and Janet Moody

Table of Contents

Maps & Charts

Preface

THE AMERICAN REPUBLIC is an interpretation of the events, struggles, successes and failures and the lives of representative leaders which have made our country great. Historians are confronted with massive collections of stories from the past and we have to be selective in the materials which are used in developing a total picture. Our concern has been to show the growth of the nation through its system of government, its politics, its ideals and specifically, through its leaders.

History is made every day, every moment. Normally, the events transpire and the participants seldom think of that fact. Some incidents do stand out in such prominence that those involved in them realize that future generations will point back to the moment as a turning point in the life of a nation. Whatever the nature of past happenings, the historian looks back at them with a purpose. We want to profit by the experiences of past generations. History can be a tool; it can help us understand our world by showing us how it got the way it is. It inspires us with determination to build a better society by informing us of the nobility and courage of those who once lived and labored here.

To illustrate, some of the current concerns that receive wide attention are the family, health, woman's rights and the status of minority groups—Chicanos, blacks, Indians, Orientals and new immigrants. Since all groups with the exception of the American Indian are modern immigrants, the record of their relationship to one another gives us a measuring stick and some guide lines for living with one another now.

Following an account of the first British settlements at Jamestown in 1607 and Plymouth in 1620, we trace the story of the development of self-government from the first legislature in 1619 to the Declaration of Independence by the Continental Congress in 1776. We have examined the impact of the Revolution upon human rights followed by what we believe to be a simple but dramatic narrative of the early national experience of freedom.

We have emphasized the Civil War in spite of its agonies, because it is necessary to examine the meaning and effect of the momentary dissolution of the Union. Observation of the destruction of the nation should give us pause to consider how reckless persons can bring disaster to millions. We hope that the accounts of the first century of freedom will arouse sufficient interest to invite further reading and inquiry into these formative years.

THE AMERICAN REPUBLIC is available in a one-volume clothbound edition and in a two-volume paperbound edition. The first volume closes with the story of reconstruction following the Civil War and Volume Two opens with the same account.

In the final chapters, we have brought the story to the threshold of the 1980s. Oil and energy crises, insecurity in the cities, a crisis in the Presidency, these realities among others, are sobering thoughts to everyone. They demand creative research into our past for answers to the questions, "Where did we go wrong?" and "What can we do to heal the wounds?" This is not to say that others may not also find answers in the present moment and glimpses into what is to come. It does infer that history can help, too.

Our national history is complex and space forbids the telling of very much of it. Thus, maps, charts, graphs and pictures carry an important part of the story in THE AMERICAN REPUBLIC. The selection of these materials gives some uniqueness to the book by registering national expansion visually through the decades and by drawing upon enough illustrative material to highlight important leaders and events.

Individual persons generally highlight the events of history, even though they are sometimes only examples of the thousands or millions who have been the real determiners of national destiny. We have sprinkled our narrative with the names of men and women who have contributed to our national greatness. Presidents like Jefferson, Lincoln, Wilson and Franklin D. Roosevelt; military leaders like Washington, Lee, Pershing and Eisenhower; other leaders like Franklin, Clay, Dewey and Eleanor Roosevelt are a few of those who come in for special notice.

Our gratitude is expressed to many scholars who have helped to make this book what it is. We express appreciation to the many experts who have read chapters of the manuscript and have given advice, insight and criticism. These include:

Keith L. Bryant, Jr., Texas A & M University; Charles Bussey, Western Kentucky University; John M. Carroll, Lamar University; John A. Caylor, Boise State University; Eric H. Christianson, University of Kentucky; Ralph J. Crandall, Northeastern University; Leonard P. Curry, University of Louisville; Bailey Diffie, University of Southern California; Harold H. Dugger, Southeast Missouri State University; James Forsythe, Fort Hays State College; Bruce Glasrud, California State University - Hayward; Mike Greco, University of Houston - Clear Lake City; Nadine I. Hata, El Camino College; George Herring, University of Kentucky; James W. Hilty, Temple University; Abraham Hoffman, Los Angeles Valley College; John Howe, University of Minnesota; Franklin Hoyt, Mt. San Antonio College; Leo E. Huff, Southwest Missouri State University; Norris Hundley, University of California - Los Angeles; David E. Kyvig, University of Akron; Lester D. Langley, University of Georgia; B. B. Lightfoot, Southwest Missouri State University; Richard Lowitt, Iowa State University; Archie P. McDonald, Stephen F. Austin State University; Thomas J. McInerney, St. Thomas Seminary College; Grady McWhiney, University of Alabama; Richard H. Marcus, University of Wisconsin - Eau Claire; Franklin Mitchell, University of Southern California; Doyce Nunis, University of Southern California; Robert Oaks, University of Texas; Patrick G. O'Brien, Emporia State University; Edward B. Parsons, Miami University - Ohio; Bradley Reynolds, College of the Canyons; Glenda Riley, University of Northern Iowa; Oliver A. Rink, California State University - Bakersfield; Richard Robertson, University of Mississippi; Peter E. Robinson, Jacksonville State University; Raymond Robinson, Northeastern University; W. Stitt Robinson, University of Kansas; Philip R. Rulon, Northern Arizona University; Terry Seip, University of Southern California; Homer E. Socolofsky, Kansas State University; Arvarh Strickland, University of Missouri - Columbia; Allen Yarnell, University of California - Los Angeles; and W. Turrentine Jackson, University of California - Davis.

To Professor Dan Irwin whose maps and charts add special luster to the book we extend our special thanks. To Howard E. Short, our editor, whose help in details and manuscript preparation was always dependable, we give our sincere appreciation. Lastly, we would like to acknowledge the assistance and encouragement of Erby M. Young, Managing Director of Forum Press, who suggested our co-authorship and directed THE AMERICAN REPUBLIC in all phases of production. May this book be both an inspiration and valuable learning aid for all teachers and students.

Introduction

As the United States approached its Bicentennial, a prominent historian wrote, "We find ourselves at this Bicentennial, for all the show-business clatter of the Fourth-of-July celebrations, an essentially historyless people. Businessmen agree with the elder Henry Ford that history is bunk. The young no longer study history. Intellectuals turn their backs on history in their enthusiasm for the ahistorical behavioral sciences." According to a 1975 report, "Confidence and interest in history are not nearly as widespread and strong among students, educational administrators, and politicians as they were only a few years ago."

Doubts about history's usefulness for the individual eager to find a job and for a society eager to solve its problems, especially doubts about its usefulness in a time of rapid change, appear to be largely responsible for the recent decline in interest in historical study and the move away from it to more "relevant" and "practical" subjects. This skepticism about the utility of history has gained renewed strength in the unusual circumstances of the past decade and has affected both curricular decisions and student choices. Increasingly free to stay away as history requirements are removed, students have chosen to do so in growing numbers for history seemed useless to them.

History does not occupy the large and high place in America's schools and colleges that it enjoyed a decade and more ago. During the first two decades following World War II, students flocked to history classes, often, to be sure, forced to do so by rules imposed by curriculum planners, school boards, and legislatures, many of whom had been alarmed by reports that many schools and colleges did not require American history. Most high school graduates had only a smattering of knowledge about it and that seemed to suggest that Americans did not understand and might lack enthusiasm for the institutions and ideals for which the war was fought. Accused by their critics of 'not learning from history and being indifferent to the past !' spokesmen of the student movement reply, "a president of the American Historical Association reported several years ago . . . there is no historical precedent for our generation." More recently, a historian was persuaded that a fundamental change was taking place, that "The people of plenty have become a people of paucity," suggested that his most useful function as a teacher of undergraduates "would be to disenthrall them from the spell of history, to help them see the irrelevance of the past."

Those who insist that history is irrelevant because we live in a time of rapid change, understand neither the nature of historical study nor the character of the historical process. History is the discipline that specializes in the study of change in human affairs, and the historical process, even when moving at its most rapid pace, does not leave all features of the past behind. "Indeed, if there is any one subject with which history is concerned," David Potter wrote some years ago, "that subject is change—how things ceased to be as they had been before, how they became what they had not been." ". . . the various branches of the social sciences and humanities often tend to produce a static view . . .," Edwin O. Reischauer points out. "History . . . is focused on change, and change is the heart of the story, especially in our day." "If there is one thing clearer than another," Dexter Perkins observed, "it is that change is the law of life, one of the deepest and most inevitable of all human phenomena;" yet, continuity, what John Jay called "the continuing tie," is also a "law of life." Human affairs are dynamic, but not all parts of the past pass away. Many remain important in the present, and features of the past and present will be with us significantly in the future. As one historian put it, "the immediate, sudden appearance of something, its creation by an individual or a group at some one moment of time, is unknown in history." Instead, as another mentioned, "each event is harnessed to the other, and the present emerges from the past." And a third agreed: "Past, present, and future are linked together in the endless chain of history."

Those who are unhappy with the present can deplore the elements of continuity—the forces of resistance and the representatives of the past, but they are inevitably present in every historical situation.

They are realities that must be recognized and that are not easily brushed aside by a champion of a vision of the future. It is a historian's duty to alert people to the elements of continuity just as it is a historian's duty to point out that all things cannot remain as they were. "The best use of history is as an innoculation against radical expectations and, hence, against embittering disappointments," George F. Will suggests. It should also innoculate against the expectations of the champions of the status quo. "No trained historian can possibly put himself in the position of the thick-and-thin exponent of the static," Perkins insisted. ". . . We have our choice . . . between the gradual reconciliation of the old and the new and the more violent processes which destroy much that is good along with much that is evil.'

As the discipline that specializes in the study of continuity and change, history promotes understanding of important realities and supplies an intellectual foundation for intelligent, effective action. "Mankind is always more or less storm-driven," Allan Nevins wrote, "and history is the sextant and compass of states which, tossed by wind and current, would be lost in confusion if they could not fix their position." If students are to understand change today and prepare to shape their own world, they must be able to appreciate their own position in time and space and understand the processes of continuity and change. If students are to make sound judgments about the direction in which they wish to go, they must know the choices open to them. The study of history is indispensable to people living in times such as ours. An understanding of the past supplies insights useful in attempts to guide the course of the present and affect the shape of the future.

THE AMERICAN REPUBLIC was influenced by convictions about the importance of these concepts—change and continuity—and the consequent value of historical study as a way of gaining understanding of human affairs. Convictions about the importance of knowing institutions, such as the American institutions of self-government, and knowing people, including American leaders from Winthrop to Carter, also affect the pages that follow. The study of American history, although it must not be merely an effort to memorize facts about the past, should supply a body of information about people, institutions, dates, and events. To function effectively, everyone needs a body of historical information—information on the experiences of people—as well as an understanding of the dynamic character of human affairs.

That information should be representative of the diversity and complexity of American life. No longer narrow, the discipline of history covers all aspects of human affairs. It now has a unique and valuable scope or range. ". . . each of the social sciences and humanities selects one major facet form a culture as a whole and then studies it in detail," Reischauer writes. ". . . Only history tries conscientiously to fit all the parts into a meaningful whole."

This book captures the experiences of a diverse and complex

people over the full sweep of their history. These pages should enlarge the range of experience available to the reader, combatting narrowness, the overwhelming preoccupation with the present narrowness, the overwhelming preoccupation with the present that is a characteristic of most people, and their tendency to learn from one set of experiences at a time, those supplied by the recent past. People need to see the present in relation to various pasts, not just one, and to draw the "lessons" of history from all significantly relevant episodes, rather than from only one set of experiences.

Although not utopian, THE AMERICAN REPUBLIC is not pessimistic or cynical. It expresses admiration for many features of American life, especially self-government, which has grown from small beginnings and gained strength from tests and trials. The book expresses admiration for the capacity demonstrated by the many different groups in American society to produce leaders who, in turn, have promoted improvements in the quality of American life. We do call attention to present difficulties, including a "leadership crisis' and the possibility that economic growth, one of the main features of the story, may be displaced by economic stagnation or decline. When that point is reached, the readers will have already studied the history of a people who have encountered more than a few difficulties without being overwhelmed by them and look toward a New America.

The
American
Republic

Europe Discovers America

For some Europeans, Columbus's voyages to the New World brought feelings of excitement and adventure that would change their lives. Those distant lands filled with Indians, gold, and precious things expanded dramatically their horizons and made the Atlantic rim of nations sailing ports for the west. Instead of turning eastward for Asian trade, they looked out into the Atlantic for a short route to the Orient, for a Northwest Passage, and for the products that could be found along the way.

The excitement of discovering new lands was part of a change of spirit. In Spain, Ferdinand and Isabella united the Spanish peoples under a strong monarchy. Their successful campaign against the Moslems not only swept them from the peninsula, but represented the first victories of Christians against Islam in decades. It strengthened the Roman Catholic Church, inspired deep religious feelings, and encouraged a spirit of daring. An eloquent man like Columbus could now point to the Indies; Ponce de León could search for a fountain of youth; Ferdinand Magellan could sail around the globe, and each could find others to join him in his ventures.

If one turned to the monasteries, and to the monks who taught in

the universities, the story was the same. Scholars practiced a new learning, taken often from rediscovered Greek manuscripts, and criticized
the institutions that they saw about them. They urged a new piety, a
reform of the church, and the use of secular languages in the worship
of God. For some, missionary work among the American Indians was
the challenge of this new spirit; for others, working for changes in the
church at home held greater importance.

With the rise of nation states in the sixteenth century, daring
men had support for their plans. Monarchs like Henry VIII of England
and Charles I of Spain offered their people vigorous reigns, and more
people everywhere shared in the exchange of products, the renewal of
trade, and the enjoyment of luxury. Throughout western Europe men
put their faith in the new monarchs, sometimes attributing powers to
them that were once reserved for the Pope. They joined with them in
optimism and in the search for a better life.

European civilization, then, was rapidly changing. The new monarchs were creating national states; the Roman Church, led on a crusade
of reform by Ignatius Loyola, was combating the stagnation of centuries; the deeply religious Martin Luther and John Calvin offered new
forms of worship; the renewal of faith, like the founding of states, excited the human spirit. The imagination of men in art, drama, and
thought gave Europeans expressions of feeling that profoundly changed
their way of life. The printing press helped spread ideas in a manner
never before realized, and the new learning, with Columbus's vision
of a western passage to the Orient, turned Europeans from the greatness of Greece and Rome to a way of life of their own making.

The First Explorers of America

While Europe was thus experiencing great change, the lands
Columbus would explore for Spain had an old civilization dating back
in some areas twenty-five thousand years. The ancestors of these people
had come across the Aleutian Islands from Asia, spread over the American continents, and developed cultures almost as diverse as those in
Europe. Perhaps as many as fifteen million Asiatic people were living on
the two continents when the Europeans arrived. The number of people
and also their culture remain clouded by the lack of sufficient records.

It is clear, nonetheless, that the Aztecs of central Mexico and the
Incas of Peru had developed a sophisticated culture. Their public
buildings and monuments, their art and architecture, their governments and social systems are impressive, and the achievements in
agriculture may have even surpassed these accomplishments. The
Aztecs, Mayas, and Incas developed corn, fibers for clothing, the potato,
quinine, and many kinds of beans. Two limitations, however, are
astonishing: they did not discover the wheel or have the use of the
horse or the ox.

Most Americans elsewhere on the continent knew the potter's art,

A Typical Scene of an Early Indian Village in Western America.
(Los Angeles Museum of Natural History)

wove fibers into cloth, and practiced some form of agriculture. Climate
had much influence upon the use of clothes, the diet, and housing, but
government was generally decentralized and was unable to cope with
a foreign invader.

Americans in 1492 were not waiting to be discovered. The European's arrival was a disaster for local culture in most cases. It brought
new diseases, war, slavery, murder, and disruption of traditional pat-
terns. It took Americans by surprise, and few recovered sufficiently to
fight for their institutions. The invasion did occur, nonetheless, and
the story is told from the viewpoint of the conquerors who left records
and scored repeated victories over the natives. From the European
standpoint their migration westward opened a new world to colonization and exploration, and few voices were raised on behalf of the Indians.

Early Voyages of Exploration

When Christopher Columbus left Palos on August 3, 1492, with
the *Niña, Pinta,* and *Santa Maria,* he hoped to discover a new route to

China and Japan. Spanish and Portuguese merchants had long fought the monopoly of Italian and Arabic traders, and were anxious to find other routes to the East for the profitable spice trade. Their explorations into the Atlantic Ocean and down the African coast had widened their travels. Portuguese sailors had discovered the Azores in the 1420s, sailed the African coast past the equator in the 1470s, and entered the Indian Ocean in the 1480s. These dangerous voyages into the unknown were part of Columbus's early life. From his youth he had been connected with trading; he had sailed into the North Atlantic, round the Mediterranean, and to the Madeira Islands. On one voyage he had been shipwrecked in Portugal and had settled there for a time. While talking with the sailors of Lisbon, Columbus had become acquainted with their voyages, and began to dream of leading one of his own. He planned to sail directly west of the Canary Islands, calculating that Japan lay about twenty-five hundred miles distant, and to give his backers a safe and short route to the East.

For eight years he sought financial support, but the learned advisors of the Portuguese and Spanish monarchs believed that his ideas about the size of the earth were incorrect. In spite of rebuffs that the project was too costly and impractical, he remained eloquent in its support, won powerful friends at court, and gained the sympathy of Queen Isabella of Castile, who considered his proposal adventurous. She and her husband, King Ferdinand of Aragon, the joint rulers of Spain faced many serious political and economic problems at home, not the least was the removal of the Moors from the country, but they finally commissioned him. Providing him with three ships, they presented him with a letter to the Emperor of China and made him governor of lands he might discover on his way west.

After thirty-three days of sail out of the Canary Islands, Columbus discovered the sandy island of San Salvador in the Bahamas. Exploring this and neighboring isles, he then visited Cuba and Hispaniola, saw natives, whom he called Indians, and examined the plants and animals. He heard stories of gold mines, picked up gold-like sand, and traded some trinkets for native jewelry. His voyage homeward was easy, and he was royally welcomed as the discoverer of a new route to the Indies. Three other voyages followed, with Columbus believing even to the day of his death in 1506 that he had found the new route to the Orient.

Columbus was impressed with the lands he acquired for Spain. On the "more than 1700 islands" he found, Spain could plant colonies and Christianize the natives, adding to her strength in Europe. This "other world," his name for America, interested his monarchs, too, if only because they received just enough return from their gamble to make them try for larger stakes. From posts in Cuba, Hispaniola, and Puerto Rico, their seamen examined the Caribbean and Gulf of Mexico. In time Columbus's theory of a short route to the Indies was disproved, when Vasco Núñez de Balboa discovered the Pacific Ocean, near the

Voyages of Discovery

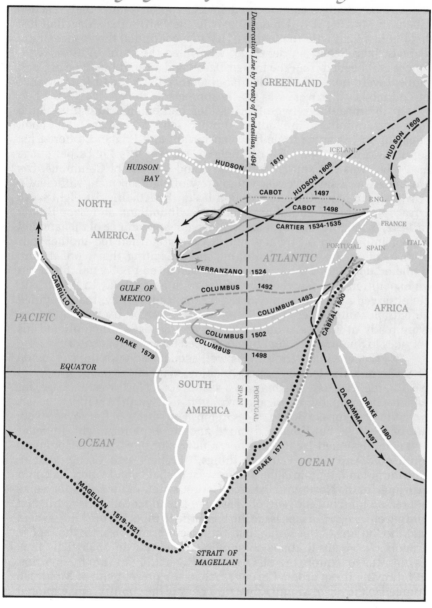

Demarcation Line by Treaty of Tordesillas, 1494

GREENLAND

ICELAND

HUDSON BAY

HUDSON 1610

HUDSON 1609

HUDSON 1609

NORTH

CABOT 1497

CABOT 1498

ENG.

CARTIER 1534-1535

FRANCE

AMERICA

PORTUGAL SPAIN ITALY

ATLANTIC

VERRANZANO 1524

GULF OF MEXICO

COLUMBUS 1492

CABRILLO 1542

COLUMBUS 1493

CABRAL 1500

AFRICA

PACIFIC

DRAKE 1579

COLUMBUS 1502

COLUMBUS 1498

EQUATOR

SOUTH

SPAIN

PORTUGAL

AMERICA

DA GAMMA 1497

DRAKE 1580

OCEAN

DRAKE 1577

OCEAN

MAGELLAN 1519-1521

STRAIT OF MAGELLAN

present site of Panama City, and when Ferdinand Magellan sailed around Cape Horn into the Pacific. For fourteen weeks Magellan's ships crossed the South Seas—without fresh supplies—until they reached Guam in March 1521. A month later in the Philippines Magellan lost his life in a fight with the natives. His men continued the voyage under Captain Juan Sebastián del Cano, who filled the sturdy *Vittoria* with spices and headed from the Indian Ocean and around the Cape of Good Hope toward home. At Seville, in September 1522, the full importance of Columbus's discovery was finally appreciated.

In the meantime, two other nations had entered into this search for a western route to the Indies. Another Genoese seaman, John Cabot, engaging in the spice trade between Levant and England, offered his services to King Henry VII of England. He won the king's patronage easily but was not supported in the grand manner of Columbus. His *Matthew* was a small vessel with a crew of eighteen men, sufficiently seaworthy to brave the late spring tides of the Atlantic. Its eight-week voyage brought Cabot and his men to Newfoundland and Cape Breton in 1497, where the fog, cold, and windswept appearance of the land left a poor impression on them. Though Cabot returned for another tour of inspection, he reported nothing more exciting than codfish and timbered country to the king. In 1509 Cabot's son Sebastian fitted out an expedition that searched the coasts for a passageway to the Orient. He observed a great bay of water, perhaps Hudson Bay, that provided an entrance into the continent. Few of his merchant backers, however, were ready to finance another voyage, and Sebastian then offered his services to Spain which kept him occupied for a quarter century.

In France, King Francis I was well acquainted with the expansion of Spain and wanted his nation to enjoy some of those advantages of wealth, too. His first scheme was a search for a Northwest Passage, for which Giovanni de Verrazano explored the North American coasts from the Chesapeake Bay to Cape Breton. The results of the voyage were not impressive, but Francis decided another explorer might do better and commissioned Jacques Cartier, a navigator of St. Malo. Hoping to "find gold and other valuable things," Francis sent Cartier first to Newfoundland, then into the waters west of that island where he could also look for the Northwest Passage. Cartier's view of the Labrador banks depressed him, but the land of Magdalen Island elevated his spirit. Not finding either gold or a passage, he had little to report to the king, except that the Indians of the Gaspé held promise of trade. Despite the report, Francis was ready to dispatch another expedition in 1535. This time Cartier was to explore the St. Lawrence River and sail into the interior. In following these orders Cartier reached the present site of Montreal, climbed to the top of Mount Royal for a view of the country, and explored on both sides of the St. Lawrence as long as the season permitted. He concluded, reluctantly, that the river was not a waterway to the Orient. Though he returned in 1541 with an expedition to establish a base for explorations, he and his men became disillusioned and abandoned the colony within two years.

Spain in the New World

The threat from these voyages of discovery did not arouse the Spanish very much. Earlier, their rivalry with Portugal had been a dangerous threat to peace. To lessen the tension, Pope Alexander VI had divided the western world between them along the Line of Demarcation. By mutual consent they later adjusted the frontier of explorations, giving Portugal more favorable treatment than at first. Portugal continued her explorations in the South Atlantic, and during the early part of the sixteenth century she moved into the Indian Ocean, established bases in India and the Far East, and had active missionaries as far distant as Japan. Her only American possession, Brazil, was accidentally discovered by Pedro Álvares Cabral who was leading an armada of thirteen ships on their way to India in 1500. Brazil was briefly explored and settled about thirty years later.

Spanish exploration of the northern coasts of South America was nearly completed before Spain began her investigation of the interior and the planting of colonies in Mexico and Peru. In 1519 Hernando Cortez inspected the Mexican coast and took a force of over five hundred men into the highlands above present-day Vera Cruz. On this natural road into the interior he heard stories of a distant city, and found the capital of Montezuma's Aztec empire. Refusing to be drawn off by bribes, he assailed its defenses and captured or killed its leaders and subdued its people. The immediate conquest in gold and silver overshadowed anything Spain had dreamt of winning by trading in the Orient. It changed her policy, excited the avarice of her conquerors, and renewed her interest in America.

In a very short time Cortez crossed Mexico and sailed along its Pacific shores, even going the short distant to Baja California where he established the post of La Paz. Everywhere he and his fellow conquerors went they heard stores of cities filled with gold, and they set out in great excitement to search for this wealth. Pánfilo de Narváez and Ponce de León entered Florida; others like Cabeza de Vaca explored Texas and the Southwest. In 1540 Francisco Vásquez de Coronado tramped through parts of present-day Arizona, New Mexico, Oklahoma, Texas, and Kansas. That same year expeditions by sea penetrated the Gulf of California and searched the California coast. Juan Cabrillo explored the Channel Islands of California, discovered San Diego Bay, and ventured ashore at San Pedro and other places as far north as Point Concepción. Neither he nor Coronado, however, found the fabled Seven Cities of Gold or anything sufficiently exciting to make them want to return to these distant lands. Spain's monarchs, however, remembered the Indians of these areas and eventually sent missionaries to St. Augustine, Florida, in September 1565. Pedro Menéndez brought

Hernando Cortez: Early Spanish Explorer and Conqueror of Mexico.
(Organization of American States)

an expeditionary force and laid plans for a chain of missionary posts from Parris Island in present-day South Carolina around the peninsula of Florida. In the Rio Grande Valley of New Mexico, Juan de Oñale established the first Spanish posts in the 1590s. Santa Fe was founded in 1610. While missionary activity in the Southwest brought Jesuits into present-day Arizona in the seventeenth century, California had to await settlement until 1769. In the southern hemisphere Francisco Pizarro and his brothers discovered the Inca empire of Peru in 1527. Their bloody dealings with the Incas gave Spain another area like Montezuma's Mexico, with enormous riches and intelligent people to exploit. Other centers of lesser wealth in the Valley of Mexico, in Guatemala, and in the Caribbean well rewarded the ambitious explorer. In each area Spain eventually established her administrative system and made the wealth contribute to the greatness of the homeland.

During these years Spain's greed was nearly insatiable and her exploitation of the natives was often cruel, but she shared her wealth with God. Spaniards by the thousands were sent into these lands to Christianize the natives, and they brought with them their monastic institutions, their art, music, architecture, and folkways. Mexico City became one seat of empire, and surrounding the administrative offices were churches, a university, monasteries, and beautiful homes. Spanish sophistication and gaiety gave the city character and splendor that swept some provincialism away and encouraged the adventurers to make their permanent homes there.

Into this new civilization the "children of the sun" were quickly drawn. While they were forced to work for the conqueror, they were instructed in the new faith and culture. Their treatment was a mixture of exploitation and paternalism, and they felt the heavy hand of Spanish supervision whether in the mine or in the church. In time the Indians came to be treated less as slaves and more as children. Some of their women became brides of young Spanish men; their bright youths were invited into the monasteries for service in the church. Indians of a second and third generation of Christianization and supervision found places in the new society, but they always remained a class apart from the native-born Spaniard and creole in this class-sensitive society.

All subjects were ruled as colonials; government was firmly held in Spanish hands, and through a strong civil and religious authority, loyalty was well maintained. All activity, economic and otherwise, was regulated by royal officials who were themselves accountable to the homeland. Even so, Spain surrounded her subjects with magnificence. The edifices of church and state in the great plaza of Mexico City are excellent examples of her energy and taste. So are the churches in the valleys and the plains, often far from the viceregal seat, where Indians were turned into Christians.

If the conquest, in spiritual and material results, astonishes the modern observer, it aroused the envy and lust of Spain's European

An Engraving by Theodore DeBrey of Conquest and Forced Labor of Indians by the Spanish. *(Library of Congress)*

rivals. It drew observers to her colonial shores, and some, like Francis Drake in the *Golden Hind*, left a trail of plunder as they captured treasure ships or sacked her provincial cities. Their invasions were sternly resisted by Spain, but her power had been spread too thin, and the attacks in Europe and America weakened her. In the seventeenth century she lost many Caribbean islands, once bases for conquest, to England, France, and the Netherlands.

English Development of Trade

Though Henry VII of England and the Bristol merchants abandoned further voyages to America early in the sixteenth century, Englishmen were no less interested in advancing their fortunes by taking to the sea. For the next half century or more, they concentrated their energy on the Low Countries, Germany, and Scandinavia. In 1548, when Sebastian Cabot returned to England, he promoted voyages north of Norway to Russia. One of his vessels successfully made the voyage, and English traders won privileges with the Great Duke of Moscow. The lines of trade were extended to Persia and planned to India, but this trade never measured up to its imagined potential. These routes to the East, moreover, did not replace trade through the port of Lisbon and through Dutch factors, or agents. Only when Spain closed Lisbon in 1585 did English merchants brave the long route around the Cape of Good Hope and seek a direct contact with the Orient. Regularizing their trade by establishing the East India Company, they received a royal monopoly and charter and, in the course of time, became a joint stock company.

Though these private ventures extended English trade in an impressive manner, they were protected by monopoly privileges, and the monopoly usually limited the potential trade. As a rule, merchants were more concerned with establishing a regular, assured market than with opening an expanding, speculative one. They quickly stabilized the market, therefore, and worked to keep interlopers out, men who might have been more competitive and aggressive than they were. This practice had the effect of forcing excluded merchants to look for other markets and of inducing a few to engage in the slave trade or in waylaying Spanish galleons. Francis Drake raided Spanish ports and stopped vessels everywhere, penetrating even the most distant areas of the world like San Francisco Bay and the north Pacific.

The Roanoke Colony

While Drake was plundering Spanish colonial cities, Sir Humphrey Gilbert and his half-brother, Sir Walter Raleigh, both courtiers and gentlemen, realized that England needed an American empire in order to enjoy trade and wealth such as Spain's. An American mart, they felt, could be stabilized. Since it would be removed from Continental intrigue and wars, it could be developed to supplement English production. Gilbert was apparently thinking of planting a colony in the West Indies, and had brought into his scheme the Richard Hakluyts. The elder Hakluyt, as a theorist and promoter, set up certain guidelines for a colony—good soil, moderate climate, a defensive position, and available sources of trade, like Indian markets and fishing. Gilbert's limited finances and his early death in 1583 delayed the execution of these plans, but in 1584 Raleigh, again with Hakluyt's guidance, renewed the explorations.

Like his half-brother, Raleigh felt the need of extensive exploration before a colony could be planted. He financed voyages that went to the West Indies, up the North American coast, and into the Chesapeake. The land by its general appearance seemed fit for habitation, and the evidence, weighed in England by the elderly Hakluyt, met his specifications. Raleigh was particularly impressed with the potential of Roanoke Island, which had good soil, fish off the coast, and a defensive position. With this evidence the promoters sought the assistance of Queen Elizabeth, and to convince her, the younger Hakluyt prepared an important paper, "Discourse on the Western Planting," which emphasized the value and safety of trade with American colonies. Her answer was undoubtedly anticipated. The queen had severely limited resources at her command, and these were deeply committed already to national defense. She was not able to finance colonial explorations along the American coasts, but she gave her royal consent to the plans.

Raleigh and the Hakluyts had to appeal, therefore, to the merchant community. To awaken an interest in a speculative venture of this kind required considerable argument and persuasion, and the elder Hakluyt, with great imagination, wrote another pamphlet. In it he described the possibility of colonial trade in terms of new products—olive oil, dyes, silk, hemp, rope, hops, and fruits—and appealed also to English nationalism. At best this plan was long range and speculative, but for immediate profits there would be Indian trade, fishing, whaling, minerals, perhaps gold and silver.

These arguments moved many merchants. Though the degree of their contribution is unknown, Raleigh was able in 1585 to win the cooperation of a good assortment of adventurers, educated men, and workmen who were willing to risk their lives by going to Roanoke Island. Bravery was only one requisite; talent and skill of good quality were also important to the promoters. The participants were expected to inspect the island, apply Hakluyt's norms of settlement, and gather evidence.

The expedition reached Roanoke Island in early summer, and John White, a fine artist, immediately began sketching scenes for the London promoters, who would have the problem of raising money and recruits for the projected colony. Thomas Hariot, an expert on navigation, busied himself with the problems of winds and tides, and a physician and apothecary studied the climate and plant life. By August a small plot of land was cleared for experimental plants, and a party of men was selected to remain for a year. Their winter was lonely, but no starvation or other privation hardened their lives. Homesickness was another matter, however, and when Francis Drake passed after a raid on Florida, the garrison welcomed the chance to return home.

Their appearance in England was obviously disappointing to the colony's promoters, but plans were already afoot to bring out settlers and lay the foundations for the first permanent base. In early July of 1587, sixty-eight men, seventeen women (two of them pregnant), and nine children arrived in good health and spirits. They were to locate their town some place on the Chesapeake Bay, about fifty miles from the open sea; apparently Hariot had recommended a better protected site than Roanoke Island. After the settlers were properly put ashore, they were left by the ship captain and crew to their own resources, but were promised more supplies and settlers in 1588. That year, formal war broke out between Spain and England, and the intended relief party was held in England. By the time ships could return, no trace was left of the settlers.

War with Spain continued through the 1590s, and the success of

A Sketch of Indians by John White ca. 1585. *(Library of Congress)*

English raids upon Spanish shipping distracted public attention from colonization. Although White's sketches were published and Hariot's observations were read by many, only the Gulf of the St. Lawrence, Newfoundland, and Nova Scotia received any serious investigation. The fishing voyages there were unsuccessful in establishing colonies, but statesmen in Elizabeth's government pondered the use of these lands as a haven for religious dissenters.

The Virginia Colony and Other English Ventures

Leaders of the London merchant community, however, particularly the affluent Sir Thomas Smith, continued to be interested in the idea of a colonial empire. Smith and his friends were involved in worldwide trade, and speculation in a colonial venture was only one part of their comprehensive plans. Included in their group was the younger Hakluyt, whose participation meant a strong emphasis upon developing a plantation colony that would supply the English market with products unobtainable otherwise except through Spanish factors. In 1606, after two or three years of planning, the promoters secured a royal

charter and brought within their enterprise not only merchants from
London, Exeter, and Bristol but also some gentlemen and courtiers.
They apparently decided also to divide the North American coast
into two colonial ventures, one on the Chesapeake and the other in
the New England area. Hakluyt's influence was evident in a provision
for government participation. Although the new monarch, James I, was
only slightly more interested in America than had been Queen Elizabeth, he agreed to the establishment of a council to oversee any problems
of ruling this far-off land. The promoters were again left largely to their
own resources in extending English territory in America. The authority
of the English king was important, nonetheless, in emphasizing to all
adventurers that the colonies lived under the law of England and that
men were expected to be obedient and loyal.

The new undertaking, like the one at Roanoke, was primarily
experimental at first; permanent settlement was to follow. That one
hundred men and four boys were gathered for the initial expedition
underscored the preliminary nature of the preparations; families would
come next. These people, sailing with Captain Christopher Newport,
were provided with excellent navigation to America. He took the precaution of going by a southern route and of stopping at Nevis, West
Indies, where the passengers could refresh themselves before undertaking their arduous duties.

Going about thirty miles up the James River in late April of 1607,
the party selected a low-lying site for its base. The marshy land that
covered some of the peninsula made this site most unattractive for
settlement. The heat of spring and summer, the dampness, and the
insect life, together with the lack of proper health precautions, turned
Jamestown into a death trap for the colonists and kept the death rate
critically high for years. The woods were hazardous, confining the
colonists to the cleared areas, and the chief of the local Indians, Powhatan, was more shrewd and daring in his relations with them than they
had calculated. Still, these slow beginnings gave way to modest growth,
as leadership, fresh food supplies, and other settlements were developed. Men like Captain John Smith and John Rolfe became leaders
and explorers, and tales of their exploits advertised the colony's potential in London.

While the Jamestown settlement in Virginia was potentially an
attractive business enterprise, it annually recorded bewildering losses.
Its difficulties puzzled stockholders, who wavered in their support and
put their money into the development of Bermuda, which, in contrast,
became an instantaneous success. In desperation, the promoters reorganized the company in 1609, solicited more funds, and recruited
greater numbers of settlers. They looked for able, intelligent leadership
that would face the wilderness with heroic virtue and turn the enterprise into success. To a degree, they were immediately successful. By
1611 more than seven hundred colonists were living in the colony,

although no more than thirty were women. Towns were planted at Point Comfort, Kecoughton, Jamestown, and Henrico. Some colonists were experimenting with silk production, and John Rolfe, who married Powhatan's favorite daughter, Pocahontas, tried his luck with tobacco.

Even with the spread of people into healthier places than James-town, the company was unable to keep the total population from declin-ing dramatically; in 1616, only 350 settlers were living in the colony. That same year Bermuda had nearly six hundred settlers, and its eco-nomic life seemed flourishing. The contrast of Bermuda with Virginia was too sharp for the London Company promoters to tolerate. In 1618 they again took stock of their position, and some old planters, forming subordinate companies, tried to rescue themselves from bankruptcy by appealing for local help. In Smith's Hundred the local company put its faith in tobacco, pooled resources of the stockholders, and brought out additional laborers. The English promoters urged a reorganization for the whole colony and, in 1619, Sir Edwin Sandys took over control from Thomas Smith. Under Sandy's direction the company mobilized tremendous support. In four years he expended vast sums on experi-mental crops and enterprises, planned a missionary college for the Indians, promised English institutions to prospective settlers, set aside lands for private development, and sent out four thousand colonists. Such effort required advance preparation in America. Unfortunately, little was done to allow for emergencies, and the company was helpless in 1622 when Indians attacked the outlying settlements and destroyed food and crops. In the massacre and accompanying starvation, thous-ands lost their lives and hundreds returned to England.

For the stout-hearted who were willing to gamble on the future, tobacco was winning popularity in England despite opposition from James I and Parliament. The expanding market made possible the importation of both white and black contract laborers. The blacks were purchased primarily from Dutch traders and treated somewhat differ-ently from their white fellows. Slavery as an institution for black labor-ers soon developed, but white and black men in these years worked side by side producing food surpluses that were sold to new Virginia settlers or, after 1633, to those making neighboring Maryland their home.

In 1624 the Virginia Company, shaken by the debacle of the Sandys regime, surrendered its charter to the crown. The shift in command was barely noticed at first, because the company left a legislature in charge of local affairs. But the rising number of inhabitants forced the royal gover-nors to look after problems of order and defense, to form county govern-ments, and to appoint local officials.

In the meantime, other merchants and gentlemen explored the coast of New England. Also driven by the desire for safe trade and a new source of products, they tried to found a colony on the Sagadahoc in 1606 and 1607. Dissension plagued the expeditions from their departure for America and, in spite of profits from furs, fish, and some other products, the settlers would not remain in the colony. The failure of the initial colony made other plans for colonization more difficult, and Sir Fernando Gorges, a principal leader of the company, turned to trading ventures of limited cost and duration. To hold their charter, the promoters granted trading privileges to other groups of merchants who wished to exploit the natural resources. One of these groups was a band of Separatists from Holland and Lincolnshire who sought an American refuge at Plymouth to practice their religion. Another group settled first at Cape Ann, then at Naumkeag, with fishing as their chief interest. But Gorges, despite his many plans for settlement, was not able himself to plant a colony. His lands fell into the hands of religious refugees, and the most impressive colonization was by Puritans who secured charter rights to Massachusetts Bay in 1628.

In supporting the migration of religious dissenters, the merchants of London, Lincoln, and Bristol provided money and encouragement. They sympathized with the plight of these people and, undoubtedly, saw possibilities for enlarged trade in the development of American colonies. But the colonies in Plymouth and Massachusetts Bay were a departure from the usual business operation. Though they used company organization for a time, their purpose was primarily that of settlement and making a home in New England.

Other British colonies developed by merchants and gentlemen promoters were Barbados, Nevis, Antigua, and the Bahamas. White colonists moved in quickly and planted those precious crops that Hakluyt recommended, but, in time, the islands imported a slave population to do the hard field labor. While most English colonials were not accustomed to slave labor, they did not resist its use; already such labor was being used in the Portuguese and Spanish empires, and it seemed natural to adapt English customs to permit the practice.

The Dutch Colonies

While Spain and England were developing their empires, the Dutch won independence in Europe and created for themselves an impressive carrying trade. These sturdy, almost fearless seamen ventured all over Europe and, as early as the 1590s, had traveled to India and the East Indies. They were fiercely competitive, pushing the Portuguese traders from bases, going into Java, Ceylon, and Malacca. They were also contenders for American territory, though they too were motivated at first by the desire to find a short route to the Orient.

Henry Hudson sailed into New York harbor in 1609, and up the river later named for him, and observed the riches of interior America. The Dutch liked the West Indies and South America better than North America, but their traders established Albany in 1624 and New Amsterdam two years later. These posts were intended primarily for trade. Dutch seamen were interested in Indian trade, and New Amsterdam also became nearly a free port, as the settlers attracted illicit trade from the neighboring English colonies. Some merchants handled the tobacco of Virginia, others sold slaves, and all were deep in the business of exchanging West Indian products for those of North America.

While New Netherland should have been extraordinarily prosperous, it was developed only as a base, with most of the vital energy being outside the colony. Its governmental authority, the West India Company, was concerned with world-wide business of which the New Netherland was only a minor part. The colony thus remained small, weak, and discontented. Many settlers begged the home government to assume control over its affairs, and won some sympathy. The company responded to these protests by appointing Peter Stuyvesant as governor. This humorless one-legged veteran of Dutch wars in the Caribbean broke up the dissent with a heavy hand and imposed severe restrictions. He enlarged the colony to include Swedish settlements on the Delaware, but was unable to provide the substance for a prosperous and balanced economy. Furthermore, his quarrels with the inhabitants over religious practices and representation in the government unsettled the colony, and hostile relations with New England lead to a loss of territory. For these and other reasons the colony did not grow in population. In 1660 it had seven thousand people while Virginia and Maryland had nearly forty thousand. Its institutions, moreover, were weak and its commerce was monopolized by a few men.

News of the colony's languishing condition gave English imperialists an opportunity which they used in 1664 to seize the colony. The English had never reconciled themselves to the existence of a Dutch colony on the Hudson. It interfered with their own plans, divided their Virginia and New England settlements, and drew off valuable trade to Dutch smugglers. Their seizure of New Netherland (which they renamed New York), moreover, generally pleased the Dutch inhabitants, who had tired of the West India Company's monopoly. The conquest was significant for England, giving her territory that would permit control of the interior of North America.

France in the New World

The presence of France in the back country was already an irritant to England. French voyages along the Maine coast and in the Gulf of the St. Lawrence had troubled her fishermen, and nationals of the two countries had occasionally confronted each other in these lands. Before 1600, however, France was too distracted by religious wars to pay much attention to exploration and colonization.

The Canadian Colony

When Henry IV of France pacified his opposition in the late 1590s, he urged adventurers to explore the North American coasts and accept

the obligation of bringing Christianity to the natives. He offered a subsidy and promised a trade monopoly to induce merchants to risk their
own capital. These favors proved to be irresistible to the merchants of
Rouen, who organized a company and engaged Samuel de Champlain,
son of a mariner, soldier, and geographer, to head their venture.

Their choice of Champlain was fortunate. This inspired patriot,
Frenchman, and Catholic ignored hardship and hazard in his quest for
knowledge, adventure, and the objectives of his merchant employers.
His selection of Quebec as a base was preparatory to an extensive investigation of the interior. He explored the upper St. Lawrence River
country in 1609, went deep into the forest, and discovered Lake Champlain and Indian trade routes. He established French trade with friendly
Indians by taking sides against the Iroquois and gained opportunities
to search even deeper into the back country.

His investigations, however, uncovered nothing like Spain's
wealth of Mexico and Peru, only a vast forested country of limited
agricultural potential. His merchant backers, with little enthusiasm
for colonization, were reluctant to commit more funds to the project,
and he returned to France in search of support. Though he secured
money for additional expeditions and lived until 1635, his backers
were not interested in settlement and found the prospects of trade dim.
The few Frenchmen who did brave the hardships of settlement discovered a severe climate and few rewards for their sacrifices. Isolation,
winter desolation, and limited growing seasons frightened off promoters, and the merchants nearly abandoned the colony to the religious
societies who were attracted by the opportunities for missionary work.

To finance their enterprises the missionaries raised funds by private
schemes and advertised the value of the missions. A group of fifty-four
soldiers, laborers, and nurses settled at Montreal in 1641, hoping to
build a hospital and Christianize the Indians. In larger numbers the
Society of Jesus established missions, sometimes laboring alone at distant outposts and living in fear of Indian uprising. The religious settlers,
however, were unable to cope with the hostility of the Iroquois, whose
raids threatened the very existence of the colony.

In 1660, the young Louis XIV and his great minister, Jean Baptiste
Colbert, rescued the colony by taking over its control. The king was
determined to protect France's economy by giving her access to overseas
supplies: naval stores, timber for masts, and unusual products that
would assure France of markets as she met the challenges of England
and the Netherlands. While Louis was more interested in the East and
West Indies, Colbert moved particularly to develop Canada.

In assuming active direction of Canadian affairs, the king recon-
structed the government and put local authority in a Sovereign Council
composed of governor, bishop, intendant, and other officials. He reserved lawmaking and appointments to his ministers. The home government eventually regulated most aspects of life in a paternalistic fashion,

in which change or direction was at the discretion of the king. The local embodiment of his paternalism was the intendant, whose vast powers over most colonial activity made him the royal leader of the colony. The arrival of Jean Talon, the first resident intendant, had an immediate effect upon life there.

Talon was an exceptional figure. Vigorous, ambitious, and imaginative, he grasped the responsibilities of his position and for nearly a decade carried out French policy. He was concerned most about Canada's small population and urged the home government to select young, healthy men and women as immigrants. Sometimes their moral quality was not first rate, and he had to correct their behavior, but in sending out over four thousand settlers France laid the foundations for a stable colony. Talon encouraged the settlers to marry early and have large families. He devised a system of rewards and punishment, providing gifts at marriage and subsidies upon the birth of the tenth child. Until young men were married they were denied the right to engage in the fur trade. Men finishing contracts as indentured servants were required to marry within fifteen days or lose their rights to engage in trade. Gentle persuasion of this kind had some effect in expanding the population.

Talon realized also that the colony had to improve its economy. He tried to increase its self-sufficiency by importing cattle, expanding agriculture, and encouraging manufacturing. A brewery, shipbuilding facilities, mines, and a tannery were opened, but the scarcity of laborers caused most of his enterprises to fail. Over the years, only the fur trade provided the profits to balance imports, and this trade, although lucrative, harmed the colony because it drew off young men to the forests and spread the colony over too great an area.

Most of the colonists sent to Talon were farmers, attracted by the promise of land, good life, and abundance. In addition, the king, playing on human vanity, encouraged wealthy people to immigrate by assuring them of a privileged position in the colony. He established for that purpose a feudal system, giving the seigneurs special powers over the church, marks of honor in the community, and minor judicial supervision. In short, they were to be Quebec's nobility. However, they never achieved the position and influence of an aristocracy, and never were permitted to rule the colony. Since they were recruited from the merchant class, often men in search of wealth, they possessed little prestige to attract colonists. Furthermore, they met fierce resistance from François de Montmorency-Laval, the powerful vicar-apostolic of the Catholic Church, when they tried to control parish affairs. Bishop Laval was determined to rule his diocese without interference and exercised, in addition, stern supervision over his flock. His authority reached down to community affairs and up to the Pope, to whom he gave filial loyalty. In cooperation with the Jesuits and other religious orders, he founded schools, charitable institutions and organized mission activity.

From the colony's founding, missionaries were sent into Indian country. Their labors were difficult, because the natives were reluctant to accept the beliefs and mores of the French; those who did were often social outcasts. War between Hurons and Iroquois kept forest life hazardous. Missionaries working among the Hurons fell with their flocks as the Iroquois attacked village upon village. Father Isaac Jogues, who lived among the Hurons, was severely tortured in 1642 and killed four years later. Continued danger from the Iroquois drove missionaries from the northern Great Lakes until the 1660s, when Claude Allouez went out to live with the Ottawas. His successes were also reduced because French officials were unable to pacify the Iroquois or strengthen the resistance of friendly Indians. Even Louis de Baude, the Comte de Frontenac, the resourceful governor-general, was perplexed by Iroquois hostility.

Frontenac was first appointed governor in 1672 and, except for a brief interruption, served until his death in 1698. Always a quarrelsome, controversial figure, he disputed policy with Bishop Laval and the intendants. He was primarily interested in the fur trade and risked the anger of the church by selling brandy to the Indians and war with the Iroquois by building a fort at Cataraqui (Fort Frontenac). At this strategic spot he hoped to draw the Iroquois under French military control, but rivalry over western trade brought a war with them that destroyed the fort in 1689.

Behind the Iroquois stood the Dutch and English at Albany, who supplied muskets, powder, and liquor and who did not invade their trading area as did the French. Without help from the English or the destruction of English posts, the French had little chance to control the Iroquois. When the English showed no willingness to join him, Frontenac staged raids in 1690 against Schenectady and Salmon Falls and into Maine. Though he did not inflict permanent damage upon English settlements, he launched bitter attacks upon the Iroquois, rebuilt Fort Frontenac, and forced the Iroquois to sue for peace.

Expanding French Territory

Even before the Iroquois menace to western travel and trade was removed, Frenchmen were pushing deep into the continent. The very nature of the fur trade made exploration necessary, and the presence of the Iroquois in the south and west meant that Frenchmen headed on a northern route into the continent. At Sault Ste. Marie, the famous Jesuit Jacques Marquette established a mission in 1669, and soon the civil authority annexed the mission as a part of Quebec, founding a trading base and fort. Father Allouez, who had worked in this area before Marquette's arrival, moved further west to Green Bay, where he built the mission of St. Francis Xavier in 1671 and explored a route to the Mississippi River. In 1673 and 1674 Marquette and Louis Joliet opened

French Explorations & Settlements

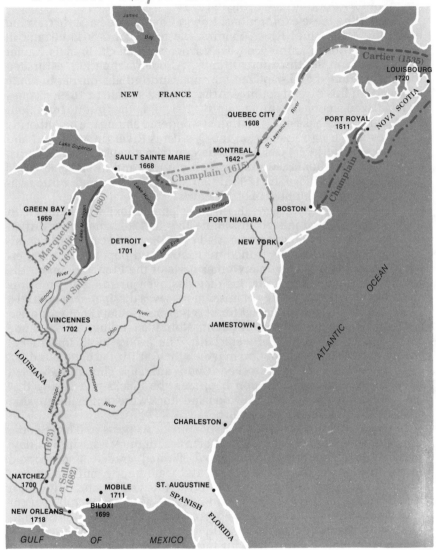

NEW FRANCE

Cartier (1535)

LOUISBOURG
1720

QUEBEC CITY
1608

PORT ROYAL
1611

NOVA SCOTIA

MONTREAL
1642

SAULT SAINTE MARIE
1668

Lake Superior

Champlain (1615)

Champlain

GREEN BAY
1669

Lake Huron

Lake Ontario

BOSTON

Lake Michigan

FORT NIAGARA

Marquette
and Joliet
(1673)

DETROIT
1701

Lake Erie

NEW YORK

La Salle (1680)

Illinois

River

VINCENNES
1702

Ohio

River

JAMESTOWN

ATLANTIC

OCEAN

LOUISIANA

Mississippi River

Tennessee

River

La Salle (1673)

CHARLESTON

NATCHEZ
1700

La Salle (1682)

MOBILE
1711

ST. AUGUSTINE

SPANISH
FLORIDA

NEW ORLEANS
1718

BILOXI
1699

GULF   OF   MEXICO

James
Bay

St. Lawrence River

the area south of Green Bay and traveled down the Mississippi River as far as the Arkansas. Marquette spent the remaining two years of his life in Illinois working among the Indians.

Extending these explorations, Robert Cavelier de La Salle traveled down the Mississippi River, naming the delta country Louisiana in 1682, and Allouez journeyed yearly from mission St. Francis Xavier to Kaskaskia in southwestern Illinois. Allouez's superiors estimated that he instructed and baptized ten thousand Indians during his long residence in this distant country. After Allouez's death in 1689, Jacques Gravier lived among the Indians until 1705, and other Jesuits from their headquarters at Kaskaskia (in Illinois) wandered among the neighboring tribes, establishing missions on the Des Peres River (in Missouri) and at Cahokia (in Illinois). As Kaskaskia grew, its clustering Indian huts, a few merchant homes, warehouses, a church, and a fort gave it the appearance of a village. In 1763 it had about five hundred white residents and an equal number of black slaves.

Settlement also was made in Louisiana. Biloxi was founded in 1699. Its population moved to Mobile Bay in 1702, and some drifted on to New Orleans when it was settled in 1718. As the capital of Louisiana in 1721, New Orleans gained in prestige and population, numbering 470 inhabitants. Like many other parts of the French domain, the colony was troubled by religious disputes over jurisdiction, and thus much of the potential energy of missioneries was dissipated in quarrels. The Catholic Church struggled for survival in a society that was often immoral, irreligious, and indifferent. Notwithstanding, schools, one hospital, and an orphanage were built. The Jesuits, with their usual energy, established a plantation in which they cultivated cotton, indigo, sugar, and fruit trees, and stocked it with animals. Though they used slave labor, they insisted upon baptizing the blacks and seeing that they were properly married. The food and stock were sent to the mission posts for distribution to the Indians.

French America was thus widely spread. At posts in Nova Scotia, along the St. Lawrence for hundreds of miles, in the Mississippi Valley, and in Louisiana, Frenchmen settled, farmed, traded, and worked among the Indians. Many prospered and were happy, but the empire attracted few people from Europe. Over the years natural increase accounted for its steady growth, and in 1763, after nearly 150 years of settlement, the population was approximately sixty thousand. Compared with the more than two million English colonials, the spacious French empire was empty. The fur trade of Canada, moreover, brought miserable returns to France compared with the gold and silver Spain took from her empire.

Europe as Seat of Empire

The century and a half after Columbus had turned attention to

America, European seamen crisscrossed the water lanes of the world. Their explorations of America covered much of the two continents by that time, but Europeans also investigated opportunities for trade in the Orient, India, and Africa. The English and French established strong bases in India, the Portuguese and Dutch in the East Indies, and the Spanish in the Philippines. In these distant areas Europeans were rivals for trade in spices, metals, and luxuries, and they fought to secure monopoly control of the trade lanes and products.

Their rivalry should not obscure the fact that world trade became a reality after 1492. Those ships full of precious products from American and oriental ports became common place in Europe, and nations vied to share their cargoes. The North Atlantic coasts of America became important in this rivalry as the search continued for products, but discoveries there did not greatly excite the European imagination. Fish and furs were bountiful and the great open spaces were heavily timbered. These northern regions held out opportunity for discoveries, but wealthy, experienced traders went elsewhere for their profits.

In developing their American empires, these European nations used varying degrees of governmental help. Spain exercised full national power, exported her institutions, and supervised her colonials. England, in letting her merchants explore and settle America, was not very successful in Virginia and New England, but her venture in Bermuda prospered. Those of her colonies that were to be populated by religious refugees were the most successful, but that story is to be told in the next chapter. Both the Netherlands and France experimented with trading companies, and both suffered failures. The overall imperialist effort of these four European nations in the West Indies and on the continent brought wealth and improved standards of living to their homelands.

SUGGESTIONS FOR FURTHER READING

Andrews, Charles M., *Our Earliest Colonial Settlements*. Ithaca, New York, Cornell University Press, 1959.

Boxer, Charles R., *The Dutch Seaborne Empire, 1600-1800*. New York, Alfred A. Knopf, 1965.

————, *Race Relations in the Portuguese Colonial Empire, 1415-1825*. New York, Oxford University Press, 1963.

Bridenbaugh, Carl, *Vexed and Troubled Englishmen, 1590-1642*. New York, Oxford University Press, 1976.

Cumming, W. P., et al., *The Explorations of North America, 1630-1776*. New York, G. P. Putnam's Sons, 1974.

Davies, D. W., *A Primer of Dutch Seventeenth Century Overseas*

Trade. The Hague, Martinus Nijhoff, 1961.

Diffie, Bailey W. and George D. Winius, *Foundations of the Portuguese Empire, 1415-1580.* Minneapolis, University of Minnesota, 1977.

Gibson, Charles, ed., *The Spanish Tradition in America.* New York, Harper Torchbooks, Harper & Row, 1968.

Haring, C. H., *The Spanish Empire in America.* New York, Harbinger Books, Harcourt, Brace & World, 1963.

Notestein, Wallace, *The English People on the Eve of Colonization, 1603-1630.* New York, Harper Torchbooks, Harper & Row, 1962.

Parry, J. H., *The Age of Reconnaissance.* New York, Mentor Books, The New American Library, 1964.

——————, *The Spanish Seaborne Empire.* New York, Alfred A. Knopf, 1966.

—————— and P. M. Sherlock, *A Short History of the West Indies.* New York, St. Martin's Press, 1963.

Penrose, Boies, *Travel and Discovery in the Renaissance, 1420-1620.* New York, Altheneum Publishers, 1962.

Quinn, David B., "The First Pilgrims," *The William and Mary Quarterly,* XXIII, 359-390.

——————, *The Roanoke Voyages, 1584-1590.* 2 vols. New York, Cambridge University Press, 1956.

Wallace, Willard M., *Sir Walter Raleigh.* Princeton, Princeton University Press, 1959.

Washburn, Wilcomb E., *The Indian and the White Man.* Garden City, New York, Anchor Books, Doubleday & Company, 1964.

2

The English Come to America

IN THE TWO DECADES AFTER 1619, ENGLAND'S colonies received major migrations of people. The population of Virginia, Barbados, Antigua, and many lesser West Indian islands mounted significantly and new areas were opened rapidly. In the 1630s, moreover, great numbers were coming to New England and the Chesapeake Bay region, and permanent settlements were now assured in nearly a dozen important areas.

Grievances at Home

These migrants reflected the deepening discontent in English life since 1603, when James I had succeeded his cousin Elizabeth I. On the surface, the accession of a new monarch released new spirit and energy, but the king was unable to solve the many difficulties affecting the nation. New classes of merchants and landholders were challenging the political order, wanting a share in ruling the state, and the king resisted their demands. They agitated from the safety of the House of Commons and used their elected representatives to give voice to their grievances. These debates over taxation, religious policy, foreign affairs, and management of the government forced James I time and time again to dissolve Parliament and call new elections. His opponents wanted the rule of king and Parliament, a government of laws, and certain rights that would shield them from unnecessary search and imprisonment.

During these contests of who should rule, who should pass the tax laws, and who should conduct foreign policy and wage war, James I was unable to command the same kind of loyalty and respect as had Elizabeth I. His ministers were poorer in quality, sometimes guilty of immorality, and the king himself seemed incapable of interpreting the emotions of the people. Many leaders who had felt the drama and excitement of Elizabeth's rule were not impressed with James's, and this intangible sense of patriotism and destiny weakened even more during the rule, begun in 1625, of his son, Charles I. In time many English people came to question the value of monarchy as an institution, finally even consenting to the execution of Charles I in 1649, when a republican government was established.

The Puritan Movement

The greatest failure of Elizabeth's successors, however, was their inability to develop a religious consensus. A movement in the Church of England known as Puritanism was challenging current religious, social, and political theories and was demanding a reform of society. Puritans were members of the established Anglican Church, which had broken from Catholicism in the 1530s. They were anxious to reform religious practice in the church still further by removing all influences of Catholicism and thereby basing the religious order upon a reinterpretation of the Bible. They did not appreciate the compromise spirit of the Church of England because it was a blend of reform and tradition. Its retention of a hierarchy, ritual, and sacramental system similar to Catholicism irritated them, and they hoped to root out these "corruptions" of centuries and renew the faith. They would eliminate all clerical orders above the minister, like the dean and bishop, set up a government of councils, and concentrate upon the sermon as an important part of the service. They drew inspiration from John Calvin, a reformer in Geneva, whose teachings had swept through Scotland and penetrated into the English universities.

For a reform of society they insisted on an end to certain kinds of frivolity. Cockfighting, stage plays, horse racing, and pageantry were frowned upon. Sundays were to be set aside for prayer, and reading matter was to be elevating and religiously inspiring. The church was to be the center of a reformed society, in which people worked hard, offered prayers through their labor to God, and modeled their conduct upon the Bible. Some reformers insisted upon a religious experience for membership and affirmed that only a few people were chosen by

God for eternal bliss. This predestination of the saints put salvation
out of human hands, and worship was generally a discovery of one's
fate and a token of appreciation to God for one's selection.

The Puritan message appealed especially to the London merchants
and to the farmers and tradesmen of East Anglia and the West Country.
It touched people educated in the universities, the learned, and men
of ideals, but it had little influence with the lower classes, with people
who would expect the church to assist them, provide social services,
and give them an emotional experience. The Puritan church, it should
be emphasized, cut itself off from the traditions of the monastery, the
architectural and musical heritage, and the social services of hospitals
and orphanages. New England Puritans (or Congregationalists)
stressed simplicity and, except for education, confined themselves
to a limited church ritual in which the sermon was the most important
part.

Puritans were a stubborn, self-righteous people, but the Stuarts
were equally stubborn. When one confronted the other with arguments,
their quarrels deadlocked politics: The kings enforced the law and the
Puritans insisted upon reforming society—according to their own interpretation of the Bible. The kings made the mistake of resisting most
reform; Charles I committed the serious error of backing the high church
(Roman Catholic) party when it attempted to reintroduce Catholic
ceremonies. Most English people were frightened by Catholicism
because it symbolized their national rivalry with Spain and France.
They regarded Catholicism as an ideology as well as a set of practices;
in the religious sense it was the anti-Christ and in national terms it
was anti-English. Charles's backing of certain Catholic practices
marked him as having weaknesses, and he was especially vulnerable
to attack because he had married a French Catholic princess.

While Charles was thus a rallying point for opposition, Puritans
themselves experienced difficulty agreeing on their beliefs. They had
many respected theologians, but every man was expected to read the
Bible and interpret it according to his own talents. A variety of religious
ideas was inevitable, even though many theologians were positive
that men of deep faith would arrive at the same interpretations. This
variety, however, did not become evident until the Civil War in the
1640s released revolutionary emotion, and men discovered that the
king was not their only enemy.

The revolution eventually touched the very core of English life,
challenging religious preconceptions, the political bases of society,
and the system of wealth. For many this churning of ideas was too
drastic, and they longed for a return of the monarchy and a religious
consensus.

The New England Settlements

Many Englishmen with Puritan sympathies were unwilling to

Signing of the Mayflower Compact, November 1620. *(Library of Congress)*

await political changes at home. Their emotion was so embittered that only an exodus from the land of their birth and the creation of a new life would satisfy their innermost feelings. They feared persecution as long as the Stuarts were on the throne.

The migration to New England began with the Pilgrims or Separatists in 1620. These humble farmers and tradespeople from East Anglia had moved to Leyden, Holland, in 1609 and organized there the first Congregational Church. Ten years in this foreign environment were as much as they could endure, and they accepted an offer from Sir Edwin Sandys and some London merchants to settle on lands of the Virginia Company. Their plans evolved slowly, but by November 11, 1620, they were anchored in the *Mayflower* off the Cape Cod coast, giving their prayers to God for the safe voyage. Because they were outside the jurisdiction of the Virginia Company, they signed a compact to govern themselves by the will of the majority. They were to petition for a charter and await a permanent determination of their government.

In the meantime, these heroic people suffered from exposure and inexperience. They had arrived at an unusually poor time, when the winds of late fall were blowing off the sea, chilling bodies already weakened by scurvy and making no activity possible on the land. By spring, over one hundred passengers of the little expedition were dead, and the survivors were emotionally shocked by their ordeal. Fortunately, there were no hostile Indians in the area, and the single Indian who ventured to the coast, Samoset, spoke English and made them acquainted with the chief of the Wampanoags, Massasoit. Another Indian, Squanto, the only survivor of the Pawtuxet Indians, agreed to teach the settlers how to fish and plant corn. These contacts with the Indians helped them to survive that first miserable year and to celebrate a thanksgiving to God in October. Shortly thereafter, the *Fortune* arrived with supplies and thirty-six additional colonists.

In spite of the good harvest the privations were not over, but under the brave leadership of William Bradford and Edward Winslow a strong foundation was laid. Few of the first settlers despaired of success and abandoned the project. They struggled ceaselessly during the next decade or two to pay off the costs of their transportation and supplies, and when other Puritans settled in nearby Massachusetts Bay, the Plymouth colonists sold their surplus livestock to the newcomers and began to prosper.

Plymouth's struggle caught the imagination of later Americans and has become part of the national folklore. From such small beginnings, as Bradford described their experience, a set of heroic symbols has formed so that Plymouth Rock, the celebration of Thanksgiving, the Pilgrim's walk to church, and the figure of the noble and generous Squanto are vivid reminders of our national origins.

But Plymouth Colony was actually a small part of the great migration of the English to America. The total population in Plymouth after a decade of settlement was about three hundred, while Massachusetts Bay received during the first year nearly one thousand settlers and thousands more yearly in the 1630s.

The Puritans who came to Massachusetts Bay began their initial settlement in 1626 at the fishing village of Salem, and then moved to Charlestown and Boston as their numbers expanded. They attracted such men of character and experience as Thomas Dudley, John Endecott, and John Winthrop, whose ability to direct the colony gave Massachusetts a good administration quickly. Like the settlement at Jamestown, that at Massachusetts Bay was governed by an English company, the Massachusetts Bay Company, but the Puritans managed to transfer their charter and company to the colony. Though they kept the company form of organization for a few years, in time modifications were forced upon the governor and assistants of the company so that the franchise was widened, annual elections held, and a two-house legislature formed. The business company then transformed itself into a charter of government. Control of the government was put into the hands of church members, yet as church membership became less the right of the elected and more the obligation of all the inhabitants of a town, most male settlers who were Congregationists in sympathy and landholders secured the right to vote.

In religious matters there was regimentation for decades. Since Calvinist doctrine separated the saved from the damned, giving no hope of redemption to the damned, society struggled constantly against this force of evil and entrusted government only to leaders of proven sobriety and piety. It justified this policy because it felt that God's will was not equally known to all men. Some people received greater inspiration from reading the Bible than others; some would not know their fate for certain throughout their whole lives. Because of this uncertainty, ministers, lay leaders, and teachers, who apparently had divine guidance, were vested with much responsibility. They were aided by laws that set the pattern of Sunday observance, church worship, and discipline so that unusual dress, instrumental music in the service, and any special identity of the church from other buildings were prohibited.

These societal norms confronted settlers arriving later, who reacted variously. Many thanked God for them. Thomas Hooker and his flock hastened off to distant Connecticut where they could follow God's will in their own way. A few, like Roger Williams and Anne Hutchinson, pushed their interpretations of the Bible beyond the point of tolerance and suffered exile to Rhode Island. Others, like the Quakers, persisted in preaching their creeds and were ousted bodily from the colony and whipped, humiliated, or executed when they dared to return.

Generally, however, life was less regimented and severe than at first glance it appears to have been. A majority of the people neglected to join the Puritan church, and the ministers, who were not united in a formal organization, rarely agreed on all doctrinal matters. The colonists themselves lived in scattered communities where working in the fields was supremely difficult and where local problems dominated their attention. They were English people, too, whose common sense modified the ways of enthusiasts. While life had a Puritan tone, later generations took upon themselves the interpretations of the Bible, changing doctrines, relaxing laws, and restoring English traditions. The community schools included much practical learning, and Harvard College, the only institution of higher learning in New England from 1636 until Yale College was founded in 1701, progressively broadened its educational objectives.

In spite of some schools and village life, New Englanders faced a raw and undeveloped land. For the ten to fifteen thousand people who ventured forth in the 1630s there was much work to do—clearing the soil of trees and rocks and making a living. While most people received ample land for themselves and their children, the rocky soil forced them to look outside their towns for other occupations. They began to engage in the fur trade, fishing, and shipbuilding, and their trade took them along the coast, later to the West Indies and to Europe.

As trade became the salvation of New England, its merchants and the towns they lived in flourished. The merchant assumed an increas-

A Portrait of a New England Puritan
(New England Historical and Geneological Society)

ingly important part in New England life, and he and the clergy, often in rivalry, bid for the support of the people as both promised a better life than the land gave them. In a material way, at least, the future was on the side of the merchants. Their contacts in the growing empire enlarged the base of New England trade until her fish, timber, and shipping services were in demand everywhere. The merchants as instruments of luxury lived in fine homes along the waterfront and imported a variety of foreign products to make the colony comfortable. Their tastes eventually ran counter to Puritan simplicity and discipline. They wanted more attractive church buildings and appreciated the architectural work of Sir Christopher Wren, whose concept of church design became the model of a New England country church. They also wanted music in church, a pleasant kind of sermon, and relaxed standards for church membership, and these innovations they successfully obtained when they established the Brattle Street Church in Boston in 1699.

These restless people provided a kind of unity for New England that the religious builders of the Bay Colony could not bring about. The builders had hoped for a unified colony and had achieved only the annexation of New Hampshire and Maine. The independence of both Connecticut and Rhode Island was too well regarded in those colonies for them to want to join forces with Massachusetts. In fact, all of the Puritan colonies during most of the seventeenth century were almost totally independent of England, conducting their own affairs as they pleased. The merchants, however, provided valuable ties of trade that drew the colonies to one another and to the rest of the empire. Often, branches of a family settled in neighboring colonies and arranged for the exchange of products among themselves. For example, the Hutchinsons, Samuel and Edward, of Boston, worked with their brother-in-law, John Sanford, and his relatives in Portsmouth, Rhode Island, and all dealt with relatives in London and Barbados. The Winthrops, too, had ties with Rhode Island, and also with Hartford and New London, Connecticut and with Barbados, Antigua, and London. Their exchanges of news, bargaining for products, and partnership arrangements had a continuing effect upon their attitudes toward the empire. Such people were less provincial in their opinions than were those working with the land, and they valued the outside contacts that trade gave them. By the last part of the century they were able to challenge the old Puritan view of life and move into positions of power in most New England colonies. They had contacts, too, with the plantation colonies in the south. Some branches of New England families chose Virginia or Maryland rather than New England for settlement—not because they were any less Puritan than their New England relatives, but because life in Virginia and Maryland seemed more promising to them, or because they wished to join other relatives or friends in a colony already well established.

Virginia and Maryland

When the Virginia Company relinquished its charter in 1624, the crown assumed the burden of providing governors and other royal officials, Charles I was anxious to rule with a minimum of interference and permitted the local government set up by the company to continue without much change. The successive royal governors who acted for the crown until 1642 left records of solid achievements, sometimes marred by quarrels with the inhabitants, but it was Sir William Berkeley who added luster to the office and is remembered today. His youthful vigor, leadership, and wisdom during his early years as governor (he served about twenty-five years) helped set the colony's direction. All the governors, moreover, worked with a council of eleven members who were the leading settlers of the colony. Together they administered the colony, acted as a superior court, and formed the second house of the legislature.

Government was, therefore, left largely in the hands of the inhabitants. Though the crown encouraged the planting of other staple crops besides tobacco, Charles I did little more through his officials than advise the colonists how best they could take care of themselves. He was uncertain about the legislature, but let it meet regularly by royal sufferance. In 1639 he instructed Governor Francis Wyatt that it should meet annually. The legislature, the House of Burgesses, to its credit, accepted the burdens of government. It levied taxes, provided for the organization of local government by dividing the colony into counties and creating offices, and dealt with the Indian problem. The title to Indian lands was purchased and steps were taken to set up a line of blockhouses from Jamestown to Cheskiack across the peninsula. Under these policies Virginia grew in prosperity and attracted thousands of colonists. In 1641 there were about eight thousand people living in the colony, scattered along the James, York, and Rappahannock rivers. Most of these people lived near the rivers, on relatively small plots of land that was cultivated by themselves and by a few indentured servants. Their wooden houses, one and a half stories tall, were surrounded by gardens and orchards, fields of tobacco and corn, and the ever-present woods. Most settlers developed small herds of cattle, kept some oxen for plowing, and raised poultry. The staple crop, nonetheless, was tobacco and it was grown in larger and larger quantities in spite of English restrictions. Some was sold directly to Dutch traders, but most went to the English market.

In trading, the settlers won a good life for themselves and were able to increase their land holdings by using profits to acquire indentured servants. They added a few black slaves as early as 1619 and continued to purchase them in modest numbers until there were five or six thousand in 1700. The spread of slavery was reflected in the growth of tobacco. Large planters used as many slaves as they could

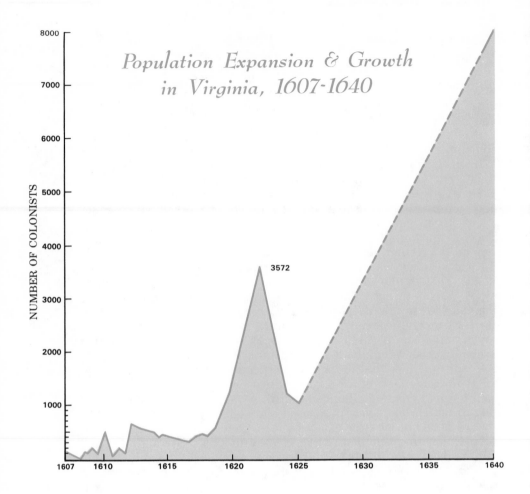

Population Expansion & Growth in Virginia, 1607-1640

NUMBER OF COLONISTS

3572

1607   1610   1615   1620   1625   1630   1635   1640

afford, and extended their fields yearly until tobacco became their largest crop, and the harvest was even greater than the market. It should be noted, however, that the labor force in the seventeenth century was still composed primarily of white Europeans, and estates remained small in cultivated land.

While the settlers constantly bettered their material life, most were also anxious about their spiritual welfare. The established church in Virginia was the Anglican, but it lost much of its structure and power in transit to America. It was not very different from its sister churches in New England and was supported by laws that kept the Sabbath holy, emphasized local control, and stressed a ceremony that made the sermon important in the ritual. Plantation owners were

Bible readers and took their inspiration from its daily reading. If Virginians had lived in towns and supervised each other's conduct, their life in the early seventeenth century would not have been much different in spirit from New England's. The lack of towns undoubtedly made a difference in religious observances, and the isolation of people, except for a few hours on a Sunday morning, relaxed the discipline.

While these people valued their religious freedom, they were Protestants and expected their fellow settlers to have the good sense to worship in the same way. They were naturally aroused when Charles I granted Lord Baltimore the upper Chesapeake Bay as a Catholic refuge. Baltimore was well aware of the possible repercussions and, in his promotional literature, opened the colony to all Britons who could finance their passage and buy land. From the first, in 1639, Protestants apparently arrived in great numbers, and the proprietors had to be ever watchful to enforce toleration.

The settlement of Maryland in the 1630s undoubtedly aided Virginia's development. The new colonists bought supplies of food and stock from farms facing the Chesapeake, and more activity in this area helped to attract shipping and outside merchants. Even though the two colonies disputed boundaries, they grew in a similar pattern and managed to live side by side in harmony.

For both colonies the development of English settlements in the West Indies was important to trade, because it kept the commercial people interested in the empire. St. Kitts was the most populous colony, with its 14,000 people, while Barbados and Nevis had together about 12,000. In these colonies planters cultivated sugar cane in great abundance and used the labor of black slaves often with greater success than that of contract English laborers. By 1660 Barbados had 40,000 slaves cultivating its cane fields, a remarkable change in the labor force since 1640.

That year the 50,000 people in the empire were drawn from England, were mostly white, Protestant, and family-oriented people who were joined in an already prosperous union.

Cromwell and the Restoration

In 1642 the Civil War in England finally broke into military engagements between Charles I and his Puritan enemies. Charles's power rapidly crumbled when the opposition's forces found superior leadership under Oliver Cromwell. The king was imprisoned, and the Puritans, meeting in Parliament, tried to interpret the meaning of the revolution. The predominant faction was Presbyterian, but most Englishmen, especially Cromwell and his army, were not ready to exchange the despotism of a king for that of Parliament under the Presbyterians. Their struggle for power persisted for four years. Then in a second revolution Cromwell purged Parliament and executed the king. His party of independent Protestants soon discovered that they, too, could not agree on national policy, and they relied on Cromwell and his army to keep the peace.

In the meantime, the breakdown of traditional authority had encouraged many groups to arise with their own political, economic, and religious philosophies. Some political theorists were republican; others found the source of political power in land ownership and through the consent of the governed in regular elections. Still others wished to divide up the land, eliminate the aristocracy and established church, and design a new society. In religion, too, a variety of ideas challenged the concepts of both Anglicanism and Puritanism. The radical Quakers, or Society of Friends, rejected a visible church, the usual scriptural interpretations, and the customs of society. They would make all persons equal in the sight of God and would separate church and state. As a rule Cromwell was tolerant of most Protestant belief, but he was harsh toward the Anglicans and Catholics, and his suppression of Irish resistance was singularly brutal.

While his toleration of Protestant idiosyncrasies disturbed many New England Puritans, his governmental policies upset them much more. Cromwell not only unified the British Isles but also interfered in colonial government. New governors were provided for Virginia and the island colonies, and his Parliament declared, in 1650, that "the colonies . . . are and ought to be subordinate to and dependent upon England, and hath ever since the planting thereof been, and ought to be, subject to such laws, orders and regulations as are or shall be made by Parliament of England." To enforce this declaration, he sent the English navy into the West Indies, and at cannon point a few colonies were compelled to submit to his authority. Further, Parliament passed the Navigation Act of 1651, which put the carrying trade into the hands of Englishmen and required that, under certain conditions, products be shipped from English ports. A few years later Cromwell waged war upon Netherlands shipping and conquered Jamaica from Spain.

Cromwell's aggressive policies, however, were resisted in Massachusetts, where the legislature refused to legalize the seizure of Dutch ships, and in Connecticut, where the trade of Dutch New Amsterdam was protected by law. Furthermore, Cromwell and his followers were unable to make their military rule permanent in England. When Cromwell died in 1658, his son proved incapable of taking over his powers, and some generals in his former staff turned instead to the exiled Charles II as a prospective successor.

Negotiations were finally successful in 1660, and England again had a monarchy, but the Restoration was not to solve the problems of the nation. Though Charles II was a pleasant, affable person at first and reduced the tension among political factions, his long rule of twenty-five years became progressively more turbulent. In the last six years he attacked English representative institutions both at home and in the colonies. His successor, James II, fell into serious trouble almost immediately and was exiled in 1689.

The Restoration in 1660 put merchants in powerful positions in the new English government, but Puritans suffered heavy penalties, and a series of laws, known as the Clarendon Code, forced many religious people to seek refuge in the colonies. The alliance of merchant and Puritan clergy was broken in these years, with the merchants becoming republicans and low church Anglicans, often backing limited monarchy and toleration.

Many of the merchants privately accepted the theories of James Harrington and the Earl of Shaftesbury, philosophers who minimized the role of the monarchy as a beneficial force in the creation of the state and accused the king of being a center of corruption in handling money and distributing offices. For Harrington the distribution of land was the primary guarantee of liberty: No man should be permitted to own vast tracts of land, and those who held land should be encouraged to participate in the government. He believed that political power followed economic power and recommended rotation of office, separation of the aristocratic and popular elements of the state, public education, and liberty of conscience as devices to insure stable, popular government. Harrington's ideas, however, were even less obnoxious to the king than Shaftesbury's, who held that government was created by men for their happiness and could be dissolved if it failed to perform that function. He felt that the king lived under the obligations of an implied contract, and the people could break the agreement whenever the king violated its provisions. Upon being threatened with bodily harm, Shaftesbury sought refuge in the Netherlands. His secretary, John Locke, extended and popularized these theories in the English revolution of 1689.

How different these ideas were from Puritanism! They were secular, egalitarian, and utilitarian. Most merchants shared in their spirit, but many were happy to have the monarchy restored and were willing to compromise and wait for an opportunity to reform the government. The king, too, was flexible in his beliefs; he was unwilling at first to risk exile. These radical ideas lingered, were raised occasionally in Parliament, and were often published in books, and only a few people suffered for their audacity.

Commercial Expansion in the Empire

In the meantime, the crown won many friends by favoring commercial activity. It supported merchants who wanted to exploit the fur trade by chartering the Hudson's Bay Company; it chartered the Royal African Company, which permitted merchants to engage in the slave trade; it engaged in two wars against the Netherlands, which destroyed Dutch trade and seized New Netherland. By a series of nav-

igation acts in 1660, 1663, and 1673 the crown reenacted many of
Cromwell's measures and, in addition, sought to make London the
center of empire trade. Most direct trade with northern Europe was
prohibited, and products for America were to be warehoused, handled,
and conveyed by English merchants. In short, English commercial
people won near-monopoly privileges in the empire, and the new laws
were enforced by flocks of custom people who were appointed by a
new supervising agency, the Lords of Trade.

These new laws point up the fact that the empire was becoming
valuable to the homeland. Colonial trade represented about £800,000
in 1660 and rose to £1,750,000 in 1696, accounting also for a larger
part of England's total commerce. The advantages of colonizing still
unsettled areas occurred to promoters, who sought a share of imperial
rewards.

Groups of speculators gained monopoly rights in 1663 to lands
south of Virginia—the Carolinas—and established some colonies there.
They drew people from the Barbados, New England, Virginia, and
France, and in spite of hardships the colonies prospered. The proprietors developed naval store, rice, tobacco, and livestock for export,
but found that the exchange of English products for Indian deerskins
was most profitable.

The Carolinas quickly divided into two colonies, both in government and in their way of life. The North drew its settlers principally
from Virginia, whose indigent population were attracted by the land
and turned to agriculture for their livelihood. For a time some settlers
took advantage of pioneer conditions by engaging in illicit trade. In
the 1680s, the company brought order to the area and granted home rule
in 1691. The South, on the other hand, developed Charleston as a trading port, exported a wide variety of products, brought in slave labor,
and accumulated some wealth. Both colonies shared similar feelings
toward their English promoters; both resisted directives from London
or their governors and petitioned the crown for a royal government.

Promoters also gained trading rights in the Bahamas, New York,
and New Jersey. Many of the same people—the king's brother, the
Duke of York, and Sir George Carteret, and John Berkeley—who were
exploring other parts of the empire were active in these provinces.
New York was given to the Duke of York, the future James II, as a royal
province, and he granted the lands lying between the Hudson and the
Delaware rivers to other proprietors. In turn, they divided New Jersey
into two provinces. East Jersey fell into the hands of Quaker promoters,
while West Jersey was exploited by Quakers, Presbyterians, and Catholics. Both provinces were later united and became a single royal
colony in 1702. In New York the duke lodged all executive power in
his governors until 1682. They encouraged trade, Anglicization of the
Dutch, and the settlement of English. Population multiplied rapidly,
and the economy flourished.

The most ambitious scheme to come out of this association of merchants and aristocrats was the development of Pennsylvania in 1680. The impetus for the colony came from the persecution of Quakers and from their great leader, William Penn. The Quakers, or the Society of Friends, at first drew their major converts from the tradesmen of England, but then reached upward into the middle class and aristocracy. Under the inspiration of George Fox, they attempted to simplify worship, hoping with less biblical emphasis, less dogma, and less external observance to discover God through meditation and prayer. They sought the friendship of all people, recognized a common humanity, and rejected external symbols and observances that would raise persons into the place of God. They refused to take oaths, to remove their hats in court, or to obey laws that regulated religious worship. They preached on the streets, used civil disobedience in obstructing laws, and accepted imprisonment as a reward. In their meeting houses they sat quietly in prayer or listened intently to the words of someone inspired by God.

Their worship attracted William Penn while he was a boy in Ireland and later as a young man in London, where he witnessed their extraordinary efforts to comfort the sick and dying during the plague. In spite of parental objection, he joined the society, preached in the streets, and like many of his co-religionists, suffered imprisonment. As the son of an English admiral and man of wealth, he used his influence at court and decided eventually to secure a refuge for Quakers in America. He first thought of making East Jersey a haven for the oppressed. Then the opportunity of settling Pennsylvania and Delaware reinforced his plans, and he organized a vast land-selling company in the 1680s that would make profits for himself and become a refuge for the Quakers.

In planning his colony, Penn wanted to incorporate into its way of life the advanced political ideas of the Puritan revolution and the religious principles of Quakerism. He gave to the colony, therefore, a written constitution, a legislature, humanitarian laws, and freedom for colonists to settle and worship God as they pleased. His colony offered a haven to the oppressed, liberal government to those tired of European absolutism. In a short time his advertising campaign enticed thousands of settlers to make their homes in the colony, and the discovery of rich land, fine harbors, and a healthful climate attracted still others. Four years after the first settlement the colonists were producing surplus crops.

Change in the Older Empire

While this commercial expansion brought considerable profits to speculators, the new laws and territories changed the relationships of the older empire to England. The most important change for everyone was the centralizing tendency of English administrators. No part of the empire was without some royal official investigating trade, government, loyalty, and customs. In a few colonies, like Barbados and Jamaica, the proprietors lost their rights and royal governments were set up; for others, like Connecticut and Rhode Island, charters were granted. To Massachusetts the Lords of Trade eventually sent agent Edward Randolph, who studied law enforcement and obedience, and as a result of his recommendations the colony lost its independence. By action of the Court of Chancery in 1684 its charter was declared forfeit and, in 1686, the colony became part of the Dominion of New England, which eventually included all the colonies from New Jersey to Maine. Under the same governor-general, Sir Edmund Andros, the colonies were expected to relinquish their independent ways and become part of England's commercial system.

These centralizing measures undoubtedly pleased some local merchants who carried on business in various parts of the empire, but there were many whose enterprises were disrupted by this channeling of trade through England. The sugar isles were severely hurt, and the foreign tobacco trade of Virginia was placed directly in the hands of a few English factors.

Virginia

Virginia protested the navigation laws through her governor, Sir William Berkeley, who described the poverty that these measures were bringing upon the colony. He took her grievances to the highest levels of the English government, but completely failed to win relief.

The navigation laws were, however, only one part of Virginia's problem. Her settlers were growing too much tobacco for both the English and foreign markets, and marginal producers were feeling a price pinch that was causing desperation. Especially was this true among smaller farmers whose market was taken over by larger plantation growers. Many farmers sold their lands and moved to the frontier; others lingered for a time and suffered still more. Most accused the government of favoring the large planter, and the governor of ruling through a clique of these tidewater planters. They also complained of high taxes, restrictive frontier policies, and, always, of tobacco prices. They were further embittered by a hurricane that destroyed most unharvested tobacco in 1667 and by the third Dutch War, which partially disrupted trade from 1672 to 1674. For all these desperate events, both natural and unnatural, the governor received chief blame.

Those farmers who for relief moved into the exposed frontier took over Indian hunting grounds and thus applied pressure upon the Indians, already made restless by the expansion of Virginia and Maryland. Other settlers aggravated these feelings by engaging in sharp trade with the Indians. Abraham Wood and William Byrd I ventured deep into the back country, peddling through their agents rum, textiles, and firearms. Their arming of Indians had immediate repercussions in the Carolinas, but tribes everywhere along the frontier also fought each other over hunting grounds. Pressure from the coast and frontier upon tribes like the Susquehannas and Doegs brought bitterness and, in 1674, open warfare between them and the colonists. Their raids in 1675 and 1676 swept down the James River and challenged the security of even the older settled sections of Virginia.

In this crisis, frontiersmen put themselves under the leadership of Nathaniel Bacon, a newly arrived aristocrat who had settled in an exposed location, and they and Bacon waged war against the Indians in defiance of the established government. Governor Berkeley pled for moderation, and promised forts; Bacon rejected these overtures and led his men against Indians irrespective of whether they were friendly or hostile. Through this crisis of authority Governor Berkeley fussed and fumed, declared Bacon a rebel, promised to hang him and his followers, and sent the militia out after him. When the House of Burgesses met in June 1676, Bacon journeyed to Jamestown as a member of the Assembly, hoping to place the grievances of the frontiersmen before it. In spite of an armed guard, he was arrested and imprisoned. However, public sympathy was sufficiently great that an apology brought his release. In a few days Bacon again challenged the governor, this time by bringing a hundred troops to the capital. The show of force compelled Berkeley to do his wishes and permit attacks on the Indians. His example of boldness aroused also the legislature, and reformers struck at the governor's power—his use of plural officeholding, his concentration of authority, and his dominance of local affairs. It provided for an enlarged franchise and elections in some local offices.

Soon after the legislature disbanded, Berkeley again declared Bacon a rebel, but the new confrontation forced the governor to flee. At the height of his power Bacon left for the frontier and met the enemy. While he was maneuvering, he was taken seriously ill and died before another leader could take his place. His followers immediately dropped the resistance, and the governor now moved to punish the rebels. In a short time he had hanged thirteen of them.

News of these disturbances had been reported to Charles II who dispatched a fleet and troops to suppress the rebellion and relieve Berkeley. But the governor did not leave until he had punished the rebels and forced the legislature to amend or revoke many of the reform laws.

Debate over the significance of Bacon's rebellion continues to this day. Certainly, for the next decade or two it left much bitterness among all Virginia classes. Berkeley's successors were not able to solve the tobacco market problem and give the colony contentment and prosperity. The home government tightened its control over local affairs. It separated the judicial power from the legislative, putting the appeal process and judicial appointments in the governor's hands, and it provided a permanent revenue for the governor's salary. Thus, it gave the governor much independence in his relations with the House of Burgesses. Though the legislature protested these restrictions, English authority was unshakable.

Discontent persisted among all classes, and many leading planters felt discouraged by Virginian life. They longed for educational advantages for their children, intellectual and urban life for themselves, and comforts of wealth and position. A letter from William Fitzhugh in January 1687 states the feelings of many planters:

> Good education of children is almost impossible and better be never born than ill-bred. But that which bears the greatest weight with me, for now I look upon myself to be in my declining age, is the want of spiritual helps and comforts, of which this fertile country in everything else, is barren and unfruitful.

In spite of this gloomy statement, Virginia was attractive to many English people. In the 1650s the first member of the Washington family arrived there; John married, increased his lands, prospered, and left a modest inheritance for his three children at his death in 1677. His eldest son, Lawrence, who was schooled in England, returned to marry and live in the colony. Lawrence's efforts as a farmer were well rewarded with good estates and money enough to permit him and his wife to travel to England. The first Thomas Jefferson also came to Virginia during these turbulent times. He moved up the James River, not far from present-day Richmond, and became a farmer, hunter of wolves, and surveyor. By his death in 1697, the same year as Lawrence Washington's, he had been married well, had fathered two children, and possessed a few slaves. Any number of persons, like William Fitzhugh (whose opinion was quoted above), arrived in the 1670s and 1680s and achieved success, gaining those "trappings and symbols of gentility" that raised them from their former modest state in English life to one of means in Virginia. By the end of the century Virginia's population had reached sixty thousand, a significant increase over that of 1670.

Both Virginia's larger population and the Restoration in England helped change the outlook of most of her settlers. Their Puritan ancestry was nearly forgotten as they struggled for land and place in the new society. Though they honored their religious obligations by attendance at the church, they were Anglicans. The church was losing its Puritan practices toward the close of the century and permitted horse races, cockfighting, dancing, and many other frivolities. The ambitions of Virginians became secularized, too, as they imitated English gentry, taking pride in their families, country seats, and offices; they studied the art of conversation and of genteel conduct. Some sent their sons to England for education, often to the Inns of Court or the universities, but always for years of experience in the sophistication of the older culture. Others gathered around them in Virginia books and furnishings that would remind them of England and of their social responsibilities. Books on statecraft, history, religion, gardening, hunting, and fishing had a utilitarian purpose, but they were there, too, to preserve civilization and maintain the traditions of England. Virginians were becoming less interested in creating something new in America than in transporting the culture they admired from home.

New England

The change in Virginia was more dramatic than it was in New England, where Puritanism lingered through the century. The first settlers left firm foundations, in their creation of towns and churches, their establishment of representative government, and their provision for an educated society. For the first two decades of settlement John Winthrop, John Cotton, Thomas Dudley, and a host of lesser men guided the destiny of Massachusetts Bay by laying down rules of worship and citizenship. In the towns, ministers often served for decades as principal figures in molding the lives of their fellow settlers, and they, with a group of deacons, enforced a test of faith upon all prospective church members. In qualifying for church membership a man then secured the right to vote and an opportunity to serve in government.

These founders did not arrive in New England with a fully developed concept of church discipline. It grew over the decade or two after 1629 and was always subject to reinterpretation. Congregational control, furthermore, deprived the churches of a provincial organization, and, except during a general crisis, ministers and their deacons solved their local problems in their own way. They were always faced with the problem of purity in selecting members and in maintaining discipline, and sometimes in trying to be pure they raised complex doctrinal problems that deeply separated their congregations.

Over the years more people failed to qualify for church membership and more people refused to seek it than were members of the church. Membership, in short, was confined to a very small part of the population in spite of a legal obligation that required the inhabitants to attend church. The exclusive nature of church membership was a constant embarrassment, and it was regularly debated by purists. Could the church ever be a society separate from the world, or must it live with impure and worldly influences?

Puritans slowly recognized that they could not indeed create a new, other-worldly society. Some clergymen, like Solomon Stoddard of Northampton in the 1680s, opened their churches to the whole town and introduced revivalism in an effort to awaken religious feelings. In time, the clergy emphasized purity of religious practice less than purity in preaching good Calvinist doctrine, and even here some

The Allyn House; Plymouth, Massachusetts. *(Library of Congress)*

clergy argued about principles. Especially were they concerned when an Anglican Church was established in Boston and Quakers were allowed to worship; their spirit of toleration was severely tested.

The most distracting changes in New England life were those arising from the activities of the merchant class. Their concentration upon wealth-getting made them particularly suspect, but their speculations on trade, pricing of goods, and dealing with money and credit aroused actual hostility. These people, nonetheless, broke through the opposition, gained colonial offices, sent their sons to Harvard College, and acted as a group to apply pressure upon the clergy and the older leaders. They encouraged their sons to seek careers in business and government instead of entering the ministry, and, as did many Virginia fathers, thought of marriage alliances for their children, luxuries, and personal power.

In the last quarter of the century the first members of the Belcher and Pepperrell families arrived in New England. Their small beginnings in trade grew into fortunes in the next century, and their connections with older settlers created political factions of power and prestige. Son Jonathan Belcher was the first of the family to attend Harvard, and he finished his formal education with a trip to England

and the Continent. Most of his mature life was spent in government service, climaxed by terms as governor of Massachusetts and New Jersey. Young William Pepperrell went directly into his father's business and emerged a wealthy man in later life, when he gave his last thirty years to politics. His achievements unlike Belcher's, were distinguished by the crown, in 1745, when he was commissioned colonel of a British regiment and made baronet.

Both merchants' interests were primarily political, while those of their contemporary Cotton Mather were religious and scientific. Mather, descended form the old leadershp of the colony, was fascinated by medicine and became in later life an amateur doctor. His interest in curing disease raised serious questions for the clergy about man's right to interfere with the world of God. Disease was apparently part of God's punishment of men. If man cured illnesses, was he not subverting the divine plan? But Mather and others, in answering "no" to the question, were discovering a natural order, in which the blood circulated through the body, the earth rotated, and diseases were caused by living organisms. They read of scientists speculating about overpopulation, the source of knowledge, and the content of space. To discuss such wonders, Cotton Mather organized a philosophic society and sent off some scientific papers to the Royal Society in London.

This discovery of the world about them enriched New Englanders and pushed Puritanism into the background. Their relations with England were forcing them to deal more realistically with political problems also. Both Connecticut and Rhode Island conferred directly with Charles II and secured confirmation of their charters. Connecticut's governor, John Winthrop, Jr., was a wise and gracious person, interested in science and people, and knew how to work with courtiers. His success was proved by a charter that unified Connecticut as well as granted her home rule. As the years passed, her independent attitude toward England aroused opposition in London and lead in 1686 to the loss of the charter.

In Massachusetts, likewise, local governmental practices irritated England. Charles II became increasingly suspicious of the colony, demanded rights for the Anglican Church, and wanted a copy of the colony's laws. He sent finally a royal commission to hold an inquiry into the enforcement of English trade laws. The confrontation was between unequals, and intelligent Massachusetts leaders tried to ward off punishment, but hard-headed clerics like Increase Mather pressed the opposition. In the end the Lords of Trade dispatched Edward Randolph, who conducted a thorough inquiry into the whole of Massachusetts life. He found trials conducted without proper procedures, men executed without legal basis, trade laws generally violated, and the oath of allegiance to the king not required. His report certainly was no surprise to anyone and the king's ministers moved against the colony. The charter was revoked and the colony became part of the Dominion of New England.

In the meantime, the Massachusetts people had undergone a deeply upsetting experience. Even as their charter was being threatened by England, their security was shaken by a fierce Indian disturbance, the first such attack since the colony's founding. Tensions between Indians and whites had been building up for years because of the encroachment of the English population upon Indian hunting grounds. Attacks had been prevented by missionary endeavors and by the settlement of some Indians as farmers. But the laws that regulated Indian affairs were severe, and the penalties, pent-up grievances, and emotional bitterness finally brought on a war.

Under the leadership of King Philip, the Wampanoags resisted in 1675, and the disturbance soon spread to neighboring tribes like the Narragansetts. For over a year the New England militia was out maneuvered and drawn into the swamps, until the Indians in late 1676 lost their food supplies and starvation forced them to sue for peace. By that time Philip had been shot by a hostile Indian, hundreds of his men were dead, and even more devastation had been suffered by his white enemies. There followed for another year or two white revenge in which Indians were executed or pressed into slavery.

The most bitter revenge, however, came from Charles II, when his Court of Chancery revoked the charter and the king made the colony part of the Dominion of New England. Massachusetts could take comfort in her misery when Connecticut and Rhode Island also lost their charters.

Happily for Massachusetts, her resistance occurred during a rising crisis in England. The aged king had become dictatorial, suppressed Parliament, annulled municipal charters, and murdered or exiled his opposition. As the crisis mounted, Charles died and was succeeded by his brother, James II. The new king, lacking his brother's flexibility, alienated most of his friends. In less than four years he lost the support of churchmen, nobility, and country people—the usual mainstays of monarchy. James fled to France. His enemies then asked William and Mary of the Netherlands, his son-in-law and daughter, to rule in his place and convened Parliament in order to legislate the "Glorious" Revolution into law.

During the Revolution, most of the colonies had overthrown James' governors and hoped now for a change of policies. No colony was more expectant than Massachusetts, who wanted a return of her charter and freedom to go her own way.

The Revolution of 1689

The Revolution of 1689 is a logical breaking point in history. The colonies to this year had accomplished much. They stretched as

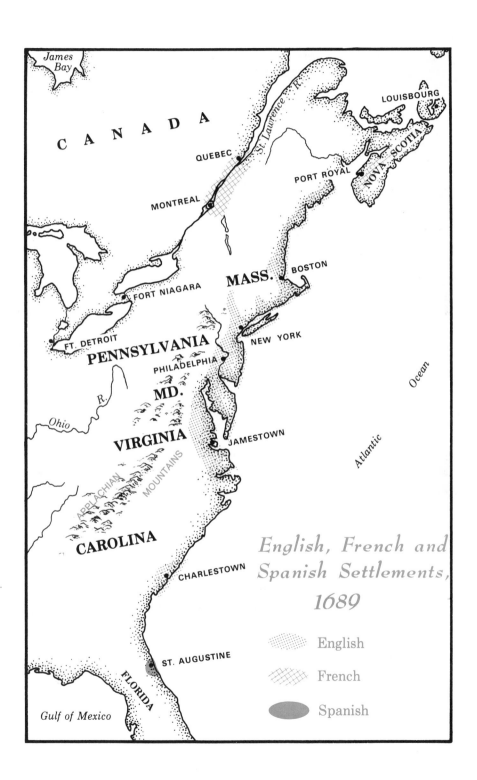

James Bay

C A N A D A

QUEBEC

St. Lawrence R.

LOUISBOURG

NOVA SCOTIA

PORT ROYAL

MONTREAL

FORT NIAGARA

MASS.

BOSTON

FT. DETROIT

PENNSYLVANIA

NEW YORK

PHILADELPHIA

MD.

Ohio R.

VIRGINIA

JAMESTOWN

Atlantic

Ocean

APPALACHIAN MOUNTAINS

CAROLINA

CHARLESTOWN

English, French and
Spanish Settlements,
1689

ST. AUGUSTINE

FLORIDA

Gulf of Mexico

English

French

Spanish

a thin line of settlement from Maine to the Carolinas. About two hundred thousand inhabitants formed an American society that was primarily agricultural, with fishing, trading, and trapping as secondary pursuits. Since most people lived on the land, they worked long hours in the fields, often in isolation from neighbors, and remained close to their homes and families. The New England towns provided some community life, but even there men were busy out-of-doors or at the hearth. Elsewhere clusters of homes, crossroads meetings, and gatherings at church gave minimum opportunities for social life. Only in Boston and New York was there available a rustic type of town life.

Nevertheless, isolation had its rewards and compensations. Food was plentiful in most settled areas. The variety, depending upon the season, was better than in England. Grains, meats, fish, fruits, and greens were regularly upon the table. Disease was undoubtedly less serious than in Europe. The scattered population, improved diet, and hearty living were reflected in the birth rate that doubled the population nearly every twenty years. The promise of life—marriage, children, the accumulation of wealth—rivaled that of the homeland.

SUGGESTIONS FOR FURTHER READING

Andrews, Charles M., *The Colonial Period of American History: The Settlements*, 4 vols. New Haven, Conn., Yale University Press, 1934-1938.

Bailyn, Bernard, *New England Merchants in the Seventeenth Century*. New York, Harper Torchbooks, Harper & Row, 1965.

Beverly, Robert, *The History and Present State of Virginia*. Ed. David F. Hawke. Indianapolis and New York: Bobbs-Merrill Company, Inc., 1971.

Bridenbaugh, Carl, *Vexed and Troubled Englishmen, 1590-1642*. New York, Oxford University Press, paperbound, 1976.

Crane, Verner W., *The Southern Frontier, 1670-1732*. Ann Arbor, Michigan, Ann Arbor Paperbacks, University of Michigan Press, 1965.

Haller, William, *The Rise of Puritanism*. New York, Harper Torchbooks, Harper & Row, 1957.

Jordan, Winthrop D., *White over Black: American Attitudes Toward the Negro, 1550-1812*. Baltimore, Pelican Books, Penguin Books, Inc., 1969.

Langdon, George D., Jr., *Pilgrim Colony: A History of New Plymouth, 1620-1691*. New Haven, Conn., Yale Publications in American Studies, Yale University Press, 1966.

McGiffert, Michael, ed., *Puritanism and the American Experience*. Reading, Mass., Addison-Wesley Publishing Co., 1969.

Miller, Perry, *Orthodoxy in Massachusetts, 1630-1650.* Boston, Beacon Press, 1959.

_____, *Roger Williams: His Contributions to the American Tradition.* New York, Atheneum Publishers, 1962.

Morgan, Edmund S., *American Slavery American Freedom: The Ordeal of Colonial Virginia.* New York, W. W. Norton, Inc., 1976.

_____, *The Puritan Dilemma: The Story of John Winthrop.* Boston, Little, Brown and Company, 1958.

Morison, Samuel Eliot, *Builders of the Bay Colony.* Boston, Sentry Editions, Houghton Mifflin Company, 1964.

Peare, Catherine Owens, *William Penn.* Ann Arbor, Michigan, Ann Arbor Paperbacks, University of Michigan Press, 1968.

Pomfret, John E., *Founding the American Colonies, 1583-1660.* New York, Harper Torchbooks, Harper and Row, 1970.

Powell, Sumner Chilton, *Puritan Village: The Foundation of a New England Town.* Garden City, New York, Anchor Books, Doubleday & Company, 1965.

Ritchie, Robert C., *The Duke's Province, A Study of Politics and Society, 1664-1691.* Chapel Hill, N.C., University of North Carolina Press, 1977.

Simpson, Alan, *Puritanism in Old and New England.* Chicago, Phoenix Books, University of Chicago Press, 1955.

Smith, James Morton, ed., *Seventeenth Century America: Essays in Colonial History.* New York, W. W. Norton, Inc., 1959.

Vaughan, Alden T., *New England Frontier: Puritans and Indians.* Boston, Little, Brown and Company, 1965.

Washburn, Wilcomb E., *Governor and the Rebel: A History of Bacon's Rebellion in Virginia.* Chapel Hill, N.C., University of North Carolina Press, 1957.

Wright, Louis B., *The Cultural Life of the American Colonies, 1607-1763.* New York, Harper Torchbooks, Harper & Row, 1962.

3

Expansion and Empire

THE VITAL INTERESTS OF THE GREAT EMPIRES clashed in-
termittently in a series of wars from 1689 to 1763. Battles for Quebec,
the Mississippi Valley, Florida, and the West Indies were part of a
world struggle that touched also Europe, Africa, and India. The Treaty
of Utrecht in 1713 and the Treaty of Aix-la-Chapelle in 1748 attempted
to settle imperial issues, but the rewards of trade were too enticing for
any permanent settlement. In 1713, Britain won Nova Scotia, Newfoundland, Gibraltar, Minorca, and the privilege of sending one
trading vessel and thousands of slaves annually to Spanish America.
She agreed in turn to the enthronement of French princes in Spain.
The Treaty of Paris of 1763 climaxed these imperialist wars, giving
Britain an empire in size and wealth that rivaled the empire of ancient
Rome.

For Britain these wars also settled the issue of succession to her
own throne and marked, especially between 1689 and 1701, a political
revolution in which Parliament passed great constitutional measures.
The coming to power of merchants and landed aristocrats set the philosophical and political tone of British and American life for the eighteenth century.

The Revolution of 1689

The Glorious Revolution institutionalized ideas that were attractive to Americans. They welcomed the new authority of Parliament, with laws for regular elections, control over the military, and power over the administration of government. But they also welcomed William and Mary, the Protestant leaders of the Revolution, to the throne and expected them to be sympathetic toward Congregationalism and other religious dissent from Anglicanism. Though Americans favored the English Bill of Rights and Act of Toleration, these measures were undoubtedly more advanced than colonial practice.

Even for England the Revolution held greater promise than Parliament or public opinion was willing to accept. William and Mary agreed to rule with Parliament, accepting the theory that the legislature was the fountainhead of law and liberty. But both the monarchs and Parliament believed that the franchise should be held by wealthy landowners and merchants, titled and untitled aristocrats, and some members of the county gentry, military, and clergy. The spirit of the age was aristocratic, and land ownership conferred rights, ennobled the owner, and symbolized purity of political aspirations. While Parliament generally reflected English wishes in its legislation, it did not directly represent most individuals. Too often it followed class interests, so that the Revolution of 1689 became a victory of great merchants and landholders who used certain revolutionary theories to consolidate their own political power.

Legislation in the 1690s reflected the aspirations of these political groups. In addition to the Bill of Rights and the Act of Toleration, laws were passed that established the Bank of England, rechartered the East India Company, and set up the Board of Trade to supervise colonial affairs. The Navigation Act of 1696, which created the Board, also tightened imperial trade regulations by erecting vice-admiralty courts and a custom organization. (Unlike other colonial institutions these offices were directly under English control.) Other laws were designed to suppress piracy and open the slave trade to additional Englishmen. These leaders of Parliament, however, were not interested in social or political legislation that would mold colonial life, in the manner of dictating religious worship, imposing censorship, or taking over internal control of American politics.

New England

The spirit of 1689 as it pervaded Massachusetts took the form of a royal charter and governor. With the franchise extended to landowners and toleration of Protestants assured by the charter, the center of politics was in the legislature. The new House of Representatives quarreled with Governor William Phips over boundaries of authority, and the crown finally had to intervene by recalling Phips to England.

New England Mercantile Life
(New England Historical and Geneological Society)

His successors developed working relations with the legislature and, except for a governor or two, lubricated the legislative process by distributing offices and military contracts and intervening with British authorities for favors. But they received little support from London and gave way to legislative pressure in such matters as the right to debate, vote taxes, and choose officers. These privileges grew in importance as the colony matured and developed leadership to handle its problems. Wealthy merchants like the Wendells and Hutchinsons offered their time and talents, serving often in a disinterested manner as popular servants. In Connecticut, Rhode Island, and New Hampshire assemblies also stood ready to act in the public interest, reflecting the desire of New Englanders to make their legislatures truly popular bodies. By mid-century, Massachusetts towns occasionally sent instructions to their representatives and, from time to time, punished them for opposing the towns' known positions.

These powerful legislatures and town meetings mirrored a vigorous standard of living. While agriculture was productive in Connecticut, and less so in the other northern colonies, interest in farm and timber land was always paramount. Companies developed tracts in Maine and western Massachusetts and colonized the areas with thousands of people. More might have gone had the menace of Indians

An Old English Spinning Wheel Used in Colonial Households.
(Library of Congress)

been less serious, but land was bought and sold, leased to sharecroppers, and held for speculation. While land on the whole was well distributed, probably a fourth of the population owned no land, and a few wealthy men like Jonathan Belcher amassed vast acreage. Belcher, in particular, used his wealth for personal power, rising to the position of governor in 1730 and scheming to put his son into the English Parliament.

Greater than the profits of land were those from the sea. From Piscataqua to New Haven, and from the other ports between them, vessels distributed their varied cargoes. Boston, as the hub of the region, cleared hundreds of ships annually. Its Long Wharf, extending a mile into the harbor, rivaled many shorter ones combined. Its ships went north to the fishing banks of Newfoundland, along the Maine coast for timber, south to New Jersey, Pennsylvania, and Maryland for food, and farther south for trade, molasses, and foreign products. Boston seamen traveled east to British ports, to the continent of Europe, and into the Mediterranean for cargoes.

As Boston grew in size and wealth, merchants built luxurious homes in the city and country mansions at Roxbury and Milton. Fine pieces of furniture, silver serving dishes, pottery, and family portraits added a touch of old England to their living rooms. Good Madeira wines, cheeses, olives, and citrus fruits gave variety to the diet, and the works of Addison, Steele, Swift, Pope, Richardson, and the Roman and Greek classics provided leisure time reading. Clubs inspired political discussions, and weekly lectures in church reflected these interests. The people laboring in the shops and warehouses had opportunity to read the Boston *Weekly News-Letter*, the *Evening Post*, and the *Gazette*, or, better, to exchange news at the taverns, which were forums of public business. The turn toward secular pursuits in Boston attracted lawyers, medical doctors, and, occasionally, portrait painters and musicians. Secular pursuits affected too the plans of young men going to Harvard College. Though the curriculum changed imperceptibly over the years, the graduate body did. Many men found careers in government, in law, medicine, and business, and fewer stayed in the clergy.

Time and fortune had allowed New Englanders to develop the tradition of large families. Population, therefore, increased dramatically decade on decade until the region had in 1750 about 600,000 people. The doubling of population every twenty-three years increased the pressures on living space. Benjamin Franklin speculated on its effect, and John Adams, as a young Massachusetts teacher, predicted that population growth would one day force Britain to move the center of the empire to America. Settlers were already taking up lands in New Hampshire and Maine, and this hunger for land was reflected in the opinions of their leaders, who wished to oust France from Canada and establish British colonies even to the Mississippi.

As New Englanders became aware of their world, they examined the defenses of the fishing banks, worried about the French post of Louisbourg on Cape Breton Island, and in 1745 arose in great emotion, while England and France were engaged in European battles, to seize the fortress. Their success brought visions of Canadian conquest, but Britain, who had at first agreed to provide naval support, was too occupied in Europe for that ambitious undertaking. At the close of the war in 1748, Britain returned the fortress to France and agreed, much to the disgust of New England, to plan a permanent boundary line between the empires.

Complicating any discussion, however, were the Iroquois nations, who managed to keep their independence. Their trade and friendship were important to both powers, and New England, recognizing this fact, sent delegations regularly to Albany to join New York in holding conferences with the Iroquois.

New York

While New England and New York were associated in exploiting Indian trade, New York City rivaled Boston in this commerce, and farmers of Massachusetts and New York living near the Hudson River disputed the colonial boundary.

Merchants like James and Oliver De Lancey of New York had created a political and economic empire by means of their strategic location in the city. Using the Hudson River as a highway into the interior, they sent cargoes to Albany. In that frontier town they had warehouses that held supplies for the rich trade with Oswego on Lake Ontario and that stored annually about £45,000 worth of furs for export to England. Safety of this trade was vital to all suppliers of merchandise, but there was a difference of opinion concerning its defense. Many merchants advocated peace with Canada, exploiting trade with the Iroquois, and speculating in land. Others like William Johnson, an Irishman with powerful English connections, who had settled near Albany, advocated fair dealing with the Iroquois and an extension of British authority over the Indians. Johnson emerged between the Indian conferences of 1748 and 1754 as the spokesman for British control of Indian affairs, with regulation of trade and movement of people as major objectives of the new policy. In 1756 he became the British superintendent of Indian affairs, a new position that recognized the importance of the Iroquois to frontier peace.

Political life in New York was more turbulent than in Massachusetts. Critics noted that leaders sacrificed orderly government while struggling over taxation, budgets, and appointments and that controversy was frequently valued over good policy. These antagonisms reflect the many peculiarities of New York life of the time. The land system concentrated vast holdings in a few hands, with tenants paying rent in products and labor. Tenants and small farmers came under the influence of the land barons, who, in turn, joined with other large landholders in business and marriage alliances. Perhaps twenty families held the economic and political power of the colony. These interconnections, however, did not necessarily mean that families associated together in politics. In fact, religious, economic, and ethnic considerations divided families so that the colony was eventually split between two factions, the Livingstons and De Lanceys. For power, these fighting families often sacrificed trade, defense, and principle, and outsiders shifted between factions to suit their personal interests. The most bitter dispute, over the founding of King's College in 1754, raised the specter of a powerful Anglican Church, and the Presbyterians fought to loosen the connection. Involved also were James De Lancey's political aspirations as acting governor of New York, and economic favors he wished for his family.

The success of patronage politics, however, should not be allowed to obscure gains made in representative government. The franchise was extended to all males who wanted the right, and nearly half of them cast their ballots in city elections. Offices were open to anyone who dared challenge the established order, and social climbing in the colony was as easy as in Massachusetts. James De Lancey's career was an example for others. The son of an immigrant, he had moved quickly in politics to be chief justice, lieutenant governor, and acting governor, and through business associations with relatives to amass wealth that made his family the most powerful in the colony.

For De Lancey, New York City provided opportunity and a pleasant place to live. Growing in sophistication, with newspapers, presses, a theater, and shops in which a wide assortment of goods was regularly available, New York was also expanding in population (eighteen thousand in 1760) and developing the appearance of a prosperous, well-kept city. A naval officer expressed in 1756 his astonishment at what he saw.

> I had no idea of finding a place in America, consisting of near two thousand houses, elegantly built of brick, raised on an eminence and the streets paved and spacious, furnished with commodious keys and warehouses, and employing some hundreds of vessels in its foreign trade and fisheries—but such is this city that very few in England can rival it in its show.

New York's prosperity, however, was peculiarly dependent upon her neighbors. Her close relations with Massachusetts ranged from cooperation at Indian conferences to financial and educational agreements among her merchants. Close, also, were her relations with New Jersey and Pennsylvania, whose politicians and merchants had common interests with her. Their economies seemed united as merchants bargained for products and associated in overseas colonies, and sons of Philadelphia and New York merchants were often enrolled at the College of New Jersey at Princeton.

Pennsylvania

Pennsylvania developed rapidly after 1689. Its Quaker founders enacted favorable political and economic legislation, and in 1701 William Penn gave the colony a "Charter of Privileges" that provided for religious toleration, an elected assembly, and direct election of sheriffs and coroners. The unicameral assembly, endowed with vast powers by the charter, held a privileged position because it was unencumbered by the check of a council. Over the years the assembly came to consider itself a parliament, and its members gave the governors and proprietors many unhappy disputes in developing policy.

These antagonisms were caused partly by the Quaker dominance of the assembly and partly by the assembly's relations with the proprietors, Penn's sons. From the beginning, the colony had drawn as immigrants all sorts of people, including Germans, Scotch-Irish, French, and Dutch, and had tolerated their politics and religion. The expanding population, from 20,000 in 1701 to near 200,000 in 1755, saw the

Quakers submerged into the minority as Germans and Scotch-Irish came to make up two-thirds of the population. The Quakers, however, retained their control over the assembly because of their affluence, their religious kinship with the Germans, and their opposition to extension of representation. The Quaker faction, or "gentleman's party," held majority power in the assembly until the 1760s. The faction resisted appropriations for frontier defense and, as a matter of religious principle, urged settler and Indian to compromise their differences. The vast number of Scotch-Irish, living on the frontier, were aroused by this callous disregard for defense, the denial of proper representation, and the doctrinal Quaker attitude. Founding the "popular" or "country" party, they insisted upon changes in the franchise and policies to give them security. Both groups occasionally joined in opposition to the proprietors, who appointed the governor, controlled large landed areas, and interfered with "legislative independence." When frontier defense became a critical issue in 1756, some Quakers resigned their seats in the assembly in order to have other colonials not bound by religious scruples vote funds for fortifications and garrisons. With tension thus reduced, the factions then waged an attack upon the proprietors, asking the home government for a royal charter. Benjamin Franklin was largely responsible for directing these attacks and gained great prominence.

In spite of recurring bitterness among politicians, Pennsylvania was generally peaceful, allowing the people to turn their thoughts to a spectrum of cultural pursuits. Men like Franklin were interested in electricity, like John Bartram and James Logan in botany, and like David Rittenhouse in astronomy and mathematics. The people supported the creation of the College of Philadelphia, a hospital, a circulating library, and a philosophical society, and scholarly lecturers regularly brought their findings to the public—sometimes before overcrowded audiences. Philosophers discoursed on a variety of topics, such as the origin and purpose of government, the nature of God, and the future of the colonies. In religion colonists could worship with little interference, and Jews and Catholics, along with independent Protestants, held public services. The moral code was less a concern of government than in Massachusetts, but the churches in their congregations exercised much control.

The secular atmosphere of Philadelphia is symbolized by no other person as well as by Benjamin Franklin, who came to the city from Boston as a youth. Poor, lacking friends, and in need of employment, he took advantage of his good sense and opportunities to make his way. As a writer, journalist, debater, and inventor, he speculated on a wide number of subjects and exploited his skills as a printer to publish his own essays. He made a fortune from job lot printing, from his almanacs, and from a miscellany of positions as official printer, postmaster, and newspaper publisher. In his leisure time he invented, studied, and experimented, letting his mind dwell on the issues that troubled the colony, America, and the empire. On retiring from business he entered politics and after establishing a political base, represented Pennsylvania, as well as other colonies, in London.

Franklin's early success was due primarily to his residence in growing, prosperous Philadelphia. The largest city in the colonies, with a population of 20,000, it offered more in amusement, variety of economic activity, and luxury than did the other American towns. Its great port, from which more ships cleared than from Boston, sent off iron ore, food stables, furs, and some manufactures, and imported, in addition to the usual supplementary food products, a wide range of luxuries like fine furniture, coaches, and household wares.

The city benefited also by the flow of immigrants who set out for the back country, and by enlarged trade with the country villages. Lancaster, founded in 1730, was followed by other frontier towns like Carlisle, York, and Easton. From Philadelphia these communities drew merchants who organized businesses and arranged credit for other pioneers. Their wagons made regular trips from the city and transported the large quantities of foodstuffs grown on the farms. This back country expansion made Philadelphia the center of an empire, in about the same way as Boston was the market center of Massachusetts, New Hampshire, and Maine. Her merchants were deeply concerned about the safety of this country trade and appreciated the precautions of the British military authorities in quartering soldiers along the frontier. Merchant anxiety was undoubtedly behind the Quaker move to a compromise position on defense, in favor of forts and garrisons.

Virginia

The Revolution of 1689 had little effect upon Virginia's development. The new monarchs chose Francis Nicholson as governor, and he served, except for a brief interruption, until 1705. During these years the town of Williamsburg was planned as the capital and seat of a new college, William and Mary. The founders hoped to create a cultural and political center for this agricultural commonwealth.

The town grew into a delightful, tree-shaded village, with a few thousand residents during the height of the social and political season. With a theater, horse racing, taverns, and the official residences of governor and legislative officers, it enjoyed a grandeur in its rural setting that was often lacking in other American towns. The college, with its building by Sir Christopher Wren, offered colony boys the opportunity of a local education, saving them from the hazards of an ocean voyage to Oxford or Cambridge universities, and provided the experience of being near the seat of Virginia's government.

Young men like Thomas Jefferson, who were tutored for college at home and then enrolled at William and Mary for advanced instruction, studied the classics, languages, logic, and oratory and joined relatives in the pleasures of the capital during its social and political season. Their residence in Williamsburg prepared most men for years of public service in the legislature, the courts of law, and local administration. By observing at work the House of Burgesses (which often included their uncles, cousins, or brothers), they became acquainted with the men who would soon be their associates. Many met during the social season their future wives, whose fathers might be, like theirs, involved in colonial affairs. For Jefferson, graduation from college was preliminary to the study of law and to other experiences; he moved in the company of a polished governor and erudite lawyers, and participated, perhaps more profoundly than others, in the discussions of literature, philosophy, and history that occurred daily in the capital.

In Virginia, as in most royal colonies, the king appointed the governor and the upper house of the legislature. The actual administration in Virginia was usually conducted by the lieutenant governor, whose talent and energy assured the colony of sensible and stable rule as he worked with members of the powerful House of Burgesses. These legislators, elected by the landholders, were often the most influential men of their counties. Over the century they served continually in office as a group, but actual control of the Burgesses fell into the hands of a relatively few individuals. Though they governed firmly, they were intelligent enough to admit new men occasionally to their circle and to encourage debate. At early ages Thomas Jefferson, Patrick Henry, and George Washington were elected to office and were drawn to the leadership of men like John Robinson or Peyton Randolph, who held the speakership from 1738 to 1775.

Most of these burgesses lived far from Williamsburg and depended upon letters and issues of the *Virginia Gazette* for their news. Some built libraries, and all relied upon the reports of travelers and meetings with neighbors to supplement regular sources of information. Conversations after sunday service were also a way of keeping informed. Church service at a crossroads chapel brought Anglican minister and congregation to worship; then there followed hours of conversation filled with politics, family matters, crop conditions, reports of runaway slaves, and anything else that seemed currently interesting. Even business was transacted, and issues of local government were settled by holding justice court or a meeting of the church vestry.

These rural conditions had an influence upon religious fervor. Most people were Anglicans, providing a minister and church were available. Otherwise, they attended other Protestant service—Presbyterian, Baptist, or Lutheran—or simply read passages from the Bible. Doctrinal positions for most people were accepted with moderation, and a spirit of toleration among Protestants pervaded society.

Tidewater Virginia

After 1730, Virginia life was divided generally into three types. The tidewater area grew into a plantation society, with the tobacco economy dominating life in the area. Plantations steadily increased in size until estates of fifty to sixty thousand acres were common, and work forces numbered fifty to one hundred slaves. The total work force for a few plantations ranged upward from one hundred to one thousand slaves. Planters grew more and more tobacco, and then put nearly their total crops into the hands of English factors. When charges for freight, insurance, commissions, taxes, and warehousing were deducted, the bountiful crops provided little profit for the planters. In addition, labor charges, such as the maintenance of the slave force, ate up most remaining revenue. It should not be surprising, in summary, to note that the planters were heavily in debt and accepted the burden uneasily.

Their debts, however, did not reflect their temperaments. An easygoing, aristocratic life, full of hunting, gambling, cockfights, and horse racing, blunted some pains of debt. Though they worked hard, they indulged in luxury and surrounded themselves with staffs that made their country seats almost villages. At Mount Vernon, Bedford, and the many other estates, the proprietors were like feudal lords presiding over attendants. Such was William Byrd II's life at Westover:

> I have a large family of my own, and my doors are open to everybody, yet I have no bills to pay, and half a crown will rest undisturbed in my pocket for many moons together. Like one of the patriarchs, I have my flocks and my herds, my bondmen and bondwomen, and every sort of trade amongst my own servants, so that I live in a kind of independence of everyone but Providence. However, this sort of life is without expense, yet it is attended with a great deal of trouble. I must take care to keep all my people to their duty, to set all the springs in motion, and to make everyone draw his equal share to carry the machine forward. But then 'tis an amusement in this silent country and a continual exercise of our patience and economy.

Byrd might have mentioned that he also had time to build a library, indulge his scientific interests, and write as a man of letters; time, also, to amass a very large estate. At his death in 1744, he held title to 179,000 acres and had patented 105,000 acres near the North Carolina boundary.

Blacks in Virginia

Byrd was sensitive about the fact that so much of this prosperity depended upon slaves. Slavery had increased dramatically in the years after 1700, when only 7000 blacks were counted in the population.

In 1721, there were 23,000 blacks; in 1774, about 200,000. While these people left few traditional records of their thoughts, sufferings, and humiliations, they were part of plantation life. They learned the English language, adapted themselves to the habits of the white man, and, in many instances, mixed their blood with the white when their women became mistresses of the plantation owners. Unlike the Indians, who moved ahead of the frontier, the blacks remained part of organized society, often as threats to the peace, sometimes as pangs of conscience, and frequently as contributors to humor and song. In writing of the blacks, William Byrd touched upon the evils of slavery:

> I am sensible of many bad consequences of multiplying these Ethiopians amongst us. They blow up the pride and ruin the industry of our white people, who seeing a rank of poor creatures below them, detest work for fear it should make them look like slaves. . . . Another unhappy effect of many Negroes is the necessity of being severe. Numbers make them insolent, and then foul means must do what fair will not.

Frontier Virginia

Tidewater planters struggled to find ways of making additional money. The most promising seemed to be speculating in frontier land. With the increasing migration of people into Pennsylvania, Maryland, and Virginia, enterprising colonists anticipated profits from the sale of land and petitioned the Burgesses for grants. Men like James Patten, John Robinson, and Dr. Thomas Walker formed companies to exploit grants of one to two hundred thousand acres. The Ohio Company, the most famous of the schemes, selected a strip of land between the Youghiogheny and the Monongahela rivers and prepared to colonize it. Here George Washington, a stepbrother of one speculator, was surveying in 1753 when he was challenged by the French. A year later, militia under his command capitulated in a brief military encounter that frightened the tidewater aristocracy. They petitioned the home government for help in turning back the French, and the resulting hostilities between French and British empires halted for a decade Virginia's penetration of the Ohio Valley.

At the end of the war a quarter of a million people moved through the Shenandoah Valley, the back country of North and South Carolina, to find homes eventually in the future states of Kentucky and Tennessee. These people were a mixture of Scotch, Irish, German, French Huguenot, and, of course, English. They cleared farms of several hundred acres, planted corn, wheat, potatoes, and tobacco, and lived close to the land in a rugged society that was composed mainly of plain people. Some were running away from debt, looking for a second chance, or dissatisfied with the crowded life of the coast. All were faced with

Perils of Frontier Life *(Library of Congress)*

hostile Indians, the privations of frontier life, and the prospect of moving farther south should they fail in making a new home.

South Carolina

The push of these people into the Carolina back country also intensified rivalry with the Creeks and Cherokees who fought to protect their homes and hunting lands. The resulting wars threatened not only settlements, but commerce that brought riches to the tidewater merchants of Charleston. Forts had to be built, relations with the Indians regulated, and law and order maintained. Frequently, the interests of settler and merchant conflicted, touching vital questions of the colony's future growth and institutions. The tidewater, possessing wealth and proximity to governmental power, won policies that deprived frontiersmen of proper defense and representation and alienated them from the coastal population.

Tidewater Carolina did not have complete control of its destiny, however. While its crops of rice, indigo, and tobacco returned good profits, production depended upon black slaves. The concentration of blacks, sometimes outnumbering whites four or five to one, was a cause for alarm, and even minor signs of unrest caused an overreaction. As preventative methods innocent blacks were often whipped or separated from their families, and some leaders were hanged.

Tidewater landowners depended, too, upon maintaining good relations with the empire. Factors in England handled their crops, and British laws regulated the flow of commerce. Generally, markets for rice and indigo were excellent, and commerce was handicapped only by distance and credit problems. Trade was aided by a fortunate choice of British governors. James Glen's long administration (1743-56) gave the people years of prosperity as he secured subsidies for the growth of indigo and naval products and helped them benefit from an earlier law removing restrictions on the sale of rice. But he occasionally showed independence of judgment. He was not content to remain at his post in the capital, and, instead, planned a system of frontier defenses to protect new settlements, gained ascendancy over the southern Indians, and extended the fur trade. His own views of empire included mediation of Indian disputes and the subjugation of French Louisiana.

His policies generally met favor with the Carolinians whose representatives joined him in the capital city of Charleston. Their winter homes in the city were centers of gaiety and culture that made Charleston the happiest city in the colonies. The city was primarily concerned, however, with business and politics. It was the entrepôt of plantation crops, trade with the back country, and products of commerce. Wagon roads and river lanes stretched distant from the city to provide necessities for Georgia and North Carolina. Like Boston, New York, and Philadelphia, it was a minor center of empire. Through the merchants and politicians, publications and schools, it exercised wide influence in the South. As the capital of the colony, Charleston was the focal point of tidewater power, the administrative, judicial, and legislative center, and the seat of the royal governor.

Frontier Colonies: Georgia, Nova Scotia, Newfoundland

South Carolina's southern neighbor Georgia, the last of the Thirteen Colonies to be settled, was founded in 1732 as a bulwark against the Spanish in Florida and as a refuge for British debtors. The humanitarian reformer, James Oglethorpe, secured a charter from the crown for these settlements in the name of "the Associates of the Late Doctor Bray." He and the Associates were interested in all sorts of charitable projects, but none was more urgent in their thoughts than plans to rehabilitate debtors. Their enterprise, they hoped, would create a land of small, prosperous farmers, living under wholesome laws that pro-hibited hard liquor and black slavery. It soon attracted many national-ities and cultural groups—Jews from Germany and Spain, Germans, Scotch-Irish, French, Italians, and Irish. By the 1770s the German groups, the largest European minority, numbered about twelve hundred in a total population of 18,000 whites. Over the years 15,000 blacks were imported into the colony which used them in agriculture in spite of earlier laws against slavery.

When Georgia became a royal colony in 1752, the inhabitants asked for institutions similar to those in South Carolina and Virginia, and a vigorous representative government soon took over colony affairs. Its most influential governor, James Wright, who assumed office in 1760, was known as energetic and efficient. He opened lands to settlement and agriculture, and politics remained stable in spite of many urgent frontier problems. Crops of rice, indigo, forest products, and corn sup-plemented extensive trade with the Indians who retreated generally from the coastal area into the uplands of the western frontier. Life in the colony was pleasant, even though often rustic and on a subsistence level. The town of Savannah, with only a few hundred people, offered public libraries, the *Georgia Gazette*, printing facilities, and a selection of taverns for those looking for sophisticated living.

Like Georgia the colonies of Nova Scotia and Newfoundland were strategic areas and both were legally parts of the empire since 1713. Nova Scotia had a small French population at its conquest, but large numbers of colonists from New England settled in the area during and after the 1750s. The French (Acadians), always a suspected people, were removed in modest numbers because of their uncertain loyalties and were scattered among colonials to the south and permitted to migrate to Louisiana. The importance of the northern colonies, in addition to their strategic position, was their extremely valuable fishing banks, where massive cargoes of fish were taken yearly. Success of the fishing season meant trading profits for New England and much food for the Caribbean and Europe.

The West Indies

This survey of the major centers of the American empire should not omit the West Indies. In the regard of British officials, these islands were most important for the sugar they produced and for their strategic location in the trade with the Spanish empire. All the islands were plantation colonies by the nature of their production and population. Jamaica, for example, probably had no more than 10,000 white inhabi-tants in a total population of 130,000, or a ratio of one white to twelve black slaves, and many of the white colonists were often absent for long periods in England or the northern colonies. Jamaica produced, in addition to sugar and molasses, impressive amounts of cotton, spices,

Founding of the English Colonies, 1607-1776

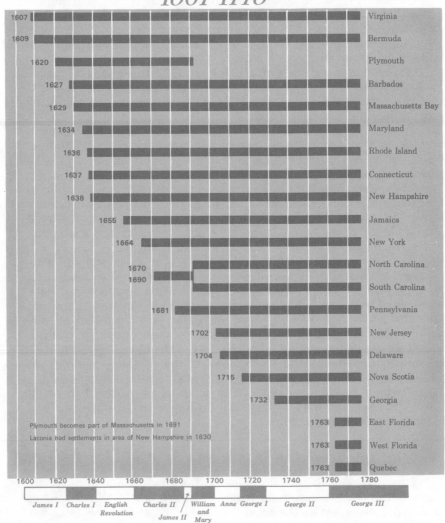

1607	Virginia
1609	Bermuda
1620	Plymouth
1627	Barbados
1629	Massachusetts Bay
1634	Maryland
1636	Rhode Island
1637	Connecticut
1638	New Hampshire
1655	Jamaica
1664	New York
1670	North Carolina
1690	South Carolina
1681	Pennsylvania
1702	New Jersey
1704	Delaware
1715	Nova Scotia
1732	Georgia
1763	East Florida
1763	West Florida
1763	Quebec

Plymouth becomes part of Massachusetts in 1691

Laconia had settlements in area of New Hampshire in 1630

1600 1620 1640 1660 1680 1700 1720 1740 1760 1780

James I   Charles I   English Revolution   Charles II / James II   William and Mary   Anne   George I   George II   George III cocoa, pimento, and ginger. Other islands like St. Kitts, Antigua, and Barbados produced great quantities of sugar and used blacks on their plantations. Barbados alone imported nearly twenty-five hundred slaves a year, mostly from the Royal African Company, which did a prosperous business not only with the islands but with Spain as a result of the Asiento agreement of 1713. This English participation in the slave trade of the Spanish colonies gave the company a market for thousands of black slaves.

British Trade Policy

As the eighteenth century unfolded, the mainland colonies fitted less well into British policies. Their populations were rapidly expanding, as were their economic bases and needs. With surplus agricultural production, some manufacturing, sizeable merchant fleets, and an extraction industry, they were becoming formidable markets. They needed customers and opportunities, but the rules and regulations of the navigation acts, if not harmful, were confining. Being forced to trade within the empire, the merchants could not maximize their opportunities for profits, and they resorted to the common practice of smuggling. Their ships took fish, wheat, corn, and timber to the foreign West Indies, and carried cargoes of molasses, fruits, and coin on the return passage. The profits were transferred eventually into British trading accounts.

The reaction of British politicans to this illegal trade was usually pragmatic. Most looked upon the trade as beneficial because it helped colonials pay for their purchases, but they relied upon the Board of Trade to regulate colonial affairs in ways that would encourage the economy. They had little interest in local affairs and urged the ministry to convey their opinion to British officials. Colonial policy for them thus became trade policy, with the growing commerce a self-regulating form of imperial government. Merchants in London joined their equals in Boston, New York, Philadelphia, or Charleston in establishing trade alliances, and often they labored together in securing favorable legislation. They frequently exchanged apprentices, sometimes took in each other's sons as partners, and occasionally sealed alliances with marriage contracts among their children. Even so, there was always tension in their relations.

The trading system worked better when Britain was spending money in the empire, particularly to support troops based in the colonies. Military provisioning put considerable specie into circulation, and merchants, thus balancing their accounts, were able to trade within traditional channels. Britain even received much cooperation from colonies like Massachusetts, which voted funds and men for the intercolonial armies.

New England, however, suffered from the strain of imperial trade regulation more than any other American area. Her merchants were primarily traders in fish, timber, and molasses. Their problems were usually severe because they were unable to secure sufficient credit to pay their accounts in England. Trade there was always greater in peacetime than were sales, and merchants were constantly looking for products to sell elsewhere for specie. They therefore resorted to smuggling with French, Dutch, and Spanish islanders, and to some direct trade with continental Europe, in order to gain products and specie. One of these merchants was Thomas Hancock, uncle of John, who traded from time to time with Amsterdam to secure favorable prices on paper and tea. But smuggling had its risks, and he avoided often direct European trade by sending supplies via St. Eustatius in the West Indies. Even less reliance was placed upon smuggling when he became military contractor for British forces in Nova Scotia during the 1740s.

New Englanders in their vast trading operations frequented the markets of Philadelphia to buy wheat and bar iron; over 103 of their vessels cleared that port in 1752. Pennsylvanians were fortunate to have a richer commercial base at home than New Englanders, and their ships also plied the seas. The city's leaders traded widely, smuggled, and prospered in their relations with merchants throughout the empire. One of their number, William Allen, used these interrelated trading interests to especially good advantage. This Scotch-Irish Presbyterian, born in 1704, studied at Cambridge in England and law at the Inns of Court and was later acquainted with the commercial techniques of his father's merchant friends. Returning to Philadelphia in 1727, he mixed a full life of business with a career of forty-nine years as assemblyman, mayor of Philadelphia, and chief justice. The firm of Allen and Turner traded widely and invested funds in distilleries, mines, furnaces, stocks, and real estate. Allen's land holdings spread into three colonies, numbering well over fifty thousand acres. His shipping facilities, as well as his political position, gave him great power in the city's market.

The merchants of Charleston also enjoyed their imperial connections. Most of their rice, indigo, and deerskins were carried in English bottoms, giving them excellent annual profits. Men like Henry Laurens owned plantations, wharves, and warehouses and were associated with English people who handled their overseas relations. Since the sale of their products took place in London, months or years after the shipments were made, credit was often tight and expensive. Laurens, sometimes at wits' end, was even forced to barter away slaves to meet operating expenses, and denounced the high fees of warehousemen and agents. Yet these were extraordinary conditions. The trade was usually profitable because of the continuing competitive demand for rice and indigo.

The planters of Virginia and Maryland, however, were less successful in their commercial relations with the British merchants. Though production of tobacco during the century had risen dramatically from 28 million pounds in 1705 to 102 million pounds by 1773, the rate of profits had declined drastically. To maintain profits the planters used more slaves, putting a heavy demand upon the market and increasing labor prices. The larger crops required more ships, warehousing, and agent services, burdening receipts with freight rates, duties, insurance, and commissions. From 1756 to 1765 few planters made production costs, and most fell seriously into debt. Some tried to extricate themselves by diversifying crops, cutting costs of tobacco production, and petitioning for help.

As pressures increased in the economic system, Americans were unable to find adequate help. With no banks or other sources of capital, the only solution seemed to be a shift from a primary activity to shipping, slave selling, trading with the Indians, or colonization. Land speculation was particularly appealing to Virginians and Pennsylvanians, but it depended upon frontier peace and British politics, and proved to be a hazardous undertaking. The slave trade, which attracted about seventy vessels a year, and the distillation of molasses into rum were profitable enterprises. Both were popular in New England, which was, as critics said, "an island in a sea of rum." Profits, however, depended upon unhampered trade with the foreign West Indies and low taxation. Unfortunately, British planters threatened to use parliamentary power to suppress the illegal traffic and to tax foreign sugar. This rivalry of colonial areas became a reality when West Indians gained seats in the House of Commons and looked after their own political interests.

English Society, Politics, and Leadership

The British state after the Revolution of 1689 passed gradually into the hands of landowners and merchants, with great men in each decade to 1760 like William III, the Duke of Marlborough, Sir Robert Walpole, the Pelham brothers, and William Pitt determining its character. Over these years they fought successful wars for empire or worked for commercial policies, both having the object of bringing prosperity. When the ruling Stuart line died out in 1714, distant relatives from Hanover were invited to the throne, and these German princes shared their royal powers with the Whig politicians.

The politics of the Whig party often became little more than the distribution of spoils from office, contracts, and monopolies. Family fortunes at times loomed greater in their plans than national interests, and society had an aristocratic quality in which there was much rigidity, privilege, and favoritism, and some people abused their position. The larger objects of peace and prosperity, in a Protestant society, were well remembered, nonetheless, and kingship, parliament, and the established church were honored and revered institutions. The Whig policies brought much contentment to the nation, and the people rallied generally to support the party in times of crisis.

The vitality of Whig institutions is illustrated by two movements. Leaders and their families interested themselves as a matter of duty in hospitals, orphanages, prisons, and homes for the poor. The founding of Georgia in 1732 was part of this spirit. Whigs also supported a great religious revival in the 1730s when John and Charles Wesley, George Whitefield, and others preached for a renewal of the human spirit. The revival spread to America, and it did much to encourage toleration and break down clerical dominion. It brought new forms of worship, many new hymns, organ music in some churches, and challenged men's inhumanity to each other. The religious revival, in turn, gave strength to humanitarian groups which worked for black emancipation and changes in the Corn Laws, to bring low food prices.

In spite of much feeling for reform, most were extremely difficult to achieve because government was not always responsive to popular wishes. Elections did not change materially the composition of the House of Commons or alter local administrations. Sometimes only open resistance would sharpen an issue. In the 1760s John Wilkes, as writer in The North Briton and then as leader of the London mob, led the craftsmen and laborers in demands for higher wages, cheaper food, and an extension of the franchise. The cry "Wilkes and Liberty" became a slogan of mass action. In America, riots along the waterfront in Massachusetts occurred frequently, sometimes to protest appointments or laws, often to resist recruiting parties of the British navy. Boston's Knowles riots of 1747 tore the town apart for nearly a week, but seamen made their point against impressment. In these years some riots may have been spontaneous reactions to oppression, more often they were the inspiration of merchants and politicians who had no other way of expressing opposition. The daring use of force, however, was not revolutionary. Most people separated local from national issues, and most regarded the nation as the best on earth. Almost all, moreover, welcomed the trade and prosperity that were enriching life.

As long as Robert Walpole remained head of the British ministry (1721-42), he opposed serious changes in domestic policy. Though his administration was often beset with war crises, economic difficulties, and political issues, he managed to compromise them after much skillful negotiation. His goal of suppressing emotional issues allowed for considerable progress and stabilized the revolutionary order of 1689. The result over two decades was peace, and the development of conservative policies that balanced political aspirations. Few English people thought of overturning the Whig politicians and bringing back the exiled Stuart family. The Hanoverian monarchs, George I (1714-27) and George II (1727-60), fitted fairly well into the new political society, especially when they let Walpole and his associates determine domestic policy. In 1739, however, Walpole faced a political crisis that eventually caused his downfall. Parliamentarians and their merchant friends forced a war with Spain as the result of illegal British trading activities in the Caribbean and in the waters off Central America.

War with Spain

The War of Jenkins' Ear was ostensibly caused by Spain's brutal punishment of an English smuggler who was violating trading restrictions, but hostilities of a less serious nature had been occurring since 1714. From the Treaty of Utrecht (1713) Britain had received a thirty-year monopoly on Spain's slave trade and the right to send a ship annually to Porto Bello in Central America. This trading privilege, itself important, was the wedge for many illegal activities, not least of which was the restocking of the annual ship with additional goods. Other vessels abused the opportunity to cruise in Spanish waters by trading with Spain's colonists whenever they had a chance. While Spanish patience was severely tried, Spain was still willing to negotiate the matter of trade grievances with Britain; to emphasize her irritation, however, she inflicted upon Shipmaster Robert Jenkins the harsh penalty of clipping his ear. An inflamed public stirred by opportunistic politicians seized upon the incident as cause enough to wage war.

The hostilities with Spain had some effect upon the North American colonies. Thousands of men joined the services, some were recruited, a few ships were repaired in the colonies, and loads of supplies were purchased from the colonies. The three politicians in power, Henry Pelham, the Duke of Newcastle, and Lord Wilmington, considered briefly the question of colonial union, then fell back on Walpole's policy of leaving the colonies alone. Newcastle set the stage for later colonial military participation, however, when he put his favorite, William Shirley, into the Massachusetts governorship in 1741 when the colony was separated from New Hampshire.

Though the North American governments generally ignored the Spanish war, many Americans like Lawrence Washington served in the British forces. British leadership of these expeditions was severely criticized because of mismanagement of supplies and services. So serious was disease that it forced the army to retreat, and the heavy loss of life weakened attacks on Santiago de Cuba, turning these expeditions into failures.

The War of the Austrian Succession

The full impact of these disasters had not yet been felt when the Spanish war became a side issue in a European dispute over the Austrian succession. The kings of Spain and France, for different reasons, were interested in unseating Maria Theresa of Austria, and Britain, in trying to strengthen the queen's position, arranged a coalition that brought

Prussia into the war. Hostilities for Britain began in 1744 and had no better results than the Caribbean adventures against Spain. The war, except in North America, was a dreary series of battles that caused heavy loss of life without accomplishing objectives. The British ministry, reorganized during the war crises of 1745, minimized opposition over its conduct, but the nation was unprepared to endure years of inconclusive battles. Only at Louisbourg on Cape Breton Island was a dramatic victory won—and that by militiamen from New England.

The French had attacked Nova Scotia in 1744, intending to arouse the Acadians, who had been propagandized by France since the colony's loss to England in 1713. But quick reinforcements by Governor William Shirley of Massachusetts prevented the conquest and persuaded most Acadians to remain neutral. Shirley had earlier persuaded the Massachusetts legislature to prepare the colony for eventual war with France. He had rebuilt forts, gathered cannon and small arms, and enlarged the garrisons. At the time of the successful Nova Scotia repulse, colonial merchants and seamen urged Shirley to send an expedition against Louisbourg. The daring idea caught the imagination of New England, and her four thousand recruits, with some help from other North American colonies, were dispatched in nearly a hundred vessels to Louisburg. The expedition, American inspired and led, was assisted by a British naval force that sealed off the fortress from the sea.

Though the capture of Louisburg delighted the English everywhere, Britain did not support plans for the conquest of Canada. New Englanders organized three additional attacks, in 1746, 1747, and 1748, but these failed because the home government withdrew financial and naval support. Her forces were occupied on the Continent, and to many leaders military engagements in America seemed unimportant.

Many Americans, however, considered the victory over Louisbourg to be the first step toward the conquest of Canada. Governor Shirley spoke of a colonial empire spreading to the Mississippi River and of a vast population of farmers who would grow products for Britain's overseas trade. Others, like George Croghan and William Johnson, were struggling to capture the western Indian trade, and Johnson achieved great influence among the Mohawks as a member of the tribe. Their interest in the fur trade was shared by the Pennsylvania woodsman, Conrad Weiser, who negotiated the Treaty of Logstown in 1748, which opened trade into the Ohio Valley. At about the same time the Ohio Company, represented by Christopher Gist as Indian trader and organizer, began preliminary surveys for a colony between the Monongahela and Kanawha rivers. Some New Englanders were bold enough to call for the western boundary on the Mississippi River. In short, British Americans were pushing westward, trading, exploring, and colonizing. They were extending colonial frontiers into disputed

country, and it could be only a few years until American would clash
with French interests.

When the War of the Austrian Succession ended in 1748, all conquests were returned, and Louisburg was again in French hands. The
powers also provided for a boundary commission to study ways of pre-
venting another war in America. Unfortunately, neither France nor
Britain halted its officials and people from moving into the disputed
regions, so that, as the commissioners debated in Paris, new causes
of conflict were created in America. In 1754 a clash near the forks of the
Ohio set off the French and Indian War, or the Great War for Empire,
though no formal declaration of war was to be made until 1756.

The Great War for Empire

Over the years France had anticipated the movement of British
colonials westward and had built an impressive series of defense posts
along the frontier. These included Louisbourg on Cape Breton, Beausé-
jour near the Bay of Fundy, Crown Point and Ticonderoga on the northern lake route to Montreal, Niagara on Lake Ontario, Presque Isle on
Lake Erie, and Fort Duquesne at the forks of the Ohio. In addition, smaller forts and Indian posts blocked the British paths into the interior.

These measures were primarily defensive, but a radical departure
from traditional policy was required if Canada was to withstand the
pressure of British expansion. The governors-general of Canada had
often speculated on the possibility of developing the Ohio Valley as
a supply center of the empire. Assured food in Quebec would encourage
a greater migration from France than was currently possible. However,
government finance and preoccupation in Europe delayed a change
of policy and the population of Quebec remained about 60,000. In
Louisiana, which had developed as a plantation colony, the promoters
were also unable to attract settlers. The energy of the colonists was
dissipated by quarrels among clergy and officials, and instead of giving
settlement of the colony priority, men vied for honor and power. Too
little thought was given to Indian relations, and the colony suffered
heavy casualties as a result, losing also most of the rich fur trade to their
South Carolina rivals. The four districts of population, New Orleans,
Natchez, Natchitoches, and the Illinois country, had no more than five
thousand inhabitants in 1745, and two thousand of these were black
slaves.

While France fortified her possessions, therefore, they were all
internally weak because of their small and scattered populations. Her
colonial government, nonetheless, provided impressive defense of
the empire, and the frightening results to British colonists of lost trade
and burned villages on the fringe of the Ohio Valley were strong evidence of British weakness in meeting the challenge. In spite of a population of nearly 2,500,000, the British Americans were almost help-

less in controlling Indians or combating the French.

To remedy this situation, the British government considered colonial reorganization, and Lord Halifax, as president of the Board of Trade, gathered evidence and recommendations. But no one was willing to impose colonial union on the colonies or take the responsibility for the reform. The British ministry finally called an intercolonial conference in 1754 in order to handle defense and Indian trade problems, calculating that the delegates would feel the need for strong government. Still, the urgency of union was only partly realized by the participants when they considered the Albany Plan of Union (presented by Benjamin Franklin), and even less by their colonial assemblies, which generally ignored the plan. Only in Massachusetts was the plan debated by the legislature, and there it was finally rejected out of fear of British interference in local affairs. Many legislators, while favoring the liquidation of Canada, were aroused by the potential peril to colonial liberty of imperial supervision. The British ministry, while still not ready to force union upon the colonies, decided to use limited military action to remove French encroachments. It hoped to encourage the colonists to consult with each other, to plan local engagements, and to fortify their harbors and frontiers. But George II and some ministers were uncertain of the importance of America to national defense, and resisted any serious commitment of military forces.

Only William Pitt in the House of Commons seriously questioned ministerial policy. That abrasive politician, in speeches and letters, tried to arouse leaders to the dangers of French aggression in America. He feared the loss of Newfoundland fisheries, Indian trade, and West Indian commerce, and he urged military support for the colonies. His words were not always appreciated because of his personality and his involvement in a mix of politics that concerned other issues. As the crisis became greater along the American frontier, however, the government responded to his pressure and sought some immediate defense measures without committing the nation's full strength.

In working out a compromise, the ministry in 1755 chose Edward Braddock as commander and gave him two Irish regiments. The aged general, with no experience in America, was provided with the secretarial advice of young William Shirley, the soldier son of the Massachusetts governor, and two additional regiments of newly recruited American militiamen. In one season of campaigning, he expected to attack Fort Duquesne (at present-day Pittsburgh), forts on the way to Niagara, Niagara itself, and eventually Crown Point and Ticonderoga. Once these French encroachments were removed, he planned to return to England.

When reports of Braddock's campaign plans became known to Governors Shirley and Charles Lawrence (of Nova Scotia), they mobilized forces to sweep French posts from the Bay of Fundy. Shirley also aroused his New England colleagues to the need for an attack upon Crown Point and Ticonderoga. Recruiting for these expeditions was, therefore, under way when Braddock reached Virginia. He welcomed the cooperation, approved the mobilization, and readied himself for the difficult march through the mountains to Fort Duquesne. Lacking adequate supplies, wagons, and Indian auxiliaries, and with the burden of sick men, unfamiliar surroundings, and hot weather, Braddock's force was exhausted by the time he neared Fort Duquesne. About seven miles from the fort, a sudden ambush of nine hundred French and Indians upset British strategy, fatally wounding Braddock and causing panic among the men. The result was a loss of momentum and, more important, the loss of effective leadership that could have turned the defeat to victory.

Expeditions to Niagara and Ticonderoga were abortive; only Governor Lawrence in the north was able to realize campaign objectives. Probably the most harmful event of 1755 was the rivalry between New York and Massachusetts, in which Braddock's successor, Governor William Shirley, became embroiled. The controversy over management of Indian affairs and war contracting reached amazing bitterness in a short time. For the sake of harmony, Britain sacrificed Shirley to expediency and reassessed the military situation.

The American crisis precipitated a debate among parliamentarians, who examined the war's limited objectives, Braddock's lack of proper staff, supplies, and equipment, and the relations between London and the colonies. After months of argument, the government finally appointed John Campbell, the Earl of Loudoun, as commander-in-chief and set up a unified military system in America. The government also decided to wage an all-out war against France, and made formal declaration in the spring of 1756.

William Pitt as Military Leader

Loudoun, like Braddock before him, was unfamiliar with American conditions, rigid in military philosophy, and quarrelsome. His problems sprang up everywhere, not allowing him to mount attacks in 1756, and the deterioration of military defense within the empire unsettled Whig politics. During the crisis, the British ministry was reorganized and William Pitt came into power with the pledge of a vigorous prosecution of the war. Under Pitt's leadership, troops, supplies, and governmental services were put at the disposal of the field commanders in order to liquidate Canada as soon as possible. Pitt gave Loudoun his full support in the hope of an early victory.

Loudoun, however, not only moved cautiously, perhaps too deliberately, but also faced obstacles that wore down his energy and patience. The home government was committed to mix colonial troops, supplies, services, and officials with those of the regular military services. Coordination of so many military efforts gave rise to questions of authority, primacy, rank, and initiative. Everywhere Loudoun turned he was forced to negotiate instead of command. In Massachusetts, for example, he was quickly confronted with questions of insubordination. His recruiters, moving through the province, were not supplied housing at public expense; some of them were suspected of having smallpox and were quarantined. The governor refused to spend public funds for housing without legislative authorization, and when he could not get the necessary legislation, Lord Loudoun threatened to occupy Boston. A heated exchange between governor and general continued for weeks, but the legislature eventually voted the funds. The House of Representatives, nonetheless, reminded Loudoun that he could not bully a popularly elected assembly and sent him a message on the rights and liberties of Englishmen. Other issues involving the discipline of colonials, the extension of enlistment periods, and the impressment of seamen also irritated New Englanders. They were relieved, however, when Pitt decided to modify British policy.

Under Pitt's dynamic leadership in 1758, the ministry assumed most of the financial and military burdens of the war—recruiting, provisioning, and fighting. Loudoun was replaced by James Abercromby, then Abercromby by Jeffrey Amherst, as new men directed the campaigns. In 1758, forts Louisburg and Duquesne were successfully besieged, in heroic actions that were widely celebrated throughout America. In 1759, James Wolfe surprised the French before Quebec and fought them fiercely on the Plains of Abraham. Although Wolfe and the French commander, Louis Joseph de Montcalm, were both mortally wounded, the British won this climactic engagement of the war and then, in 1760, took Montreal.

In the hearts of Americans, William Pitt was at this time a great hero, and when George III succeeded to the throne in 1760, the celebrations for the new king symbolized the love, appreciation, and dependence of Americans upon the power of this, "the greatest of empires."

British armies also won significant victories in Florida, the Caribbean, Africa, and India. Though Britain's allies in Europe—Prussia, Bavaria, Russia, and some cooperating German states—did not win comparable victories, they kept France and Austria occupied and insured the balance of power for Britain on the Continent. The cost of subsidizing Frederick the Great of Prussia and of maintaining Hanover was a severe burden, however, with heavy land and excise taxes meeting part of the expenditures and public borrowing the rest. At the close of the war the national debt had reached the staggering sum of £129 million. Englishmen were tired of war and anxious for peace.

The Fall of Pitt

In mobilizing national resources for war, Pitt had depended upon the cooperation of such Whig magnates as Newcastle, Hardwicke, and Devonshire, King George II, and the lack of an organized opposition. As secretary of state, he had gathered around him brilliant military experts, and within his hands held the power to execute policy. At the king's death in 1760 Pitt lost the help of an experienced, appreciative monarch; in the king's place was a young man of twenty-three, ignorant, obstinate, and anxious to govern. George was wise enough, however, to realize that war was growing unpopular, and he questioned Pitt's policies. Pitt's desire to carry the war to the Spanish empire was soon challenged by the new king's chief advisor, the Earl of Bute, and the argument over military policy brought Pitt's resignation and a split in the Whig coalition.

Though Bute and associates concluded successfully a peace treaty in 1763, the Treaty of Paris, they were severely criticized in the press and House of Commons. The loss of Pitt's service at this point must be regarded as most unfortunate for the nation, because there were present critical issues that would challenge creative leadership in any age. Leaders faced at home a large public debt, resistance to taxes, and demobilization of the armed forces. In the empire there were problems of Indian massacre, a large alien French population, a massive territorial area, and a restless colonial population. It required the wisdom of Solomon, but Britain had Lord Bute, a young king, and William Pitt who did not appreciate the seriousness of the approaching imperial crisis.

During Pitt's secretaryship the colonies prospered. British purchases of raw material and military subsidies gave them money to maintain trade balances and buy luxuries. Even so, American appreciation of his policies was ungenerous. Colonials deserted from the army, opposed restrictions on commerce, and traded with the enemy. Such scandalous dealing finally drove Pitt in 1760 to order tighter controls on smuggling, with naval inspection and on-shore searches of warehouses. The reaction of New Englanders was immediately hostile to the enforcement of his orders, and James Otis, Jr., as the spokesman of some Boston merchants, challenged the use of the search warrants and raised constitutional questions that related these seizures to a violation of a subject's natural rights. The Boston community rewarded Otis's efforts by electing him to the House of Representatives, where he became a critic of trade regulation. The navy, nonetheless, maintained its vigil along American coasts, with more than forty ships patrolling the sea lanes. Ship captains, who took a third of any seizure as personal profit, worked assidously, sometimes trapping even innocent traders. Bostonians, as well as New Yorkers and Philadelphians, were furious over these incidents and organized local protests. Their reaction became particularly serious as markets for military purchases declined, business activity dropped, and problems of meeting trade deficits became acute.

The Great War for Empire is one of those watersheds in history. The old colonial system may have ended in 1756 when Pitt assumed control of military policy and Britain and France turned to war to resolve their boundary problems, or it may have ended when the idea of colonial union was rejected 1754 by Americans. The elimination of France in Canada and in the Ohio Valley put Britain in the position of maintaining peace in that vast territory, and her policies became in time as controversial as those of France had been. She had Indians to pacify, trade to regulate, and lands to distribute, with an additional problem of sixty thousand alien French to rule. For Americans, the end of the war brought the first opportunity in a decade to consider their political institutions, and they reacted with uneasiness about the future. The Whig Revolution of 1689 was gaining a new meaning, a discovery of English life and history, and the works of Algernon Sidney, James Harrington, and John Locke offered interpretations of political institutions that few Americans previously had dared to make. Americans compared their colonial institutions with those in England, claimed for themselves equality of legislative power, and worried about tendencies in British politics to attack their liberties. Men like Franklin and the young Worcester teacher John Adams dreamed of the day when the empire's seat would be in America, and James Otis spoke of American rights that were outside the limits of parliamentary power. Since 1689 the population of the colonies had grown each decade, reaching the two million mark in 1750. Surpluses, comforts, and a variety of occupations were improving the quality of life, and most Americans were proud of their British ties.

SUGGESTIONS FOR FURTHER READING

Becker, Carl L., The Heavenly City of the Eighteenth-Century Philosophers. New Haven, Conn., Yale University Press, 1964.

Bell, Hugh F., Points of Power in Early America. St. Charles, Mo., Forum Press, 1975.

Bonwick, Colin, English Radicals and the American Revolution, Chapel Hill, N.C., University of North Carolina Press, 1977.

Breen, Timothy, and Stephen Foster, "The Puritans' Greatest Achievement: A Study of Social Cohesion in Seventeenth-Century Massachusetts," Journal of American History, LX, 5-22.

Bridenbaugh, Carl, Cities in Revolt: Urban Life in America, 1743-1776. New York, Capricorn Books, G. P. Putnam's Sons, 1964.

_____, Myths and Realities: Societies of the Colonial South. New York, Atheneum Publishers, 1963.

Crane, Verner W., Benjamin Franklin and a Rising People.

Boston, Little, Brown and Company, 1954.

Christie, Ian R. and Benjamin W. Labaree, *Empire of Independence: A British American Dialogue on the Coming of the Revolution.* New York, W. W. Norton Company, 1976.

Cunliffe, Marcus, *George Washington: Man and Monument.* New York, Mentor Books, The New American Library, 1960.

Dishman, Robert B., *Burke and Paine on Revolution and the Rights of Man.* New York, Charles Scribner's Sons, 1971.

Franklin, Benjamin, *Autobiography,* ed. Leonard W. Labaree, New Haven, Conn., Yale University Press, 1964.

Greene, Jack P., *The Quest for Power: The Lower Houses of Assembly in the Southern Royal Colonies, 1689-1776.* Chapel Hill, N.C., University of North Carolina Press, 1963.

Hall, Michael G., *Edward Randolph and the American Colonies, 1676-1703.* Chapel Hill, N.C., University of North Carolina Press, 1960.

Hall, Michael G., Lawrence H. Leder, and Michael G. Kammen, eds., *The Glorious Revolution in America.* New York, W. W. Norton & Company, Inc., 1964.

Hawke, David F., *Franklin.* New York, Harper & Row, 1976.

Heimert, Alan, *Religion and the American Mind.* Cambridge, Mass., Harvard University Press, 1966.

_____ and Perry Miller, *The Great Awakening, Documents.* Indianapolis and New York, Bobbs-Merrill Company, 1967.

Hindle, Brooke, *The Pursuit of Science in Revolutionary America, 1735-1789.* Chapel Hill, N.C., University of North Carolina Press, 1956.

Jacobs, Wilbur R., *Wilderness Politics and Indian Gifts.* Lincoln, Nebr., University of Nebraska Press, 1966.

Malone, Dumas, *Jefferson and His Time: Jefferson the Virginian.* Boston, Little, Brown and Company, 1966.

Schutz, John A., *William Shirley: King's Governor of Massachusetts.* Chapel Hill, N.C., University of North Carolina Press, 1961.

Smith, Abbot Emerson, *Colonists in Bondage: White Servitude and Convict Labor in America, 1607-1776.* Chapel Hill, N.C., University of North Carolina Press, 1947.

Tolles, Frederick B., *Meeting House and Counting House.* New York, W. W. Norton & Company, 1963.

Wright, Louis B., *The First Gentlemen of Virginia.* San Marino, Calif., The Huntington Library, 1940.

4

The Struggle
for American Rights

PEACE IN 1763 WAS WELCOMED by most Britons. For two decades crises and wars had troubled everyone with high taxes, irritating restrictions, and thousands of men in the military; the people now expected some relief from these heavy burdens. Relaxation of wartime controls seemed to be the first order of business. But the peace was complicated by the great spoils of war as well as by the great responsibilities of empire—vast new territory and many new people. Governing the enlarged empire raised anew old questions of imperial supervision and loyalty and the desirability of using the resources of the empire to pay the costs of administration. The peace occurred, moreover, in a period of political transition, with an inexperienced young king, George III, on the throne and a new prime minister, George Grenville, taking on the responsibilities of government.

The Grenville Reforms

Most historians now agree that English leaders were right in worrying about American dependence. For decades the Board of Trade had considered reforming colonial government, but had hesitated for various reasons, mostly out of fear that reform might raise inflammatory political issues. One problem of obedience had its origin in the assemblies which had resisted almost everything ordered from London. They refused to vote money for salaries and defense, unless they were given their way in policy making, and they forced British officials often to violate the expressed will of the ministry. Their arrogance reflected the growing power of the colonies in population and wealth. But Americans gave Britain also cause to wonder about their republican sympathies and their criticism of the Anglican Church. Their writings against the pomp and circumstance of English life was irritating, especially when England was accused of being corrupt and decadent.

England reacted only in a modest way to American criticism, but reformers in the Board of Trade and in Parliament had long stressed the need for drastic changes in colonial government. The peace of 1763, however, awakened interest in colonial administration, and George Grenville agreed that something had to be done to provide effective supervision of American problems. But he also was impressed by new problems arising from the late war—by the tremendous size of the Canadian and Floridian conquests, the turbulence there of Indian-White relations, the presence of a large foreign population, and financial burdens for the United Kingdom of imperial government. Especially was he concerned about the protests at home over high taxes and the need to find other sources of revenue.

In broad outline Grenville interpreted the imperial problem as requiring an involvement of England in American affairs—to regulate Indian trade, to supervise western migration and settlement, and to force Americans to pay some costs of imperial government. More specifically, he issued a proclamation in 1763 limiting settlement west of the ridge of the Appalachian Mountains because of Indian disturbances, and he had a large number of British regulars garrisoned at various frontier posts to compel the obedience of Indians and frontiersmen. He had units of the navy cruise in American waters as auxiliaries for customs agents. His famous Revenue Act of 1764 and Stamp Act of 1765 were designed to raise money for this program of reform.

Both tax acts irritated Americans, but they did not like the whole program of imperial regulation. Nothing frightened them more, however, than law enforcement by means of military force and through admiralty courts where judges instead of juries made the legal decision.

The American reaction to the Stamp Act was immediate and explosive. In Massachusetts rioters attacked the homes of customs officials and the lieutenant governor. In Pennsylvania elections removed those sympathetic to these laws, and in most colonies the stamp distributers were forced to resign or seek safety by hiding. In Virginia, Patrick Henry urged the House of Burgesses to pass resolutions denying Britain's power to tax the colonies and declaring that "this ancient and loyal colony" had the right to manage her own internal affairs. Virginia's resolutions received great publicity when other colonies, in registering protests, used them as models. At the same time, the House of Representatives of Massachusetts urged other legislatures to send delegates to a congress at New York where a joint protest could be written. For twelve days in October 1765, delegates from nine colonies argued, debated, and composed a declaration of thirteen articles. Its major point was a denial of parliamentary taxation and of legislation that took away basic liberties like trial by jury. These three articles set the tone of the declaration:

III.   That it is inseparably essential to the Freedom of a People, and the undoubted Right of *Englishmen*, that no Taxes be imposed on them, but with their own Consent, given personally, or by their Representatives.

IV.   That the People of these Colonies are not, and from their local circumstances cannot be, Represented in the House of Commons in *Great-Britain*.

VII.   That Trial by Jury, is the inherent and invaluable Right of every British *Subject* in these Colonies.

The protest itself should not obscure the significance of this union of colonial sentiment. Probably at no time in their history had colonials been so embittered over a common issue, and their response was indicative of the seriousness of the occasion. Riots and violence had erupted in seaboard communities in every colony. In Boston, during two nights of violence, the homes of four distinguished officeholders were destroyed. In Philadelphia, the people let loose their anger upon the ruling party and threw it out of office; mobs threatened the stamp distributor with physical harm; and merchants put flags at half-mast and tolled the church bells to show their feelings. In most colonies, even the isolated Bahamas, the stamp distributors were compelled to resign their commissions.

Pitt's Second Ministry

In England, George III reacted to the rising opposition by looking for a new prime minister. He first turned to William Pitt, who might have formed a popular government, but was still bitter over the treatment he had received from the king and the Whigs. All knew that as long as Pitt remained outside of government, ministries would be weak, and politics would be fluid. The king, nonetheless, had to find leadership, and he turned to the Marquis of Rockingham, an heir to the traditions of Robert Walpole. The Marquis wanted peace, perhaps a return to the old-time trade policies of the Walpole era, but he was bewildered, as Grenville was, by American violence and put troops on the alert. His merchant friends, the traditional allies of the Whigs, urged repeal of the revenue acts and conciliation of the colonies. Before he could act upon their advice, Pitt revealed his own position in an address to the House of Commons. He denounced the Stamp Act, asserted that Parliament had no power to tax America, and shocked his colleagues by declaring "I rejoice that America has resisted."

His voice may have awakened some romantic notions about the Revolution of 1689, when Parliament in March 1766 repealed the revenue acts and emphasized its lawmaking supremacy in the nation. But there remained the nagging problem of taxation, governmental responsibility, and English rights in colonial lands, and few people were wise enough to offer solutions.

In July 1766, George III finally persuaded Pitt that the nation needed him, and the great man, old, infirm, and haughty took office. He brought with him a motley group of officeholders, united more by desire for power than by a feeling for this moment of crisis. Pitt's health soon broke under the pressure of colonial disobedience and financial stringency, and he even considered the use of force in America. As leadership slipped from his hands, it fell into the hands of less able people who lacked wisdom and tact. To Charles Townshend, the Chancellor of the Exchequer, however, fell the responsibility of finding new sources of revenue and initiating measures that were intended to tighten colonial administration.

The new taxation—upon glass, lead, paint, paper, and tea—was no more acceptable to Americans than the Grenville measures had been. In this confrontation, however, the colonists were prepared for resistance. The Massachusetts agitators, James Otis, Samuel Adams, and James Bowdoin, purged local offices of pro-British sympathizers and put on a campaign of terror to mobilize public opinion. Using economic pressure also by withholding trade, they sought local substitutes for tea and cloth. Boston led and New York, Philadelphia, and Charleston followed, so that by 1770 trade with England was drastically cut. Those who would not comply with local demands were publicly ridiculed, and some found themselves wearing coats of tar and feathers.

At the passage of the Stamp Act in 1765 Parliament had also extended the Mutiny Act to the colonies and clarified their responsibilities regarding military provisioning. The New York assembly denounced the Act as a tax, disobeyed it openly, and invited reprisals from Britain. In defying the law, the legislature irritated even its parliamentary friends who approved of a law to suspend all legislative activity in New York until the assembly recognized the Mutiny Law. The colony plainly faced a crisis, but the assembly, frightened by the possible consequence of resistance and a lack of support from other colonies back down. By means of strategic retreat, then, the legislature voted the funds without reference to the Act, and the ministry adroitly accepted the compromise. A crisis was narrowly averted.

The ministry, however, continually introduced innovations. New commissioners of customs were sent to America in 1767; a Secretary of State for Colonies was appointed in 1768. The secretary was Lord Hillsborough, an Irish peer of little tact or understanding, who excited great feeling almost immediately by issuing a circular letter on British policy. He warned the colonies in a haughty tone not to follow the lead of Massachusetts in advocating resistance against the Townshend Acts and threatened suspension if they did. His letter served as an abrasive in an already tender situation in Boston, but it did not frighten the Massachusetts legislature, which voted by a margin of ninety-two to seventeen to let its own circular letter go forth. Though the punishment of suspension was prompt, leaders called a convention that underscored in address and declaration the right of the legislature to protest illegal taxation. The convention was itself illegal, as well as a challenge to constituted authority and seriously weakened British authority in Massachusetts.

In Boston the intensity and bitterness of feeling reached nearly a climax when the home government ordered four regiments of the British army into the province. The presence of so many troops threatened representative institutions and aroused the traditional antagonism of Britons to a standing army. Although the British government withdrew two regiments in 1769, those soldiers remaining were a constant irritation to Bostonians, who accused them of crimes and of breaking the peace. For years the city had experienced some disorder and crime; now it blamed the troops for these. There were frequent clashes in dark alleys, petty attacks of citizen upon soldier and soldier upon citizen. A time or two, troops had to rescue soldiers from rough treatment, and in moments of calm the Boston selectmen expressed fear of a serious incident. Governor Bernard, who retired in disgust to England in 1769, told his British superiors that he had lost control of the government and despaired of the future. His successor, Thomas Hutchinson, felt that kindness, understanding, and firmness might restore order, but violence continued.

On the night of March 5, 1770, a group of boys, sailors, and laborers assaulted the sentries of the customs house. The captain in charge of the garrison ordered out reinforcements, who were, in turn, menaced by the mob with clubs, knives, and anything close at hand. In the confusion of whistles, bells, and screams, someone shouted "Fire!" and the excited soldiers emptied their muskets into the mob. Quieted by the shots and smoke, the mob was further sobered by the sight of five of its number dead or dying, and everyone then tried to reconstruct what had happened.

In the investigation that followed, citizens demanded a public trial of the soldiers, removal of the garrison from the city, and solemn funerals for the victims. In November, when quiet had returned to the city, Robert Treat Paine and Samuel Quincy prosecuted eight of the soldiers before a special session of the Superior Court, and John

A Contemporary View of the Boston Massacre Engraved by Paul Revere.

Adams, Josiah Quincy, and Sampson Bowers defended them. The prosecution used the testimony of a score or more witnesses to prove that the soldiers were guilty of murder, but Adams, in a minute examination of the evidence, successfully challenged the allegations. "The law," he said in concluding his plea, "will not bend to the uncertain wishes, imaginations and wanton tempers of men. To use the words of a great and worthy man, a patriot, and hero . . . and a martyr to liberty; I mean Algernon Sidney . . . 'The law no passion can disturb. 'Tis void of desire and fear, lust and anger. 'Tis *mens sine affectu*; written reason, retaining some measure of the divine perfection.' " The pleas of Adams and his colleagues had their impact. Of the eight soldiers charged with murder, the jury freed six and gave two reduced punishments.

The trial, however, had served its purpose for the radical leadership of Boston, who never permitted the people to forget that it was the military who had menaced the lives and liberties of Americans in what they called the "Boston Massacre." They instituted for March fifth a public oration, in keeping with the solemnity of the occaison, to revive the feeling of Boston over the martyrdom of its citizens.

Massachusetts had gone through a tremendous emotional experience since the end of the Seven Years' War. The violence of the Stamp Act protest, the nonimportation agreements, the occupation of Boston by soldiers, and the critical issues in the legislature were the major episodes. But these should not obscure subtle changes that were occurring: the use of terms like Whig and Tory to separate friend and foe; references to colonials as Americans; the resort to violence against pro-British citizens; the lack of reverence for the governor as representative of the king, and the growing bitterness toward the home government. The slogan "Taxation without representation is tyranny" became a matter of principle, one of emotion, and a cry for resistance against England. In dress people of substance wore homespun and abandoned the fashionable wig and, for drink, served substitutes for tea and favored whiskey over rum.

American episodes of protest and violence were not isolated from the larger debate of the day. Since 1760 when George III had become king, there had been a political struggle among leaders for control of the English state. A succession of politicians had taken places in government, vying for honor and prestige but rarely raising their eyes to the important issues troubling the empire.

Politics were primarily heated by the activities of John Wilkes and his friends. This son of a distiller, friend of Pitt, and antagonist of Lord Bute had dared criticize in 1763 the king, the queen mother, and the ministry. When Grenville succeeded Bute that year, he was determined to prosecute Wilkes. To procure information, Grenville secured general search warrants and used the evidence gathered to have Wilkes arrested while he was a member of the Commons. But the courts found the writs illegal and the arrest a breach of parliamentary privilege. Grenville then resorted to the dubious tactic of having the Commons expel Wilkes, which put the ministry in a poor light. Politicians ridiculed Grenville's tactics; publicists cynically exposed them for what they were. The reputation of Parliament as a bastion of liberty was compromised and its leaders made to appear unconcerned about issues of equity and justice. Wilkes chose to escape to France rather than stand trial and receive certain punishment.

Wilkes remained on the Continent as an outlaw until desperation drove him home in 1767. With the help of the press, he advertised his cause, aroused considerable feeling, and dared the government to fine and imprison him. Only when his cause had been made known to all did he give himself up to the authorities. The courts quickly found the charge of outlawry improper and convicted him on the lesser charge of blasphemy and seditious libel, eventually sending him to prison for twenty-two months.

Public reaction to his punishment was frightening to the ministry, which had hoped to ignore him. Organized demonstrations and riots kept London excited, and during an encounter with some marchers the police shot and killed a few participants. The "Massacre of St. George's Fields" aroused public passion still more. The cry "Wilkes and Liberty!" became a haunting expression of the people's contempt for the politicians and for the corruption of Parliament. There followed the formation of the Bill of Rights Society and demands for reform—annual elections, destruction of rotten boroughs, the secret ballot, and extension of the franchise.

"Wilkes and Liberty" became the toast of Americans as they chose their heroes, and it reflected their disgust with the Townshend Acts. For many, the corruption at home brought about speculation on its source in the state. The Whigs had often pictured the pure society as that of ancient Germany and Anglo-Saxon England, when men of the forest lived sturdy, independent lives. The monarchy, the army, and the aristocracy, sometimes the sophistication of society itself, were seen as the bringers of corruption. The writings of Jean Jacques Rousseau, the distinguished French philosopher, idealized a reformed society in which people would throw off the chains of the present civilization. James Burgh, the propagandist and writer, denounced the low political morality of the day. "Luxury and irreligion," he wrote, "are inseparable companions, are the characteristic vices of the age, and ... our degenerate times and corrupt nation have the unhappiness of being singular in this respect."

Apart from contemporary writers on the corruptions of society, translators had made the works of the ancients available. The contrast of republican virtue with the venality of Rome's decline gave rise to speculation on the decline of nations. Could Britain then in the hands of "a motley race of English traders" be facing collapse? Could America be the rising empire? The virtues of Cato the Younger, known to many Americans through Joseph Addison's famous play, were extolled. Cato, says a character in the play, is like Mount Atlas—though storms break at its base, the mountain stands unshaken. And Cato reminds his associates:

> A day, an hour, of virtuous liberty
> Is worth a whole eternity in bondage.

Rather than bow to the conquering Caesar, he committed suicide, a martyr to republican virtue. So Cato became the figure of steadfastness, honor, integrity, as one challenged British policy.

Americans in Virginia, the Carolinas, and Maryland were undoubtedly more influenced by these currents of thought than by any feelings of open resistance to Britain. They read themselves into the rebellion as they followed events in distant Boston and London. Though they boycotted British goods through nonimportation laws, corresponded with other colonists, acted in their legislatures, and published their protests against taxation, they were caught up in the developing revolution chiefly by British innovations threatening their way of life. Their mental reactions to events elsewhere were strikingly similar to those of people in Boston and New York; in responding to critical reports they called for a "common cause," and in resisting taxation without representation, for a "unity of action." The pamphlets of Richard Bland and Thomas Jefferson emphasized that the present British state was corrupt ("these Days of Venality"), and that its imposition of taxation was out of harmony with the ancient principles of English liberty and the Constitution. In *A Summary View of the Rights of British America (1774),* Jefferson noted:

> Scarcely have our minds been able to emerge from the astonishment into which one stroke of parliamentary thunder had involved us, before another more heavy, and more alarming, is fallen on us. Single acts of tyranny may be ascribed to the accidental opinion of a day; but a series of oppressions, begun at a distinguished period, and pursued, unalterably through every change of ministers, too plainly prove a deliberate and systematical plan of reducing us to slavery.

The Mounting Crisis

Even as Parliament repealed most Townshend duties, the king asked Frederick, Lord North to form a new government. Though North was inwardly friendly to the colonies, and a man of peace and moderation, he adopted firm policies of trade law enforcement which did little to relieve tension or bring good will. Late in 1771 more inflammatory incidents occurred. Authorities captured a vessel entering the lower Delaware, but before the ship was safe in port, men with blackened faces seized the cargo and damaged the ship. In June 1772, the revenue ship *Gaspee,* while searching the coastal waters of Rhode Island, ran aground. During the night prominent men of the colony, acting without disguises, boarded the vessel and set it afire. This contempt for a king's officer and men, not to mention the king's ship, required special attention. To underscore the gravity of the incident, the crown established a court of inquiry and appointed colonials of position and ability as judges. In spite of its prestige the court could not penetrate the wall of silence erected by the witnesses that protected the leaders of the mob from prosecution.

One of the judges, Peter Oliver of Massachusetts, now became a central figure in another controversy. The home government had decided to pay the salaries of colonial officials—the governor, secretary, and justices. News of the decision aroused the leaders of Boston, recalled traditional arguments against established salaries, and caused a full dress debate between the House of Representatives and Governor Hutchinson, in which they exchanged views on British rights and liberties. Though the controversy at first served to heighten emotions, later it became a struggle between Oliver and the legislature over the legality of the chief justice's acceptance of the British salary. The legislature initiated impeachment proceedings, accused Oliver of "high crimes and misdemeanors," and demanded that the council and governor hear the charges. No one was certain of the procedure, but the representatives insisted upon Oliver's removal, while the governor tried to avoid a confrontation. Their argument reached the point eventually where the courts could not longer conduct their business.

To make matters worse the representatives published personal letters of Massachusetts officials to British correspondents. The letters, obtained by Benjamin Franklin, provided concrete information that had great propaganda value. Hutchinson's letters, in some unguarded sentences, revealed his known hostility toward opponents of British laws. For some readers the visible evidence of his British loyalty may have convinced them that he was the wretch, the evildoer, and the plotter they had been told. His reputation was irreparably destroyed.

But what drove him from Massachusetts was the public hatred aroused by the controversial excise on East Indian tea. The so-called Tea Act was passed in May 1773, granting the East India Company special privileges in the American colonial market. The company, facing bankruptcy because of accumulated debts from the military campaigns of the 1750s, had been long in financial trouble. Its employees had plundered the company, its management was in turmoil, and its stockholders demanded high dividends. In addition, since 1767 it had been compelled to pay the government an annual subsidy of £400,000. Under the Tea Act the East India Company was permitted to ship tea directly to the colonies, thus eliminating middlemen, warehousing fees, and spoilage, and the government lent it £1,400,000 with which to defray outstanding obligations. Besides being able to meet immediate dividends and expenses, the company was presented with longterm market conditions of exceptional value. Tea could be sold at half its former price, less than even the smugglers could offer. The Act, too, gave the ministry, which calculated that the colonists would drink cheap tea regardless of expressed principles, an opportunity to reassert British sovereignty in America. A drink of cheap tea, said one wit, would make taxation easier to swallow.

The Tea Act brought a spontaneous reaction from Americans, who objected to the new regulation and the threat to their economy that it represented. Their hostility appeared early, but the company ignored the warnings of its friends; even though reports of probable violence made shipping scarce and frightened some merchants, who refused to receive consignments, it prepared without regard to the danger large quantities of tea for shipment. By the end of the summer, the ships were on their way across the Atlantic, and the consignees nervously awaited their arrival. Violence broke out first in New York and Philadelphia, the centers of tea smuggling, where merchants forced the consignees to renounce their contracts and turn the ships homeward.

In Boston, the consignees were Governor Hutchinson's sons, sons-in-law, relatives, and friends, who refused, even in the face of huge town rallies, to resign their posts, seeking instead the safety of the island fortress, Castle William. Boston's first cargo of tea arrived on November 27, and was joined later by two additional cargoes. The vessels were held at the docks. The governor would not permit their return passage, nor would the patriots permit their unloading. During the evening of December 16, a group of men disguised as Indians dumped their cargoes into Boston Harbor. The violence of Boston's "Indians" was severely criticized elsewhere in America because it seemed unnecessarily provocative. Again in March 1774, the Bostonians tossed tea into the harbor, as if to emphasize their contempt for British taxation.

That month George III summoned Parliament to consider these serious disturbances. Not fully realising the gravity of the situation, the king and Parliament dealt with the colonies as dependencies and applied punishment much as one would to a child. The punishment was selective, mainly for the erring Massachusetts people, and harsh in its application. These measures, known as the Coercive Acts, closed Boston Harbor, revised the Massachusetts charter, tampered with local government and the jury system, and revised the British Mutiny Act to compel quartering of troops in Boston. In addition, Parliament passed the Quebec Act, which provided government under Quebec officials for the Ohio Valley and Illinois Country as well as legalized the old French law and Roman Catholic worship. The Quebec Act, though not actually a Coercive Act, was considered as one by many Americans because it threatened rights of expansion that they had long claimed. Many Americans felt the act imperiled the Protestant religion and their English civil liberties. Though a calmer examination of the Act would have shown this to be untrue, at this moment of excitement it aroused deep emotion and prejudice. In Massachusetts the British government replaced its civilian governor Hutchinson with a military man, Thomas Gage.

These intolerable acts invited open colonial resistance. The only question in many minds was what the protest should be. Some New York merchants, in a "Solemn League and Covenant," supported a trade embargo, while others proposed a continental congress. As early as June 17, the Massachusetts legislature had sent out a call for an

British Cartoon of the Coercive Acts *(Library of Congress)*

intercolonial conference. This idea was supported by John Dickinson, the famous author of *Letters from a Farmer in Pennsylvania,* who considered the congress less radical than an economic boycott but who, with his colleagues, was convinced that some new form of imperial government was necessary.

On September 5, fifty-five delegates from all the colonies except Georgia assembled at Carpenter's Hall in Philadelphia and began deliberations that continued until October 26. The First Continental Congress was undoubtedly the most distinguished gathering of Americans in their history, and it represented a cross section of the groups that had governed the colonies. With leaders like John and Samuel Adams, John Jay and James Duane, Patrick Henry, and Richard Henry Lee, it had men committed to some innovative action—not revolution, but a vigorous form of protest. Joseph Galloway, the distinguished leader of Pennsylvania, presented a plan of union providing for an American imperial government, with representatives from the local legislatures, a president-general appointed by the king, and power over commercial, criminal, and civil affairs. In short, the American legislature, he wrote, "shall have power to chose their speaker, and shall hold and exercise all the like rights, liberties, and privileges as are held and exercised by and in the House of Commons of Great Britain."

Galloway's radical plan caused some debate, but the delegates were less concerned with governmental union than with making an effective protest. They formulated, therefore, a declaration of rights and resolves in which they stated their constitutional position and reasons for objecting to various British laws. At its end they projected a course of resistance that became the basis of the Continental Association of October 20. In combating the "destruction of lives, liberty, and property," they planned to embargo trade with Great Britain and ask all Americans to be frugal. They would also invite their fellow Americans to set up committees in every community to supervise trade, encourage manufacturing, and maintian loyalty. The congress concluded its deliberations with a final petition "of reverence and loyalty" to the king.

The delegates returned home. While they had not declared the colonies independent, they had made it difficult for moderates to resist the revolutionary groups, which collected arms, harassed pro-British subjects, and obstructed commerce. They isolated British General-Governor Gage in Boston, cut off nearly all trade with England, and turned America from thoughts of peace to thoughts of war. While many people were unwilling, even then, to plot the future course of resistance, men like John Adams, in his *Novanglus* of January 1775, came near to declaring America independent:

> We owe no allegiance to any crown at all. We owe allegiance to the person of His Majesty, King George III, whom God preserve. But allegiance is due universally, both from Britons and Americans to the person of the king, not to his crown; to his natural, not his politic capacity.

Into Revolution in Arms and Thought

The position of the colonies disturbed Britons too. In the ministry, as the country was prepared for military combat, only Lord North and Lord Dartmouth, the Secretary for Colonies, favored conciliation. They risked parliamentary censure by pushing through the famous Conciliatory Resolution of February 20. But the resolution offered Americans little, save that they could tax themselves in paying costs of defense and administration. The ministry tempered even this action by approving a hard policy toward the colonies—reinforcements for

Gage, economic restrictions, and a declaration of rebellion against Massachusetts. Gage received the help of Major Generals William Howe, Henry Clinton, and John Burgoyne as well as orders to arrest revolutionary leaders and seize military stores. He was instructed to make some lightning raids that would undermine morale, take prisoners, and relieve besieged Boston.

Lexington, Concord, and the Siege of Boston

When Gage received these London dispatches on April 14, he hastened to comply with his orders. It seemed to him that Concord, the meeting place of the legislature, would be a strategic town to attack, with some leaders still there and probably with large military stores. He expected to sweep down with a few troops and accomplish much with little risk. As Gage prepared for the expedition, however, news of his activities became known to the patriots. Hours before his men left for Lechmere Point across the Charles River, Paul Revere and William Dawes were making their midnight rides, and minutemen were preparing to assemble on the Lexington Green.

As Gage's troops marched along Concord road early on the morning of April 19, 1775, they met some seventy militiamen drawn up on Lexington Green. The militiamen moved quickly toward a distant fence as the troops came within musket range, but someone opened fire. In the exchange that followed, eight Americans were killed and ten wounded, and a few were pursued into private homes and captured and killed there.

The militiamen scattered, and the troops advanced cautiously toward Concord. Musket shots and church bells signaled their progress on the road and brought out a force of nearly four hundred men to await them at Concord's North Bridge. The forces exchanged fire briefly, but then the troops, fearing for their safety, fell back from Concord.

Their return march to Boston was a terrible ordeal, as Americans fired on them from walls, houses, and trees. A relief party of twelve hundred men was sent to join them, but the Americans, undaunted, kept up their fire all along the way until the British were again in Boston. Dead were 273 British and perhaps as many as 95 Americans. The sudden clash, with all its bitterness, aroused the countryside, and thousands of Americans rushed to join in the siege of Boston.

Most Americans were shocked by the news of Lexington and Concord, especially by reports of atrocities, which were vividly exaggerated by the patriots. The propaganda put Britain in the position of an aggressor, a foe of liberty and humanity, and an enemy. Waves of emotion spread across the colonies and brought the collapse almost everywhere of royal government. They also doomed Lord North's Conciliatory Resolution, which arrived in the colonies about the

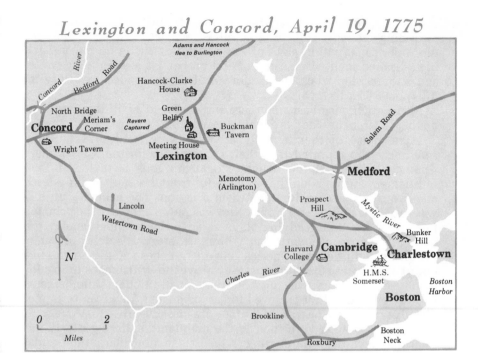

Lexington and Concord, April 19, 1775

time of the clash and made military preparedness the first business of the Second Continental Congress, convened on May 10 at Philadelphia.

This Congress rivaled in luster the first, with Benjamin Franklin, George Washington, and Thomas Jefferson among the distinguished new members. As in the earlier Congress, the members hesitated to adopt war measures and voted instead an "Olive Branch Petition," urging the king to guard their rights against the encroachments of Parliament. But they also turned to the practical business of defense, raising money and forming an army. The most immediate task was the choice of a military leader who would reflect their own cautious attitude and also would symbolize, in word and deed, the American cause. Such was Washington, a moderate in politics, a man of wealth and position, and an amateur soldier whose personal qualities were recognized by a unanimous vote of the Congress. He was to need their full confidence, for already the Americans were engaged in another bloody battle in Massachusetts.

Gathered around Boston in June 1775, the militiamen had sealed off the city from the countryside, although the British were free to come and go by sea. General Gage did not have sufficient troops for

another expedition and occupied himself with defensive measures—
disarming citizens, collecting supplies, and stationing cannon—and
the Americans, within sight of these batteries, made no move. Lacking seasoned men, siege cannon, and proper leadership, they waited
and suffered the trials of inaction until Gage decided to fortify the
hills above Charlestown.

The Americans hastened there and on Breed's Hill threw up a re-
doubt, dug trenches, and brought in powder and arms.

The noise of their activity at night was heard by the British
sentinels, who reported it to their superiors in Boston. Gage's major
generals laughed at the haughty, contemptuous behavior of these
militiamen and decided that a powerful frontal assault, with a lesser
attack at the rear, would teach them a lesson. The general's attitude
was equally haughty, and Howe, who was put in charge of the principal
force, took his time readying his men, spending as much energy preparing the garrison's quarters as with the strategy. His delay in staging
the attack permitted the Americans to dig trenches and pile up mounds
of dirt. From these fortifications, they drove the British back from a few
bloody assaults. Gage was forced to send for additional reinforcements,
and the pressure of his renewed forces exhausted American resources,
already unequal to the task. In the face of a massive drive, the Americans
retreated to Bunker Hill, then to the mainland, suffering nearly four
hundred casualties but inflicting on the British more than a thousand.

The heavy losses stabilized military activity for the next nine
months. Washington, taking charge of the siege in July, began recruiting men for the regular army, while the besieged British debated the
value of Boston as a base. Washington also used these months of stalemate to have heavy cannon moved from Ticonderoga and placed
upon the heights of Dorchester in March 1776. The threat of such
fire was sufficient to convince William Howe, who had succeeded
Gage, that Boston was no longer defensible, and he evacuated immediately the thousands of soldiers and Loyalists to distant Halifax.
Howe's departure was actually a preliminary regrouping of forces
for a new campaign. With reinforcements on their way, he awaited
the opportunity for an assault upon New York, where he would have
the advantages of Loyalist residents, water routes into the interior,
and food supplies. His plans were obvious to Washington, who reassessed the military situation and decided to move his own forces
southward.

In the meantime, the British government rejected the "Olive
Branch Petition" and, refusing any thought of compromise, proclaimed
America in "open and avowed rebellion." The declaration caused
debate in Parliament between friends and foes of the colonies. The
reality of war, with the prospect of punishing American leaders as
rebels, raised questions of justice and liberty, but Lord North called
upon his overwhelming majority in Parliament to brush aside all

Signing of the Declaration of Independence
(Iverson Collection University of Kansas)

warnings of disaster. In rapid succession, laws were passed providing for a naval blockade, impressment of Americans, mercenary troops, and the creation of an expeditionary force that would reach thirty-four thousand men in 1776.

The Declaration of Independence

These measures also caused public debate in America. Many loyal colonists were perplexed as to how they should react to British war preparations, and larger numbers of patriots reluctantly accepted mobilization, even independence, as the only alternative to suppression or total submission. Britain had not stated her war aims, and the Loyalists often found themselves in the perplexing position of having to choose between extremes.

For many patriots like John Adams, George Washington, and Thomas Paine, a declaration of independence seemed the only course of action to clear the political atmosphere. The publication in 1776 of Paine's *Common Sense* and Adams's *Thoughts on Government* hastened the movement for a pronouncement, and Congress, modifying a document written primarily by Thomas Jefferson, gave that pronouncement to the states in July 1776. It began with this statement of philosophy:

> When in the course of human events, it becomes necessary for one people to dissolve the political bands which have connected them with another, and to assume among the powers of the earth the separate and equal station to which the Laws of Nature and of Nature's God entitle them, a decent respect to the opinions of mankind requires that they should declare the causes which impel them to the separation.

> We hold these truths to be self-evident, that all men are created equal, that they are endowed by their Creator with certain unalienable rights, that among these are life, liberty, and the pursuit of happiness.

The Declaration of Independence set forth the reasons for separation from Great Britain and laid down a broad philosophical basis for revolution that aroused not only many Americans but also people of like spirit in Europe. It may have unfairly indicted George III for the evils that were separating the two peoples, but the personalization of the conflict had a psychological impact that forever damaged the cause of monarchy in America, and it turned Americans to thoughts of establishing a republican government.

Toward National Union

This was the first time most of the people had pondered the implications of independence. Many had long felt that America was different from England; the thought of independence gave them the inspiration to speculate on the structure of the new government, its place in the world, and its institutions. To trace these origins of nationalism and republicanism would be difficult, but these forces had a great influence at this time in determining the future character of the evolving nation. Men like Benjamin Rush, the influential medical doctor of Philadelphia, believed America was being given a unique opportunity in the history of the world, a chance to develop new institutions, refine old ones, and build a nation upon principles of liberty and justice. His view of the Revolution as part of a world movement was symbolic of how American thought had shifted—from causes of revolt, like taxation and representation, to the duty of creating a new order.

Though Americans searched for the significance of what they were experiencing, few had yet interpreted the Revolution in terms of a united American nation. The Declaration of Independence, however, obliged Congress to consider this important question, and a committee, with John Dickinson as an important member, finally drew up the Articles of Confederation. These articles provided for a republican government, a national legislature, a loosely organized federal structure of government, and certain powers for the union, like the postal service, coinage, and Indian relations. While Congress lacked the powers to raise taxes and regulate trade, these were probably less important at this point than the act of laying the foundation of a union. As the national government came to be appreciated, it could grow in power to meet the need. Even the limited powers of the Articles, however, seemed excessive to some people, who held up ratification until 1781.

Sentiment for union, of course, was forming. From the organization of the army, the battles of the war, the sacrifices of life and treasure, and the help of foreign nations, strength was given to the cause. From the devotion of Washington as commander-in-chief, the people gained inspiration. Modest and unselfish, he assumed the responsibilities placed upon him with integrity and dignity. He avoided quarrels and intrigue, asked no salary or financial benefits for himself, and lived up to the ideals of republicanism, even when the power thrust into his hands could have made him king. A modern Cato, he ennobled the cause.

The Campaigns of 1776 and 1777

Upon the British evacuation of Boston in March 1776, Washington transferred his headquarters to New York. The town was full of Loyalists, and nearly defenseless without extraordinary cooperation from its people. Its riverways and bays made its fortification exceptionally difficult without naval support and experienced soldiers. Even though Washington had some feeling for his peril, he stationed troops at strategic locations and had fortifications hastily thrown up. His plans were not equal to the British threat which was awesome in appearance: 29,000 British troops, thousands of mercenaries from Hesse-Kassel, Brunswick, and elsewhere in Germany and, in addition, a naval squadron of frigates, ships of the line, and transports, perhaps totaling two hundred vessels. Washington was fortunate, nonetheless, to gain something when the Howe brothers, Admiral Richard and General William, did not immediately test the defenses.

Admiral Howe brought with him a peace proposal that promised pardons to Americans if they would submit to British authority. In an informal conversation with the Americans, Howe expressed his friendship for America and offered "to converse and confer." While he sidestepped the important political and philosophical issues of the conflict, he promised peace through submission to what was described as the best of empires and the gentlest of kings. But he could not conceal the

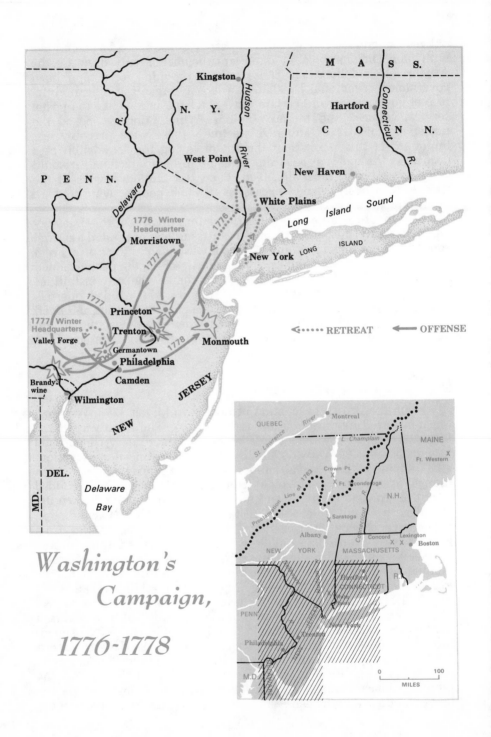

Washington's
Campaign,
1776-1778

fact that he lacked power to negotiate terms for peace. The American envoys accepted Howe's wine and dinner, but emphasized that further discussions were useless.

Howe also expressed the futility of continued talks by landing 20,000 men at Gravesend on Long Island and striking Washington's army of 8000 men at Flatbush and Brooklyn Heights. Howe's superior army forced Washington to retreat across the East River. With the aid of a driving rain and fog to cover his evacuation, Washington success-fully regrouped his forces in Manhattan, but further retreats were neces-sary to prevent his army from being surrounded, and positions were taken at Harlem Heights, then White Plains. Washington left garrisons of nearly 7000 men at Forts Washington and Lee as he moved north-ward to Peekskill. In making these moves, he had good fortune; Howe followed up advantages slowly and gave Washington time to get his supplies to safety. Howe's swift attack on Fort Washington, however, captured not only the fortress with its 3000 men but also irreplaceable arms and equipment. The emergency forced Washington to abandon the New York area and flee into New Jersey.

With more energy and imagination, Howe could easily have made short work of Washington's armies. Instead of pursuing them with his whole force, however, Howe sent 6000 troops to Newport, Rhode Island, and ordered preparations for winter quarters. He let Lord Charles Cornwallis pursue Washington south of New Brunswick, New Jersey, and engage him in battle. But Washington retreated so fast that he exhausted the British forces and lessened the pressure of attack. Reaching the Delaware River, he seized boats for miles on either side of his proposed crossing and then moved his troops into the safety of Pennsylvania just as Cornwallis neared the river.

The weather was brutally cold, and rather than prepare ships for the crossing, Cornwallis decided to garrison some men for the winter and pull the major forces back to New Brunswick. But the fighting season was not over for Washington. Reassembling his men and collect-ing some Pennsylvania volunteers and regulars under John Sullivan, he planned a surprise attack on Trenton. With about 2400 men, he crossed above Trenton and hit the town at dawn. The Hessian mercen-aries, having neglected orders to fortify their positions, were caught off guard, and most of the garrison was captured. A few days later, with more good luck and courage, Washington's men took the Prince-ton garrison.

These victories, though minor, heartened Americans everywhere and encouraged resistance in 1777. On the other hand, the British had expected the campaigns of 1777 to end the war. The success British arms had had in 1776 was undeniable, and Washington had to count fortune as an ally for his success at Trenton and Princeton. The British now planned to open the new season with an attack upon Philadelphia, retaining some forces in Rhode Island and New York City as garrisons, and then to end the summer by cooperating with the northern campaigners. A Canadian army under John Burgoyne was to march south from Montreal, and lesser units to move eastward from Oswego on Lake Ontario. Together these British forces were to split the colonies, allow Britain to fight one part at a time, and finish the conquest in 1778. In Philadelphia Howe would be able to call the Loyalists to the colors and enlist their aid as the rebellion was gradually suppressed.

But British strategy was complicated by problems of communication and distance. With not one but three successive campaign plans suggested, the field commanders were often confused as to which plan was being followed, and because they held independent commissions their movements were often uncoordinated. In addition, serious errors were made in timing the campaign and deploying troops and materiel. For example, Howe delayed his voyage to Philadelphia until July 23, then left Henry Clinton to defend New York with 7000 men and without authority to assist Burgoyne, who was to come down the Hudson River in late summer.

Though there was considerable debate among Howe's staff over the objectives of the campaign, they did not turn Howe's mind from Philadelphia as a major objective. Their arguments undoubtedly delayed his departure, but he easily reached the Delaware River in July. When he realized that Washington had thrown up defenses along the river, he sailed for the Chesapeake and disembarked his men at its head on August 25. The long voyage, perhaps justified to avoid American fire, wearied his men and delayed the campaign. Howe was confronted by repeated attacks as he left the Chesapeake. Time and time again he was successful in pushing Washington back. At Kennett Square, Brandywine, and Germantown, the Americans suffered heavier losses than the British, but they fought, occasionally with brilliance, and kept Howe occupied until October.

Though Howe won many battles, he achieved no real victory, even after he entered Philadelphia. He encountered hostility everywhere he turned, and found few Loyalists to join the army; rather, they enjoyed the social life of his regiments and the profits from supplying his troops. Indeed, the longer he stayed in the city the less cooperation he received.

In northern New York along the water-land route south of Lake Champlain, Burgoyne's army was slowed down on the frontier path by Americans who threw brush into the line of march, and was resisted fiercely as it approached the settled regions. When his food supplies were nearly depleted, Burgoyne sent troops foraging into Vermont. The deeper they penetrated, the more local opposition they encountered. At Bennington, a rising of farmers supported by veteran troops broke up the expedition and inflicted heavy losses. Their victory occurred while other British forces, under Barry St. Leger, were pushing eastward across the Mohawk Valley. There also savage resistance forced the British to turn back. These defeats left the principal British army without food or hope of reinforcements. In addition, its position was severely tested by Americans, who resisted its every move and then surrounded it when it stopped. Accepting the inevitable, Burgoyne surrendered his army to Horatio Gates, the senior American general, on October 17. That day about five thousand regular troops surrendered, and the shock of defeat put the British momentarily on the defensive.

The American victories during 1777 changed the character of the war. Foreigners were impressed with Washington's ability to hold his army together, exchange blow for blow, and make strategic retreats. They hailed the destruction of Burgoyne's army as evidence that the Americans would fight until they had won their independence. The determination of the Americans fitted into France's plans for avenging her losses in the Seven Years' War, and she consulted her ally, Spain, on how both nations could best support the Revolution.

Americans had come a long way since the end of the Great War for Empire in 1763. In their fight against taxation and for constitutional rights, they had become less and less colonial in their political views and more and more national in their aspirations. For men like Benjamin Rush and John Adams their Revolution seemed to have world significance; indeed, the presence of Benjamin Franklin in France as an American minister was symbolic of the change in America's position. "His reputation," said Adams, is "more universal than that of Leibnitz or Newton, Frederick or Voltaire, and his character more beloved and esteemed than any or all of them."

SUGGESTIONS FOR FURTHER READING

Adair, Douglass and John A. Schutz, eds., *Peter Oliver's Origin & Progress of the American Rebellion.* Stanford, Calif., Stanford University Press, 1967.

Adams, Randolph G., *Political Ideas of the American Revolution,* 3rd ed., with commentary by Merrill Jensen. New York, Barnes & Nobel, 1958.

Bailyn, Bernard, *The Ideological Origins of the American Revolution.* Cambridge, Mass., Harvard University Press, 1967.

Bridenbaugh, Carl, *Mitre and Sceptre.* New York, Oxford University Press, 1967.

Brown, Gerald Saxon, *The American Secretary: The Colonial Policy of Lord George Germain, 1775-1778.* Ann Arbor, Mich., The University of Michigan Press, 1963.

Douglass, Elisha P., *Rebels and Democrats: The Struggle for Equal Political Rights and Majority Rule During the American Revolution.* Chicago, Quadrangle Books, 1965.

Flexner, James Thomas, *Washington: The Indispensable Man.* Boston, Little, Brown and Company, 1974.

Gipson, Lawrence Henry, "The American Revolution as an Aftermath of the Great War for the Empire, 1754-1763," *The Political Science Quarterly,* LXV, 86-104.

_____, *The Coming of the American Revolution.* New York, Harper Torchbooks, Harper and Row, 1962.

Guttridge, George H., *English Whiggism and the American Revolution.* Berkeley and Los Angeles, University of California press, 1966.

Kollenberg, Bernhard, *Origin of the American Revolution, 1759-1766.* New York, Collier Books, Crowell Collier and Macmillan, 1961.

Labaree, Benjamin Woods, *The Boston Tea Party.* New York, Oxford University Press, 1964.

McIllwain, Charles Howard, *The American Revolution.* Ithaca, New York, Great Seal Books, Cornell University Press, 1961.

Main, Jackson Turner, *The Social Structure of Revolutionary America.* Princeton, N.J., Princeton University Press, 1968.

Morgan, Edmund S., *The Challenge of the American Revolution.* New York, W. W. Norton and Company, 1976.

_____, and Helen M., *The Stamp Act Crisis.* New York, Collier Books, Crowell Collier and Macmillan, 1963.

Pole, J. R., *Foundations of American Independence, 1763-1815.* Indianapolis and New York, The Bobbs-Merrill Company, Inc., 1972.

Rossiter, Clinton, *The First American Revolution.* New York, Harvest Books, Harcourt, Brace and World, 1956.

Smith, Paul H., *Loyalists and Redcoats: A Study in British Revolutionary Policy.* New York, The Norton Library, W. W. Norton and Company, 1964.

Van Alstyne, Richard W., *The Rising American Empire.* Chicago, Quadrangle Books, 1965.

The Struggle
for Republican Government

MOST AMERICANS WAITED UNTIL 1775 to call their dispute
with England a revolution. Even then, some regretted the decision
and urged additional effort to settle the "family argument." Calling
the conflict a "revolution," nonetheless, raised for them interesting questions of its causes, objectives and character, and Americans searched
English and Ancient history for examples of the phenomena. Americans
realized very quickly that they had an opportunity should the conflict
be successful of developing a new order. Sometimes, indeed, they
became so absorbed in plans for changes that the battlefield seemed
less important than the legislature.

French Help

The need for foreign help was roundly debated on ideological
grounds, but Americans were confronted immediately by military
demands for powder, muskets, and cannon. France who was the enemy
in times past now seemed a possible source of help, and agents were
dispatched to seek military support.

The entrance of France into the war, however, awaited also the

American definition of their conflict with England. France had shown interest in a possible war between the Colonies and England early in the 1770s, but had hesitated to interfere openly until American determination was tested on the battlefield. Her great foreign minister, the Comte de Vergennes, had as early as 1775 followed with satisfaction British inability to suppress the Revolution. Sending agents to America and using the help of Caron de Beaumarchais in France, he provided some money for munitions and arms and interested Spain in the cause. These supplies arrived in increasing quantities during 1776 and were certainly an essential part of the American victory at Saratoga in 1777. Vergennes also revealed his sympathy for the American cause by receiving formally commissioners from the new government and permitting them to remain in Paris.

These new contacts with France and Spain represented a momentous shift in American attitude. From traditional enemies in politics and religion these countries had come to be accepted as friends or at least as allies in the revolutionary struggle. Somehow, prejudices against French religion, law, customs, and power, long sources of hostility, were brushed aside or tolerated and minimized as Americans took French arms. A few Americans, nonetheless, were reluctant to bring Europe into the conflict itself, and their delegates in the Continental Congress wanted to avoid permanent alliances and to separate the new American order from the politics and corruption of Europe; the decision to ally with Europeans seemed to them to compromise basic principles, but they were won over by assurances that any alliances would be terminated at the end of the war.

The Continental Congress was not content to wait until the French ministry made up its mind concerning recognition and open participation. It instructed Franklin, as the chief American envoy, to popularize the revolutionary cause and to attach himself to French intellectuals. Franklin played his part well as scientist, legislator, and rustic American and won invitations into French society. Using his Masonic connections, he fraternized with his brothers in the French lodges, and by dressing simply he exploited the popular rumor that he was a Quaker.

Thus both France and America calculated the advantages of an alliance, and France finally moved openly when the victory of Saratoga was virtually certain. The Treaty of 1778 assured America of French military participation and eventually obtained a second front in Europe to divide British forces, the active help of Spain in Florida, and the armed neutrality of the better part of Europe. Moreover, French financial backing of the Revolution, without which a continuation of the war would have been nearly impossible, was put on a regular basis. The alliance, too, encouraged the enlistment of many professional soldiers in Europe. France, for her part, was assured that America would not make a separate peace and would remain a loyal ally. The French alliance changed drastically the strategy of the American war. It gave the states a naval force, striking power in the West Indies and Europe, and a divisive issue to separate Britons.

For a time Parliament considered peace proposals and, indeed, authorized a commission under Lord Carlisle to treat with any patriotic group and concede home rule. To ease the situation, Lord North offered to resign in favor of another leader or the opposition Whigs, but George III threatened to abdicate rather than have the hated Whigs in office. In the meantime, the British ministry made some military changes. Henry Clinton replaced William Howe as commander-in-chief, and because of a possible French attack, he was ordered to consolidate the British military position. He was given permission to evacuate Philadelphia and, if necessary, New York, but was told to hold Newport, Rhode Island, as a possible base for operations against New England. He was to maintain a defensive position in the North while other British forces invaded Georgia and St. Lucia.

Britain's reassessment of the military situation did not help Washington, who had quartered his troops at Valley Forge. There was almost nothing to feed an army, for most grain and cattle had been consumed during the last campaign and Congress had not brought in additional supplies. His men suffered from cold, insufficient food, and loss of morale. Many in desperation deserted to their homes or took the honorable alternative of resigning their commissions. Washington also was troubled with opposition from some generals and from Congress. A few of the delegates accused him of incompetence for not whipping Howe at the gates of Philadelphia; others feared that he might assume dictatorial power. They wanted Gates, the victor of Saratoga, as his successor, but Washington's friends rallied to his support. Congress eventually appointed a quartermaster general, Nathanael Greene, who found supplies for the hungry army and promised bonuses to men who would serve until the war's end. Europeans like Baron von Steuben lifted morale by providing special services. The army was thus in much better condition when it challenged Clinton's forces in June 1778.

Evacuating Philadelphia, Clinton took about ten thousand troops by land across New Jersey. Washington, making use of the opportunity, attacked the rear of the slow-moving army. The daring assault brought an immediate reply, which Washington met by taking a superior position and driving off Clinton's attacks. Both sides were cautious when face to face, and both claimed partial victory after a clash or two. The Battle of Monmouth was indecisive, and represented a lengthy stalemate that affected military action in the north. In 1779 and 1780 Washington was never strong enough to attack New York, and Clinton awaited a Loyalist uprising in the southern states before he moved again. On the sea, however, thousands of Americans engaged in privateering, and the cost to British shipping was serious; perhaps as many as two thousand ships were sunk and twelve thousand seamen were captured. John Paul Jones won glory as a sea captain in his famous seizure of the *Serapis*. The British navy retaliated with raids ashore that plundered New Haven, Fairfield, and Norwalk, Connecticut, and created anxiety along the shores of Chesapeake Bay.

America During the Revolution

While Americans traded blows with the British on land and sea, and Congress found European allies for the states, the Revolution took on a political form. The battles of the war were sometimes far from the thoughts of patriots as they overturned British rulers and colonial charters. For a time they governed their states by committees of safety and conventions; they wanted orderly, constitutional governments, and within a few months after the Declaration of Independence the process of writing new constitutions, or modifying old ones, was completed. Since the Revolution was fought primarily over the issue of taxation and representation, these constitutional changes were initiated by the state legislatures. Some people in Massachusetts, however, were opposed to this method fo constitution-making and demanded a special convention and a vote of the people. Protests by the people of Concord and Pittsfield were part of a movement that led in 1779 to a special convention and the submission of the proposed constitution to the people.

These revolutionary constitutions were similar. Generally they included a bill of rights; elected legislatures, usually of two houses; an elected governor, and courts separated in powers from the executive and legislative branches. The franchise was limited in most states to property-owners or to taxpayers. Most revolutionary leaders generally accepted the political order established in the old colonies. Among individuals there were variations of opinion on representation, freedom of worship, and slavery, but most leaders wanted to achieve the political goals set by the chief philosophers of the age. With the Englishman John Locke, they wished government to be an instrument for human betterment and with the Frenchman Montesquieu they planned for a separation of powers which would guarantee stability in the political order.

The more conservative leaders resisted excessive change. While they wished to republicanize the old colonial system, they wanted to retain control of government in the hands of the educated, propertied, and socially qualified. Majority rule, or popular rule, was despised and feared because it might lead to anarchy. They valued pomp and ceremony, family connections, and titles as devices to hold the general population in its place. Many conservatives were reluctant revolutionaries. When the old order was threatened by changes in legislative control, they gave their support to the national government. In Pennsyl-

vania the merchants, like the tidewater aristocrats of Virginia, turned
to a national government to protect their interests against the rising
power of the frontiersmen in the state.

The radical leaders, though not always democratic in philosophy,
insisted upon a greater extension of the franchise, more power for
the legislature, less dependence upon legal arrangements that favored
the eldest son over his younger brothers and sisters, and more educational opportunity. Generally, the popular tide was with the radicals,
but for the moment the opening of the West, with its abundance of
cheap land, took the people's mind off of social revolution. Those
who felt oppressed moved out of the range of government and, instead
of fighting for change, took advantage of the breakdown of British
authority to move west.

In Massachusetts and Pennsylvania, with their larger settled
populations, more democratic progress was achieved than in other
states. Societies to abolish slavery, to agitate for religious toleration,
and to make demands for a broader franchise were important movements. Their leaders formed societies advocating emancipation and
worked to have slavery eradicated by law. The Quakers had been in
the forefront of this movement, forming the first abolitionist society
in 1774; their work, however, was interrupted by the war, when Philadelphia was occupied and communications with other states became
difficult. Throughout the North they had found much sympathy for
abolition, and even in New York City leaders had cautiously backed
a program of reform. In the South, the concentration of slaves frightened some plantation owners, who feared a revolt, but influential
leaders like Washington, Jefferson, and Patrick Henry favored abolition and joined societies to promote the cause. In backing abolition,
however, most white reformers were limited in their appreciation of
the black man's future in a white man's society. Equality of opportunity
was not seriously considered, but Americans in general welcomed
blacks into the army and appreciated their service.

If toleration for blacks was still distant, in religion much more
was accomplished during the Revolution. Before the break with
Britain, most colonies had granted religious freedom to Protestants,
even though there were tax-supported Anglican and Congregational
churches in nine colonies. Roman Catholics and Jews were discrim-
inated against in all colonies except Rhode Island, and among the
rest, only in Maryland, Pennsylvania, and Delaware were the laws
sufficiently mild for Catholics to live comfortably. With the Revolution
the movement for disestablishment made great progress, especially
in the southern states where Baptists and other dissenters were superior
to the Anglicans in vigor and numbers. The Anglican Church in Virginia, however, had better support and was able to wage a ten-year
fight against liberalizing legislation. In the end, a statute of religious
liberty, drawn up by Thomas Jefferson, was passed. Its rhetorical first

section warned against the state's putting itself in the position of God by compelling religious worship:

> Truth is great and will prevail if left to herself, . . . she is the proper and sufficient antagonist to error, and has nothing to fear from the conflict, unless by human interposition disarmed of her natural weapons, free argument and debate, errors ceasing to be dangerous when it is permitted freely to contradict them.

Jefferson was rightly proud of his part in securing religious liberty for Virginia. Tax-supported churches, however, continued in some New England states for another fifty years, and various kinds of written and unwritten restrictions disturbed the religious community for decades. Full religious toleration for Roman Catholics would not be a reality until the twentieth century.

For women there was new respect. The war gave them responsibilities as they managed farms and businesses and supervised their families while their husbands were away. They served often as nurses, hostesses, and messengers, even as spies, and they won champions like Benjamin Rush who urged education fitting their position in the new republican society. Women, nonetheless, spent most of their time at home, in raising large families and in looking after household matters. John Adams' wife, Abigail, was such a woman. Her letters reveal concerns for the education of the children, the farm, the rights of women, and the progress of the Revolution, and they were an inspiration to her husband. Mrs. Adams was an example of a thoughtful person who felt deeply about the problems facing her sex and the nation.

The liberal course of the Revolution had also its effect on the distribution of land. Almost everywhere in America there were landless people, perhaps as high as twenty-five percent of the population in the more settled areas. Since 1763 British policy toward the West had discouraged migration, and the speculative land companies of the 1740s were unable to exploit their vast tracts. Even so, thousands of people settled in the Tennessee region along the Watauga River, made their homes, and created prospering villages. In the Kentucky area, too, pioneers founded settlements near the present-day city of Lexington. With the Revolution these western areas were incorporated into the states of Virginia or North Carolina by the establishment of county governments. But distance, isolation, and inadequate government made these arrangements unsuitable. Frontiersmen went their way as the states argued among themselves over title to the West. At length all parties looked to the Continental Congress as an arbitrator in their disputes.

The internal revolution may not have brought great changes to American society, but the colonial order was gone. New men were taking governmental positions everywhere; new ideas of republicanism and nationalism were uniting Americans. Almost everyone real-

Abigail Adams *(New York State Historical Association)*

ized that his safety depended upon common action and that the Continental Congress was the appropriate central body. In waging war, maintaining diplomatic relations, providing governmental services like paper money and a post office, and declaring the colonies independent states, the Congress certainly took important steps toward national unity. Perhaps the most valuable of all its accomplishments was the creation of a national leadership—military, legislative, diplomatic, and administrative—with leaders who, from time to time, felt the obligation of returning to their states in order to accomplish some necessary task there. So John Adams left diplomacy temporarily and accepted the arduous responsibility of drawing up the 1780 Massachusetts constitution, and Thomas Jefferson left national affairs for service as governor of Virginia.

Over the years of the Revolution, the Continental Congress attracted men of talent and integrity. They toiled in committees, working for the common good, and carried out most of the executive functions of the central government. Their record of service, though marred by the weaknesses of the Confederation, was good. They cooperated with George Washington, gave him leeway in reaching decisions, and backed him in crises. They sought foreign alliances, and with Franklin, John Adams, and John Jay they successfully obtained the money and supplies to win the Revolution. They kept a government in being, even when they had to retreat from Philadelphia, and they drew up the first United States Constitution.

The Articles of Confederation

Congress struggled to gain the approval of the states for the Articles of Confederation. Ten of the Thirteen States had ratified the Articles by July 1778, but Maryland, New Jersey, and Delaware insisted that Congress should be given authority over western lands before they would ratify. Maryland held out for nearly two years, forcing an evaluation of western land grants. Finally, Virginia generously ceded to the Union her trans-Ohio River lands, stipulating only that land speculators like those in Maryland were to receive no advantage. Connecticut, too, promised to give up some of her western land. With these concessions and under pressure from France, Maryland at last ratified the Articles, and on March 1, 1781 the American Union was formally established.

Union was not the only problem facing the states. The home front was troubled by civil conflict. The states were unable to impose controls or compel loyalty, and at no time were the full resources of the states thrown into the Revolution. Not only did the war bring disruption to ordinary routines of life, but the invasion, blockade, and division of the country at times had a detrimental effect on the economy. All the governments issued excessive amounts of paper money; the Continental Congress before 1780 had put out nearly $200 million. The serious inflation forced some governments to fix prices. Many merchants took advantage of scarce products to evade restrictions or engage in privateering for personal profits. Some fortunes were made in this business, like that of the merchant Stephen Higginson of Massachusetts, but opportunities to make hugh profits were readily available also to military commissaries and those serving in government.

No part of the population suffered so much as the Loyalists, or Tories. They came from nearly every class, rich and poor, educated and uneducated, native born and recently arrived, Congregationalist and Anglican. At the beginning of the war, there were undoubtedly large numbers of Loyalists, but over the years the failure of British military policy and the brutalities of American treatment brought many to the revolutionary side. But there remained those who assisted the British army and provisioned it, propagandized for the British cause, and acted as spies. Some enlisted into British regiments, formed their own provincial units, or raided patriot settlements; a few tried to arouse the hostility of the Indians. As their activities became known, bitterness toward them increased. The states passed laws denying them civil rights and imposing harsh fines, penalties, and restrictions. Most Loyalists were driven from their property and, almost everywhere, physical harm was threatened. Only a few suffered death, but great numbers were forced into exile; perhaps as many as 100,000 fled to Nova Scotia, New Brunswick, Ontario, or England and a few settled in the West Indies and Bermuda. More might have been hanged, whipped to death, or tarred and feathered if American authorities had not feared retaliation. But at times hatred was intense, and some Loyalists were fortunate to escape abroad British warships.

Concluding the War

The Loyalists always had boasted that if they had the chance to fight, they would give Britain victory. In 1778 Henry Clinton was ordered to mount an offensive in Georgia and South Carolina and call them to help him. In a matter of weeks and a few easy victories, Georgia fell into British hands and royal government was restored. The attack on South Carolina took longer, but in May 1780 the British, employing a combination of naval and land forces, seized Charleston.

The capture of the city, with five thousand soldiers and much heavy equipment, was a serious blow to American prestige, but these losses sharpened Carolinian resistance. Leaders like Thomas Sumter, Francis Marion, and Andrew Pickens executed well-planned raids, making the back country dangerous to British forces, and Congress sent Horatio Gates into the state to command regular troops. Although the troops were poorly equipped, hungry, and sick, Gates was determined to attack Camden, in the heart of hostile country. Meeting the British army of over two thousand regulars, Gates was outflanked and outfought, and his men fled in wild disorder.

The British victory tempted her commander, Lord Cornwallis, to invade North Carolina and Virginia, even though this would mean disobeying his orders to hold Charleston and to keep his troops available as a striking force. Weighing the dangers of a distant march, he recklessly decided to take matters into his own hands and launched his campaign. But in North Carolina he discovered that the Americans were fighting harder than they had been in South Carolina. Fewer Loyalists volunteered, and those who joined Tory forces in the battle of King's Mountain in October 1780 were badly whipped. Cornwallis discounted the setback when he received reinforcements and learned that other British forces under Benedict Arnold, the American traitor, were operating in Virginia. He also failed to weigh the military consequences of the change in the American command, when General Nathanael Greene replaced the bungling Gates.

Greene infused immediately into the southern army vitality and daring that were reflected in its fighting. While cautious in tactics, he was courageous, and he set out to harass Cornwallis in any possible way. Greene permitted Daniel Morgan's riflemen to attack and run, frequently by prearranged routes. Sometimes they drew British forces into unfamiliar territory and stood on favorable grounds. Other times they met the enemy at a river or hill, hit him as long as they were winning, and then retreated. Their toll on men and supplies weakened Cornwallis, who found himself, as at Guilford Courthouse in March 1781, unable to follow up attacks. In the end he drove north toward Yorktown, Virginia, where the British army could reinforce him.

As Cornwallis marched north, General Greene and a host of irregulars, operating sometimes together and sometimes independently, moved against British forts and garrisons. The Americans were not always successful in meeting the British, suffering heavy losses at times, but they continued their resistance and turned the countryside against the British. In three or four months of hit-and-run attacks, they had driven the British into garrison positions primarily at Charleston and Savannah, towns that remained in British hands until the end of the war.

In Virginia, Cornwallis moved slowly, collecting other British fighting units as he went toward Yorktown. When he entered Petersburg on May 23, 1781, he had seven thousand men. News of his march disturbed the cautious Clinton who feared the loss of bases in the South and the threat to his army in New York. Since Cornwallis was scheduled to succeed him, however, he deferred to the other's judgment. Cornwallis chose to build a base at Yorktown during the summer instead of combating the patriots. His presence on the peninsula attracted various American regiments, who took up positions to block his movement by land.

The significance of what was happening was quickly apparent to the French, who had long planned to use their great fleet in American waters. In the spring of 1781 they had twenty-eight warships in North American waters under the command of the Comte de Grasse, who was looking for a combined sea and land assault. The British navy, expecting De Grasse to split his fleet, did not have its own at full strength. Both Washington and the French army commander, the Comte de Rochambeau, had considered employing their forces against New York and other possible targets like Newport and Charleston. Cornwallis's exposed position offered a new possibility for attack, and after some hesitation Washington agreed to abandon the New York campaign and move 2000 of his regulars with Rochambeau's army southward into Virginia.

The change of objective was not fully understood by Clinton until the armies were well on their way. When he realized the gravity of the situation at Yorktown, he prepared to take a relief party of 4000 men there by sea, but while these reinforcements were on their way, De Grasse entered the Chesapeake and isolated Cornwallis. When the British ships tried to force an entry, they were turned back. The great peril to Cornwallis's army was obvious to Clinton, who refused to accept defeat and hastened another relief party to the Chesapeake. His mounting fear of tragedy drove him to accompany the fleet on this second attempt to run the French blockade. But even before they reached Virginia, they learned that Cornwallis had bowed to the inevitable on October 19. On that day more than 7000 men had given up their arms, while the British military band played "The World Turned Upside Down" and the French responded with "Yankee Doodle." Britain had experienced her darkest day of battle. When Lord North in England heard the fateful news, he exclaimed: "O God! It is all over."

Peace and Independence

Though the war was to continue for almost two years, the Battle of Yorktown was decisive. Joy spread across the land and a *Te Deum* was sung in Notre Dame Cathedral in Paris. In London, events moved swiftly, as Lord North was replaced by Lord Rockingham as prime minister and problems of peace came to dominate politics. The new ministry exchanged Clinton for Sir Guy Carleton and instructed Sir Guy to take the defensive. It also dispatched an envoy to Paris, with power to open negotiations with Benjamin Franklin. The United States reacted cautiously, but drew to Paris its other European envoys, John Adams from the Netherlands and John Jay from Spain, and they pondered with much wisdom the British proposals. The ministry had hoped not only to split the American-French alliance, but also to persuade Americans to consider a new kind of political union with Britain.

It counted heavily on American hostility to Spain as a wedge for breaking up the coalition.

Since the 1760s the government of Charles III of Spain had been taking defensive precautions against foreign invasion and had ordered financial and administrative reforms. In 1769 it had sent Franciscan missionaries under Junípero Serra into upper California, founding San Diego and Monterey that year, and in the next decade had encouraged immigrants to found the towns of San Francisco and Los Angeles. In Sonora and Arizona, Indians were pacified by Francisco Garcés, who founded Tucson in 1776 as a Spanish outpost of empire. In Texas the settlements at Goliad, Nacogdoches, and San Antonio were given additional colonists, and in Mississippi Valley Spain slowly brought her new colony of Louisiana into the empire. During the American Revolution the Spanish governor, Bernardo de Gálvez, provided some assistance to George Rogers Clark for expeditions into the Ohio Valley and led expeditions himself into the Floridas, which he recovered for Spain.

Throughout the Revolution, Spanish politicians remained suspicious of the Americans, fearing their republicanism as well as their expansionism. They refused in 1779 to ally themselves with the United States or to recognize her belligerency, and for their aid to France bound her to continue the war until Gibraltar was captured. They never received John Jay during his years of residence in Spain, regularly opened his mail, and generally maintained an icy attitude toward the Revolution. Both sides were unable to reconcile their territorial aspirations in the West, especially when the Americans demanded all British territory from the Atlantic to the Mississippi River. Even though Jay secured some financial help to relieve his personal distress, the Spanish court made its attitude toward republicanism painfully clear to him.

France, too, did not fully support American territorial ambitions. Her officials, moreover, favored Spain in a clash of interests between Spain and the United States, and France generally backed Spanish pretensions to territory in the Southwest. During the fall and winter of 1780, the Comte de Vergennes, her foreign minister, even pondered the possibility of negotiating peace, with the United States to get little more than a truce with Britain. But France was caught between the aspirations of her allies and merely managed, often not too skillfully, to hold her course.

American negotiations with Britain, therefore, were affected by suspicions of Spain and France and by a desire to win independence by a separate treaty, if necessary. But Franklin refused to break with France and insisted that negotiations by all parties proceed at the same time. He pointed out to the British envoy the advantages of American friendship if Britain were liberal in her concessions, and Lord Shelburne, known for his pro-American ideas, backed early negotia-

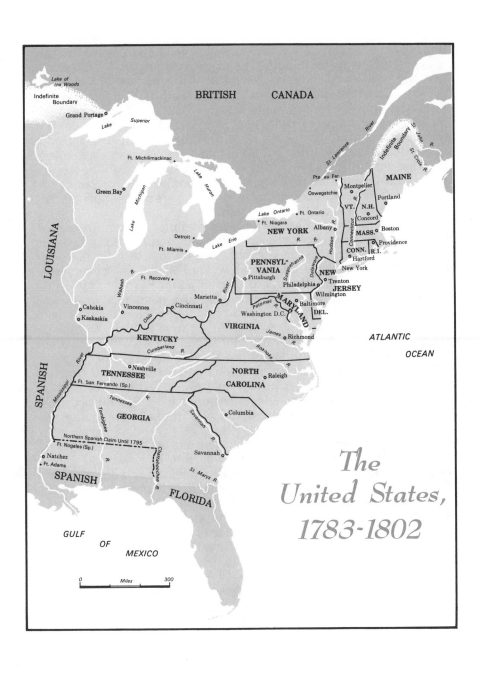

Lake of the Woods

Indefinite Boundary

Grand Portage

Lake Superior

BRITISH   CANADA

St. Lawrence River

Indefinite Boundary

St. John R.

St. Croix R.

Ft. Michilimackinac

Lake Huron

Green Bay

Lake Michigan

Pte. au Fer

MAINE

Montpelier

Oswegatchie

Portland

VT. N.H.

Concord

Lake Ontario   Ft. Ontario

Detroit

Lake Erie

Ft. Niagara

NEW YORK

Albany

R.

Connecticut R.

Boston

MASS.

Providence

Ft. Miamis

Hudson R.

CONN. R.I.

Hartford

Wabash R.

Ft. Recovery

PENNSYL-
VANIA

Susquehanna R.

Delaware R.

NEW
JERSEY

New York

Pittsburgh

Trenton

Philadelphia

LOUISIANA

River

Marietta

Ohio

Cahokia

Vincennes

Cincinnati

Wilmington

MARYLAND

Baltimore

Potomac R.

DEL.

Washington, D.C.

Kaskaskia

VIRGINIA

James R.

Richmond

ATLANTIC

OCEAN

KENTUCKY

Cumberland R.

Roanoke R.

Mississippi River

SPANISH

Nashville

TENNESSEE

Ft. San Fernando (Sp.)

NORTH
CAROLINA

Raleigh

Tennessee R.

Tombigbee R.

GEORGIA

Savannah R.

Columbia

Northern Spanish Claim Until 1795

Ft. Nogales (Sp.)

Natchez

Ft. Adams

R.

Chattahoochee R.

Savannah

St. Marys R.

SPANISH

FLORIDA

*The
United States,
1783-1802*

GULF

OF

MEXICO

0   Miles   300

tions as a prelude for an alliance. Indeed, when he succeeded Rockingham as prime minister in June 1782, he refused to grant independence in a last rigid stand for some sort of British-American union. Weeks passed as negotiations for a peace treaty were stalled. To break the deadlock, John Jay hinted to the British envoy that the United States might agree on a separate peace treaty and grant other concessions if its independence were conceded. Lord Shelburne reluctantly agreed to negotiate along these lines, but let the discussions move along toward a settlement. Within a few weeks the envoys agreed upon the wording of the peace treaty, and they signed preliminary treaties on January 20, 1783. The war was thus concluded. Within fourteen months the final treaty of peace was ratified by all parties.

But the final treaty left serious uncertainties concerning western boundaries, issues of prewar merchant debts, and Loyalist claims and treatment, and there was the problem as well of forgetting the late bitterness. At this critical time, unfortunately, Lord Shelburne was succeeded by a coalition of the followers of Charles James Fox and Lord North. Though Fox carried out some of Shelburne's plans, his government adopted instead the popular course of applying the mercantile laws. The ports of the West Indies were mostly closed to trade, and the old triangle of commerce was nearly eliminated by the new regulations. Instead of building up a union of peace and trade, walls of separation were erected. Britain refused to abandon frontier bases on American soil or to treat the first American envoy, John Adams, with the respect due to a delegate from an independent, friendly nation. Republican America received ridicule in the press and was frozen out of conferences with the ministry.

America's relations with Spain were no better. Boundary difficulties in the South arose over the ownership of a vast area west of Georgia and South Carolina. For the fifty thousand settlers of present-day Tennessee and Kentucky, the disputed boundary also raised questions about the free use of the Mississippi River or, more specifically, access to the ocean for their agricultural products. The confusion permitted the Indians to hold the balance of power. For nearly a decade, Alexander McGillivray of the Creeks used this opportunity to collect arms and tribute from Spain and defy the United States. In the meantime, Americans debated the value of the West, and statesmen like Jay suggested the possibility of trading the right of navigation for a treaty of commerce with Spain.

These disputed claims to the West should also be seen in terms of Indian interests. Numerous Indian tribes inhabited the vast area, for longer than any Indian could remember, and they had their homes, villages, and hunts there. Perhaps a half million Indians inhabited the area, but their interests became incidental to those of the invading settlers. The bitter clashes, nonetheless, made the west hazardous and slowed the advance.

The Young Nation

Even though difficulties with Britain and Spain were to drag on for a decade, Americans welcomed the opportunities of peace. Merchants loaded their shelves with goods and their ships again searched the West Indies for markets. Vessels also went into the Pacific, trading with Hawaii and China and exploring the Pacific shores north of California. Speculators formed land companies like the Ohio Company and the Scioto and sold thousands of acres of land to purchasers from along the East Coast and in Europe. Others chartered banks, formed stock companies, and invested in depreciated state bonds. Perhaps the most noticeable happening was the movement of people—into Vermont and the back country of New Hampshire and Maine, into New York's Mohawk Valley and the water route to Oswego, into present-day Tennessee and Kentucky. People were migrating, and frequently, as in Vermont and the Southwest, they insisted that the Confederation government provide adequate defense and order. When such services were not quickly granted, their loyalty wavered, sometimes to Spain and to Great Britain.

The experiences of the war also brought some changes in American society. In religious worship, men were willing to tolerate sects and traditions, and some, like Thomas Jefferson, wanted separation of church and state. The churches were reorganizing themselves, and the Roman Catholics, Episcopalians, and Methodists separated from England by erecting bishoprics and modifying their prayer books. In education, the Revolution brought some secularization of the curriculum; chairs of law and modern languages replaced those of divinity and Hebrew. Benjamin Rush and his colleagues at the Pennsylvania Medical School used their wartime experience to publish papers on tetanus, asphyxia, and inoculations. Many new colleges—Hampden-Sidney, Dickinson, Transylvania, and Georgetown—were founded in the 1780s from the desires for more educational opportunity and for neighborhood institutions. Two preparatory institutions of future eminence, Exeter and Andover, attracted students by their devoted faculties.

During the war, agitation against slavery had grown as blacks joined in the revolutionary cause and Americans were confronted by the implications of the natural rights philosophy. If the Revolution was a struggle to free men, how could color hold them in bondage? Five thousand black soldiers had participated in the war, and some had lost their lives; their sacrifice, however, probably had only a minor impact on the abolitionist movement. In Massachusetts the ideals of the Revolution were the foundation for a court decree in 1783 that brought black emancipation, although black political rights remained clouded as the legislature often passed racist laws. In Vermont the constitution of 1777 abolished slavery, and legislative enactments in

Pennsylvania (1780), Rhode Island (1784), and Connecticut (1784 and 1797) provided for gradual abolition. The struggle for full emancipation was carried forward by the Pennsylvania Quakers and the New York Manumission Society, which had such national leaders as John Jay and Alexander Hamilton as members and officers. Much was accomplished in these years, but equality with the white man was not granted to men of color.

News of the antislavery movement, as well as of other social issues, was aided by an extraordinary number of new publications. About ninety newspapers offered various kinds of service, including dailies in New York, Philadelphia, and Charleston. Even more magazines were published, and two of them, the *Columbian Magazine* and *American Museum*, had national circulations. The book trade, too, was revived, as was book publishing. Histories of the war, treatises on religion and medicine, geographies, and physics texts, as well as efforts in belles-lettres, appeared. Probably Joel Barlow's *Vision of Columbus* was best known, and Noah Webster's spelling books and grammars the most widely used among practical books. Painters like John Trumbull and Charles Willson Peale memorialized the scenes and heroes of the war.

The judgment of those surveying American progress during the 1780s was affected by their residences and occupations and, perhaps, by their wartime experiences. Most accepted the national republic as the solution for separation from Britain. Some people longed for the return of colonial times, and in New York and Philadelphia some admitted their Tory connections, but the overwhelming majority of Americans were happy to have their national independence.

Many heroes of the war saw the problems of unity, government weakness, and financial confusion as serious impediments to progress. They criticized the Confederation government for its lack of power over commerce, its inability to pay the current costs of administration, and its record in foreign affairs. They pointed to the rising foreign debt: New loans were negotiated in 1784, 1787, and 1788, making the total foreign debt $9.7 million, and in addition there were heavy obligations outstanding to Beaumarchais for his service during the Revolution. Critics also noted that most American trade drifted back into old channels with Great Britain, but that Britain refused to negotiate a commercial treaty or send full diplomatic representation. British violation of American borders by maintaining bases at such places as Oswego, Niagara, Detroit, and Michilimackinac irritated many, as did her refusal to return some 3000 slaves carried away by her armies during the evacuation. Diplomatic relations with other countries were not such serious problems, but they did not offer any bright opportunities. Commercial treaties with Sweden, Prussia, and Morocco were more frustrating than useful. Not even trade with France prospered as expected. Plainly, the national government was not measuring up to the people's new assessment of its role in politics, and something more dynamic in policy formulation had become possible. The national structure seemed only half complete.

Internally, the states were slowly meeting their problems, but mounting debts and declining tax receipts were burdening economic life and delaying full recovery from the war. In Massachusetts, heavy debts and taxes hurt private credit by undermining property values, and court actions by speculators increased public desperation. In Worcester County over 2000 lawsuits were filed to recover debts, forcing many debtors into prison. Rebellion of a sort broke out in western Massachusetts when Daniel Shays and his debtor friends closed the courts. The uprising alarmed people throughout the United States and pointed up, better than any other event, the source of the corruption. Noah Webster described the crisis in these words: "So many legal infractions of sacred rights—so many public invasions of private property—so many wanton abuses of legislative powers." Legislatures had fallen into the hands of wicked men and mobs were doing their bidding.

When the Congress had power, however, its members did an extraordinary job. Its creative program for the West was remarkable and republican. As western lands passed under its control, Congress tried to pacify the Indians, regulate trade, and supervise settlement, and within the limits of its resources it accomplished much. Two of its acts, the Ordinances of 1785 and 1787, were landmarks. The first provided for orderly surveys of the West, for the sale of relatively small tracts of land, and for donations of land for public schools. The second, the great Northwest Ordinance, promised statehood to the western territories as each area passed through defined stages of development. When any territory reached 60,000 inhabitants, it was ready for statehood. The act set the form of western penetration that the United States was to follow permanently, which was characterized by a spirit of equality and anti-imperialism.

The debates in Congress were conducted in a sophisticated, parliamentary manner. The delegates spoke their minds on the nation's problems and put men of considerable talent into places of trust. No hard evidence of corruption, bad faith, or excess marred the conduct of Congress. Its officers were surprisingly loyal to the United States, and the aministrative force that developed over the years continued to provide service for Washington when he became President.

But Congress was obviously feeble. More than anything else, the Confederation government proved that more national power was necessary and desirable. Power to regulate commerce, power to tax, and power to regulate credit were essential to the growth and security of the nation. Unfortunately, Congress was divided over the nature and extent of amending the Constitution, and the state legislatures feared national supervision of their internal affairs. By the fall of 1786, many nationalists had undoubtedly decided to work outside the Congress. Virginia's government was finally brought into their plans, and it called a convention of the neighboring states at Annapolis, Maryland, for September 1786. The delegates there quickly perceived that nothing could be done to the Constitution without representation from the other states. Their opinion was presented to Congress, and the states, and Congress somewhat reluctantly, issued invitations for a convention in Philadelphia. In a letter to John Jay, George Washington revealed his own thoughts about the need for a change in the Articles, and these thoughts were shared by Alexander Hamilton and Jay:

> We have errors to correct. We have probably had too good an opinion of human nature in forming our Confederation. Experience has taught us, that men will not adopt and carry into execution measures the best calculated for their own good, without the intervention of a coercive power. I do not conceive we can exist long as a nation without having lodged somewhere a power, which will pervade the whole Union in as energetic a manner as the authority of the State governments extends over the several States.

The Federal Constitution

In 1787, while some delegates were still traveling to get to the Philadelphia convention, others who had arrived early explored the possibility of making changes in the Articles of Confederation. Most of them soon agreed that fundamental reforms were necessary and that these would require a new form of national government. On May 25, when a majority of the seventy-four delegates was assembled, the convention formally opened its deliberations in the Old State House where eleven years earlier independence had been proclaimed.

The delegates met in an atmosphere of crisis. Men like Washington, Hamilton, Franklin, and many others of this revolutionary leadership felt that the Union was imperiled by weakness and selfishness, caused to a large degree by an erosion of ideals. The states were selfish, holding on to the taxing power and erecting trade barriers; the people in the back country, especially in Daniel Shays's Massachusetts, were rebellious, and many city dwellers were less attentive to the needs of the nation than to their private speculations in land, banking, and commerce. While the United States prospered, it was not measuring up to the expectations of its founders, to the promise of a new order, and a serious threat of disunion hovered over it.

Many of these Philadelphia delegates were holders of securities, almost all were landowners, and most were substantial citizens of their states, people with a stake in the success of the United States as an independent country. Of the fifty-five delegates who attended the con-

A Portrait of George Washington *(New-York Historical Society)*

vention, thirty-one were college educated, and many were professional men like college professors, lawyers, legislators, and officials. Their average age was near forty-two years, with a range from thirty years for Charles Pinckney to eighty-one for Benjamin Franklin. Almost everyone of significance in American leadership was present, save John Adams, John Jay, and Thomas Jefferson, who were occupied with government business. The delegates, as a whole, were devoted to the revolutionary cause, idealists to the extent that they accepted republicanism as a form of government, but realists in approaching the problems before them. Some had undoubtedly selfish motives in coming to Philadelphia: to secure their bonds, to win office, and to safeguard the reputations gained in the struggle for an independent nation.

Two days after the convention convened, Edmund Randolph of Virginia presented his famous plan. The Virginia Plan, or "large-state plan," which brought up such issues as the structure, powers, and philosophy of a national government, was debated point by point for approximately two weeks. It provided for an executive, a judiciary, and a two-house legislature, with members of both houses elected according to population. The executive, to be chosen by the legislature, would be ineligible for reelection, but would have an absolute veto over all bills. The judiciary, too, would be selected by the legislature. It would be entrusted with the enforcement of federal authority, including crimes on the high seas, impeachment proceedings, and questions of peace and harmony. While these provisions for a strong national government were an improvement over the Articles of Confederation, they did not satisfactorily set the bounds of authority between the central and state governments. George Mason of Virginia described the problem in these words:

> The State Legislatures also ought to have some means of defending themselves against encroachments of the National Government. In every other department we have studiously endeavored to provide for its self-defense. Shall we leave the States alone unprovided with the means for this purpose?

Seeking to answer the question, William Paterson presented the New Jersey, or "small-state," Plan, which was modeled after the Articles of Confederation and incorporated very few improvements on the Articles. However, it did contain a significant idea of constitutionalism, basic to the discussions—that the Constitution was to be the supreme law of the land. Paterson's plan, moreover, was productive of considerable debate, forcing the delegates eventually to accept a national structure of government with one supreme power of three branches (executive, legislative, and judicial), and to recognize in the Union the existence of large and small states. The so-called Great Compromise provided for equality of the states in the Senate and recognition of their population size in setting the membership of the House of Representatives.

Rivalry among the states and delegations then shifted to other issues. The degree of popular participation in government was important to men like Elbridge Gerry and James Wilson, who did not like the plans for indirect election of the Senate, President, and Supreme Court. Issues relating to the West and its place in the nation, the slave trade, the regulation of commerce, and the collection of imposts inspired debate and were settled by compromises. At no time did these questions threaten the unity of the convention. By September 17, 1787, after a committee on style had polished its phrasing, the Constitution was ready for signature. Only thirty-nine members signed it; some denounced it as too aristocratic, too aloof from the people, and too radical to win national favor. Some delegates like Gerry hoped for a new attempt at constitution-making; others left Philadelphia in disgust, not waiting to register their dissent. However, the majority made allowance for this opposition by providing that the Constitution be submitted to special state conventions and be put into effect when nine of them had ratified it.

The Constitution submitted at this time, or Federal Constitution as it is generally known, created a strong national government, acting directly upon the citizen, and complete in its delegated or assigned powers. It was not created by the states to do their work, but provides instead for a separate, distinct government that can demand from the states cooperation in laboring for the common good. "The judges in every state," Article Six provides, shall be bound to honor the Constitution, the laws of the United States, and treaties as the 'Supreme Law of the land." State officials are bound to support the Constitution, the police power of the states is required to enforce national laws, and the President has the power to call out the militia in times of crisis.

The nature of this federal union has always been a subject of great debate. The passing years have changed the scope of its powers, and the partnership has taken new forms, but the states in no sense are subordinate corporations. With them rests the primary responsibility for local government, the health and welfare of the people, the administration of law and order, the control of education, and a multiplicity of other matters. It is well to emphasize that this union is no voluntary agreement among states; it is a permanent association of separated and shared authority that cannot be broken unless three-fourths of the states act to amend the Constitution.

The meaning of this union must be found in United States history, because the Constitution itself is the barest outline of a governmental structure. The document has been given content by tradition, by the experiences of public officials, by the decisions of the courts, legislature, and executive, and by events themselves. A reading of the Constitution is absolutely important as a first step, but then an understanding of history, reference to the deecisions of the Supreme Court, and a study of the will of Congress are needed to put flesh on the skeleton.

Since the Constitution has received over the years constant interpretation, a review of its major features is not essential at this point. However, some important provisions and concepts must be mentioned.

1. In the selection of President and Vice President the Constitution did not allow for the development of political parties, and this omission raised serious political difficulties in the 1790s. The Constitutional plan provided for electors in the quiet of a conference room to select the best men in the nation for those offices, and the first and second choices in the national balloting became, respectively, President and Vice President. When parties came to nominate candidates, they chose partisan figures and waged campaigns. The people, in turn, assumed the right to name the victors, and the people instructed the electors to vote the popular choice. Men of talent certainly were elected to these high offices, but they became partisan figures.

2. The rise of parties created problems for Congress in lawmaking and for the President in administration. The national interest sometimes has been subordinated to the party interest. Parties in control of committees and offices of Congress have challenged the power of the President, or have created stalemates and confusion. The President as party leader may use the veto power, his presence as a national spokesman, and his administrative force to favor a partisan position. Too often, control of the party is decentralized so that there is not a responsible voice; claims may be heard from Congress, the President, the governors, or the business world.

. The Constitution created two levels of government, the national and the state. For decades the division of powers between them has been uncertain, and no sure formula has ever been worked out. Disputes arise over the better place for responsibility; frequently vested interests measure the advantages of control that can be enjoyed when they argue their position for national or local administration. Tradition, in general, favors local government. The closer to the people the closer to responsibility has been the golden rule.

4. The Constitution is a brief document that needs to be interpreted and implemented to be made workable. Power for this purpose was vested in the Congress, the President, and the courts. Over the years each has developed traditions, rituals, and procedures that have anticipated most problems. From time to time, however, constitutional issues have arisen, and the Supreme Court has assumed that it has the authority to make these important determinations. This assumption of power has not gone unchallenged, but the fathers of the Constitution plainly intended that such power should be vested in the Supreme Court. In recent years the decisions of the Court have been attacked because they seem to have developed a new philosophy of government. Questions such as representation in state legislatures,

religious liberty, human equality, censorship of motion pictures, and loyalty have been decided often by departing radically from long-established practice. The opposition has frequently asked the Court what materials it consulted in the process of making its decision. Such materials may be the debates of Congress, the historical record, the English common law, past decisions, and evidence from social and political documents. In the end, the judges must decide what seems to be wise, just, and proper. Since interpretations of the Constitution are not permanently binding, the Court can reverse itself, and frequently does.

5. The Constitution did not create a national standard of citizenship, nor extend the rights of citizenship to everyone. The blacks early realized this inadequacy in the Constitution and, in 1857, the Supreme Court even raised the question whether black males could ever be citizens. Women, too, found themselves without full rights and have had to wage a fight to this day for equality. Immigrants, freed prisoners, and those who have deviated from societal norms have had problems exercising their rights. To solve these problems, the Supreme Court has found constitutional interpretations and the people have added amendments. The process, nonetheless, has been long, continuing, and costly in American history.

Ratification of the Constitution

During the ratification process the Constitution was well interpreted by its friends. Alexander Hamilton, James Madison, and John Jay published a series of essays later entitled *The Federalist*, which examined most of its provisions. The information, passed by newspapers and orators across the nation, had a powerful influence, yet it should be emphasized that those backing the Constitution had an uphill fight to win ratification.

Probably most Americans were opposed to the Constitution and suspected that it would eventually destroy republican institutions. They could point to its weakening of state authority, its lack of guarantees like a bill of rights, and the complex national government it set up. Fear of an all-powerful government was genuine, as men saw the threat of losing liberty to a distant tribunal. "Large and consolidated empires," editorialized the *Massachusetts Gazette*, "may indeed dazzle the eyes of a distant spectator with their splendour, but if examined more nearly are always found to be full of misery." A poet of the *South Carolina State Gazette* caught this fear of creeping imperialism very well:

> When thirteen states are modulated into one
> Your rights are vanish'd and your honors gone;
> The form of Freedom shall alone remain,
> As Rome had Senators when she hugg'd the chain.

Engraving of Alexander Hamilton, First Secretary of the Treasury
(Library of Congress)

To combat this fear the advocates of the Constitution had the counteracting influence of Washington and Franklin. They had youth, vigor, and organization. Perhaps they had luck, too, for Delaware and Pennsylvania quickly ratified the Constitution. In Philadelphia, lawyers and merchants, associates in business and town affairs, gained control of the convention, and upon the motion of Thomas McKean the members began a warm debate whose outcome never was in doubt. The Constitution was approved by a 46 to 23 vote, in an open convention that was well reported in the newspapers.

News of these great victories spread to New England. In Massachusetts the contest was doubtful at the beginning, for John Hancock and Samuel Adams seemed to be opponents of the Constitution, and most Boston newspapers occasionally printed hostile articles. However, the Antifederalists lost seriously in the elections when Elbridge Gerry was defeated, and their confusion was compounded when Hancock and Adams were persuaded by promises of political patronage to lend their immense prestige to the Constitution. The Federalists swung the campaign decisively by promising to support a bill of rights, a strategy that undercut the opposition sufficiently to win on February 6, 1788, a favorable vote of 187 to 168.

The winter and spring brought more victories. On the first day of summer in 1788 New Hampshire became the ninth state to vote approval, and the Constitution was at last ratified.

Four states remained: Virginia, New York, North Carolina, and Rhode Island. Without the first two, the Union could not succeed, and the Antifederalists of Virginia were well organized and counted heavily upon George Mason, Patrick Henry, and Richard Henry Lee to turn the tide. Yet as the debate was joined, Henry's oratory seemed almost desperate, as James Madison and his Federalist supporters returned logic for emotion. Henry spoke day after day; his courtroom oratory swayed many listeners; his meandering course of exposition permitted his colleagues to press uncommitted delegates. In the end, however, the Antifederalists were defeated by a vote of 89 to 79, and the delegates then asked the new Congress to adopt amendments that would give the nation a bill of rights.

The approval of Virginia helped to undermine opposition in New York, where Governor George Clinton had lent his prestige and power to the attack. The skillful maneuvering of Hamilton and Jay put the delegation of New York City behind ratification, and victory was finally achieved by a vote of 30 to 27. North Carolina ratified later in 1788. Rhode Island did not even convene a convention until 1790, and finally ratified on May 29 of that year, about thirteen months after George Washington became President.

The Triumph of the Constitution was the result of a well-organized campaign, good arguments, influential support, and much luck. The Antifederalists were outmaneuvered by the Massachusetts plan for a bill of rights and by defeats in state after state. The press, public information, and letter-writing supporters undoubtedly helped the Federalist cause. The first ten amendments, or Bill of Rights, were formally adopted in 1791, although Massachusetts failed to ratify them.

In the decade since the Declaration of Independence in 1776 much had happened in America. Imperial ties with Great Britain were severed, and while attempts to find ways of re-establishing them were often made, nothing occurred of significance. Lord Shelburne in England and others in America had hoped for a new and peaceful union, but the cause of empire gave way to the cause of independence in the thinking of more and more people. The new order as it took form in their plans became a republican society of peace and justice separated from Europe. It would require, however, a reorganization of society, not just a revolt against Britain, and the creation of a new constitutional order. Only a few men were ready to accept changes, even when violence threatened state governments. Their solution was the Constitution of 1787. It could provide little or great changes depending upon popular inclinations. Whatever the future held, nobody in 1789 was able to predict, but men of goodwill, even many who had fought the ratification of the Constitution, hoped a new order was beginning.

SUGGESTIONS FOR FURTHER READING

Alden, John Richard, The American Revolution, 1775-1783. New York, Harper Torchbooks, Harper & Row, 1963.

Becker, Carl L., The Declaration of Independence. New York, Random House, 1942.

Billias, George, ed., George Washington's Generals. New York, Apollo Editions, Thomas Y. Crowell Company, 1964.

Boyd, Jullian P., Anglo-American Union: Joseph Galloway's Plans to Preserve the British Empire, 1774-1788. Philadelphia, University of Pennsylvania Press, 1941.

Brooks, John, King George III. New York, McGraw-Hill Book Company, 1972.

Brown, Marvin L., ed., Baroness von Riedesel and the American Revolution. Chapel Hill, N.C., University of North Carolina Press, 1965.

Brown, Robert E., Middle-Class Democracy and the Revolution in Massachusetts, 1691-1780. New York, Harper Torchbooks, Harper & Row, 1969.

Caughey, John W., The American West: Frontier and Region, eds. Norris Hundley and John A. Schutz, Los Angeles, Ward Ritchie Press, 1969.

Chambers, William Nisbet, Political Parties in a New Nation,

1776-1809. New York, Oxford University Press, 1963.

The Federalist Papers, ed. Ray P. Fairfield. New York, Anchor Books, Doubleday & Company, 1966.

Jensen, Merrill, *The Articles of Confederation*. Madison, Wisconsin, University of Wisconsin Press, 1966.

Kenyon, Cecelia, *The Antifederalists*. Minneapolis, The American Heritage Series, Bobbs-Merrill, 1966.

McDonald, Forest, *The Formation of the American Republic, 1776-1790*. Baltimore, Md., Pelican Books, Penguin Books, Inc. 1965.

Main, Jackson Turner, *The Anti-Federalists: Critics of the Constitution*. Chicago, Quadrangle Books, 1965.

Rutland, Robert Allen, *The Ordeal of the Constitution*. Norman, Okla., University of Oklahoma Press, 1966.

Wallace, Willard M., *Appeal to Arms: A Military History of the American Revolution*. Chicago, Quadrangle Books, 1964.

Wood, Gordon S., *The Creation of the American Republic, 1776-1787*. New York, W. W. Norton & Company, 1969.

6

The Federal Experiment

To FIND THE FORMULA FOR DIVIDING POWER between the states and the federal government became the great problem of politics in the first thirty years after the writing of the Constitution. The states, always jealous of their rights, were often ready to leave the Union when federal obligations disturbed their interests. Their citizens talked of secession, issued resolutions, held conventions, and conspired to organize new governments. No section of the nation was free from these divisive forces, and few leaders were so sanguine as to believe that the Constitution would long endure as the law of the land. They regarded the Federal Republic as an experiment; even if it was radical, unnatural, and republican they were willing to take the chance. Perhaps, they thought, men could progress in wisdom and guide their own destiny; the risk was worth taking.

The New Government

Soon after Virginia approved the Constitution, the Confederation Congress scheduled elections for presidential electors and represen-

tatives and instructed the states to choose senators. It set March 4 for
the inauguration of the new government, but the first session of Congress did not get under way until April, when the electoral ballots
were counted and George Washington and John Adams were officially
named President and Vice President of the Republic. They took office
on April 30, 1789.

The President on that momentous day stepped out onto the bal-
cony overlooking Wall Street in New York, dressed in a suit of brown
broadcloth, and took his oath of office. To one observer he seemed
uneasy, embarrassed, and agitated, but the crowd was most impressed,
standing silent, reverent, and awed. Though he had privately admitted that the burdens of office would challenge his skill and abilities, with a prayer to God and a plea to the people for help and patience,
he committed himself to his new responsibilities as the leader of
nearly four million Americans. An observer described the brief ceremony as "one of the most august and interesting spectacles ever exhibited on this globe."

The transition between the old and new governments was made
relatively easy by the near collapse of the old. The Confederation Congress had had no quorum for months, and almost everyone waited for
the new government to get under way. The congressional elections
brought into office large numbers of former delegates who had served
in the state and national constitutional conventions, and Washington,
with great caution and deliberation, selected many Confederation officials to advise him. Secretary of War Henry Knox was continued in
that capacity in the Cabinet; John Jay was moved from foreign affairs
to the Supreme Court; some lesser officials were asked to continue
their work as staff members. Washington invited his friends Jefferson
and Hamilton to be Secretary of State and Secretary of the Treasury,
respectively, and Edmund Randolph to be Attorney General. Most of
his appointees were well known in national affairs, men of integrity
and public spirit who were devoted to the cause of the Union. Congress,
too, was full of men like James Madison who were ready to strengthen
the foundations of the new national government.

With their help Washington set out to give form and life to the
government. Since the Constitution was purposely vague in providing
guidelines, he moved carefully in establishing policy, but events
forced him to make certain decisions. In the course of handling problems of western defense, he asked the advice of the upper house (the
Senate) and was well received. However, some procedural difficulties
and some strain in their relations arose; the Senate displayed independence in the way it wanted to offer its advice and some reluctance
to commit itself. These consultations with the Senate gave Washington
insight into the operation of the new government, and from this time
he abandoned the old colonial practice of using the upper house to
give advice and consent. Thereafter the position of the Cabinet secre-

Engraving of the Inauguration Ceremony of George Washington
(New-York Historical Society)

taries in presidential decision-making became of utmost importance.

The Treasury was the largest department, with thirty clerks and a thousand custom officers and agents. It had the awesome task of raising money, establishing credit, and planning for the payment of the huge national debt. Although it was aided materially by the tonnage and tariff rates of the first revenue act, still a tariff of five percent and duties of fifty cents per ton on foreign shipping were not sufficient to meet the financial problems facing the nation. Washington was fortunate to be able to enlist the genius of Alexander Hamilton in solving these problems. Then only 34 years old, an ardent nationalist and superb administrator, Hamilton infused his political philosophy into the legislation that he recommended. He fervently believed that it was the business of government to weave into policy the ambitions and interests of the people and to make their passions the servants of government. With little faith in the good will of men, he thought government alone could develop conditions of peace, prosperity, and happiness, and that only a strong government could use passions. He consciously aligned merchants, creditors, and manufacturers in the governing class and favored their interests with a legislative program.

The House of Representatives in September 1789 asked him to report a plan for adequate public credit. He complied four months later with a daring, comprehensive program. It recommended that the foreign and domestic debt of $50 million be funded at par; that the war debts of the states, approximately $22 million, be assumed by the federal government; that a national bank be chartered, with the privilege of establishing branches throughout the United States. These policies were to be backed with special tax levies and guaranteed by a sinking fund. Hamilton argued that his plan would organize the financial resources of the United States. In particular, he pointed to the benefits of credit regulation and banking facilities. For the benefit of trade, he cited the advantages of common credit conditions like interest rates and bank notes. On the whole, his recommendations received favorable consideration by Congress; some were modified slightly and others were heatedly debated before being accepted. Their practicality was quickly proven as United States bonds sold at par on European markets and the stocks of the United States Bank became a popular investment.

However, some people suspected that Hamilton was favoring speculators who had bought up the deeply depressed bonds of the states and national government and later received par prices for them. Virginians in particular denounced these measures as an insidious plot to destroy the South. With Patrick Henry leading the attack, Virginians claimed that the nation's agricultural country was being sacrificed to the moneyed and commercial interests of the North. A serious split soon developed in the ranks of the Federalists as they argued over the value of Hamilton's program.

The Rise of Parties

The price Hamilton paid for the financial support of the North was excessive. He allowed the states to inflate their debts at the expense of the nation and let speculators make personal fortunes on the bonds. In 1792 he recommended a second assumption of debts, in which creditors in South Carolina and Massachusetts benefited greatly. This class legislation angered farmers, debtors, and southern leaders, and especially awakened sectional antagonisms in which the control of the federal government became a political prize.

In this fight Hamilton's opponents were Madison and Jefferson, Virginians and close friends, both deeply committed to a republican America. Madison, in supporting the Constitution and nationalistic policies of the First Congress, had favored the tariff, tonnage duties, and establishment of the United States Bank, but the threat of Hamilton's policy made him reconsider his actions. Perhaps Jefferson's return from France had some influence upon him, because Jefferson had even before his return expressed doubts about the concentration of power in the national government. With great faith in education, the rationality of men, and their innate sense of justice, Jefferson wanted to diffuse power, provide for a democratic base, and allow for environmental conditions that would draw out the goodness in men.

Unlike Hamilton, who wanted a commercial nation, Jefferson wished to develop a nation of farmers and landowners, unencumbered by the restrictions of government. "The less government the better" may not precisely describe his rule, but "a few plain duties to be performed by a few servants" were his words for minimal government. In effect, he desired an agrarian republic of simplicity and equality, where men would live close to the soil, draw from it the strength of an independent livelihood, and grow in virtue. The man with a plow, a house of his own, and a hundred acres around him was the ideal citizen. Jefferson was an optimist, cheerful of the future, unafraid of revolution, and certain that the people could find leaders to rule them.

Jefferson became Secretary of State in March 1790, about six months after Hamilton had taken office, when most of the financial program was before Congress. He did not like the idea of a national bank, believing it violated the general spirit of the Constitution by enlarging federal power at the expense of the states; he did not think the bank was necessary, and felt that it could be used as a source of corruption and a wedge for monarchy. He also depored Hamilton's association with speculators, of whom some, like William Duer, were involved in bond and land sales of doubtful legality.

His rivalry with Hamilton spread quickly to many issues. Both eventually took their ideas to the people, castigating each other in the press. Hamilton used the *Gazette of the United States*, the largest circulating newspaper of Philadelphia, to tell his story. The paper had contracts from the Treasury, and the editor, John Fenno, sang Hamilton's praises. Jefferson retaliated by backing the *National Gazette*, with Philip Freneau as editor, and by giving Freneau a job in the State Department. Though Jefferson managed to keep himself personally out of the attacks, he supported Freneau and even sought to have Hamilton censured by the House of Representatives. The charges, however, were voted down by substantial majorities.

Jefferson and Madison laid plans for an opposition party. They defied prejudice, even challenged tradition, when they sought an alliance with George Clinton's faction in New York. Since the Constitution had made no provision for parties, and the general spirit of the 1787 convention had been antiparty, they had to move cautiously. Disguising their motives, they traveled up the Hudson River in 1791 on a "botanizing excursion" and reached an understanding with Governor Clinton, who was to be their choice for Vice President in 1792. In that year they adopted the name "Republicans," letting Hamilton's friends denominate themselves as "Federalists."

Federalism to 1792 was less a party than a political position. The name was used to represent those favoring the Constitution and the new federal government. Federalists were primarily local workers for the Union, though they belonged to a national movement and corresponded occasionally on matters of mutual concern. They were property owners, plantation owners, and officeholders; they had a stake in the community. They lived, usually, on the coastal plain and in the cities and had the support of profesisonal and laboring classes. Many, like George Washington and John Adams, felt their movement was patriotic, not factional or party, and subscribed to this philosophy: "If we mean to support the Liberty and Independence which it has cost us too much blood and treasure to establish, we must drive far away the daemon of party spirit and local reproach."

The Republican party of Jefferson and Madison was built upon the prejudices of the people who feared strong government, banks, speculators, and commercial wealth. In the South they sought to protect slavery and a way of life bound up with plantation society. But the Republicans were concerned, too, for the white masses, the small landowners and representative institutions, and somehow the Virginia aristocratic leadership wove these unrelated, even hostile, elements into a philosophy of agrarian republicanism. They were able to accomplish this because they put the interests of the farmer first and believed that government should do as little as possible. A simple, frugal government was their idea of a good one, and it appealed to many New Yorkers and Pennsylvanians, who were small landowners, workers, and tradesmen. Their leader often was Aaron Burr of New York, an ambitious lawyer and politician, who became United States Senator in 1791.

The French Revolution

While local issues gave rise to political parties, the most dramatic event of the 1790s, the French Revolution, aroused emotion and separated the people into two camps. At first the Revolution brought public rejoicing, drawing France close to America in spirit, but the increasing radicalism and violence of the French revolutionaries soon alienated many conservatives. The riots, the executions, the irreligious outbursts, and the anarchy awakened fears, and Hamilton for one wanted the alliance with France suspended. Fisher Ames, the Massachusetts Federalist and influential orator in the Senate, was frightened: "Behold France an open hell, still ringing with agonies and blasphemies, still smoking with sufferings and crimes, in which we see . . . perhaps our future state."

The excitement in France led to an invasion of neighboring countries and to a European war. The hostilities had an immediate impact upon the United States because of its alliance with France. The Cabinet debated American obligations to France, particularly whether the United States should defend the French West Indies and whether France should be permitted to mount an attack from American soil on Spanish Florida and Louisiana. The debate involved treaty interpretations, foreign policy, possible war with Great Britain, and political philosophy. Washington weighed the arguments and decided early that a policy of neutrality was the only practical course, allowing for trade and peaceful relations and time for the United States to develop as a nation. Washington's famous declaration in 1793 advised foreign nations that the United States would "pursue a conduct friendly and impartial toward the belligerent powers," and he instructed citizens to restrain from unneutral acts which would be prosecuted.

The Western Frontier

Washington actually had few alternatives to neutrality. The United States military forces were deeply committed in the Northwest, where the British still held frontier posts and the Indians were offering fierce resistance to American authority. In 1789, shortly after Washington had become President, he had sent Josiah Harmar and about fifteen hundred militiamen on a raiding expedition. The task seemed easily accomplished, but on his return Harmar was ambushed and had to retreat. In 1790, he was reinforced and ordered to retaliate. He went deep into the present state of Ohio and left a trail of burning villages and fields, but with success nearly in his hands, he was again surprised and forced to retreat, this time with heavy casualties. Even as a court of inquiry took note of his courage and acquitted him of laxity, Washington ordered the governor of the territory, Arthur St. Clair, to assume the command of the army. In 1791 St. Clair's troops were ambushed in the forest, shot down, and scalped in heavy, bloody fighting. Over nine hundred American casualties were recorded.

Though St. Clair was investigated by Congress and exonerated, Washington turned for new leadership to the Revolutionary War hero, Anthony Wayne. Readily understanding the seriousness of frontier fighting, Wayne ordered his rag-tail army drilled, kept under strict discipline, and taught how to yell and fight like Indians. In the spring of 1794, while Wayne's men were moving into position, the President sent agents into the Indian villages promising peace, concessions, and grants of money. His envoys were merely humiliated by the overconfident leaders of the Miamis, Shawnees, and Ottawans, and Wayne was allowed to begin operations. Moving north from the Ohio River in a slow, cautious drive, he fought an indecisive battle at Fallen Timbers (near the present Michigan state line), destroyed Indian villages, and settled down for the winter. In early 1795 he called for an Indian conference, which resulted in the famous Treaty of Greenville that released two-thirds of the present state of Ohio to settlement. The boundary, however, was only a temporary line; in the next decade the Indians were compelled to concede more and more land, until all of Ohio and much of Indiana and Michigan were open to settlement. In the wake of the Indian retreat came thousands of Americans who, in 1803, would form the state of Ohio.

The Southwest frontier, though not so chaotic as the northern, was dangerous to the peace in the 1790s. The southern boundary was disputed, and travel down the Mississippi was handicapped by Spanish custom officials in Louisiana. Perhaps the continuing disloyalty of men like speculator, duelist, and troublemaker James Wilkinson was more serious than the uncertainty of the boundary; they plotted and schemed and sold their services as revolutionaries to the highest bidder. In the 1790s they turned gradually against Spain, continuing to take bribes and sell their fantasies but joining the new governments forming in the region. Kentucky became a state in 1792; Tennessee received territorial status and then statehood in 1796. These frontier areas achieved more peaceful conditions after Alexander McGillivray died in 1793; the powerful Creek nation lost his leadership and the advantage of pitting Spain and the United States against each other.

The northeastern frontier faced less dangerous perils in the 1790s than the Ohio and southern frontiers. For a time the Allen family did flirt with disloyalty by soliciting British trade and friendship. But the reluctance of Britain and the flood of loyal Americans into Vermont changed political conditions, and Vermont became a state in 1791. Thousands from Connecticut and Massachusetts were moving northeast also into frontier New Hampshire and Maine (which was still part of Massachusetts).

Party Rivalry and the Jay Treaty

These conditions on the frontier had their importance, therefore, in Washington's assessment of United States power. He was also troubled by serious relations with the belligerents, particularly with Great Britain, which seized American merchant vessels trading with the French. The British were not willing to let the United States define the rights of a neutral, even though these principles were held by some European countries. By an order in council of November 6, 1793, Britain detained American ships trading with the French West Indies and executed the order in a harsh manner. Admiralty condemnations became routine, with little or no relation to judicial rules of evidence. These condemnations aroused American traders, angered Hamilton, and brought demands for retaliation by the Republicans, who wished to impose a trade embargo. However, timely action by the Pitt ministry brought a revocation of the order in council, and Washington decided to explore the possibility of conciliation by sending the chief of the Supreme Court, John Jay, to Britain as a special envoy.

At about the same time, Congress authorized the building of naval vessels, but the lack of appropriations held up the construction of the *U.S.S. Constitution, United States,* and *Constellation* for more than three years.

While Jay was abroad negotiating with the British, the administration was disturbed by a large-scale rebellion in western Pennsylvania. The Whiskey Rebellion, or Gallatin Rebellion as John Adams called it, was a reaction against the Excise Act of 1791. The Act levied high duties upon whiskey to the disgust of frontiersmen, who denied the federal powers to levy taxes. Excise officers attempting to enforce the law were beaten and threatened, and opposition spread into Maryland, the Carolinas, and Georgia. Though there was sufficient anger and plenty of oratory, the persuasion of Albert Gallatin, a rising politician of the area, and the reluctance of the Pennsylvania governor to employ force helped to dampen the fire. But the President was unwilling to let this contempt for federal authority go unchallenged. Ordering to arms thirteen thousand troops, he accompanied the army into Pennsylvania, where the resistance was quickly broken. Washington's aim was to suppress the opposition as soon as possible but to use moderate means. The expedition captured a few prisoners, frightened some leaders, who escaped into the frontier, and held for federal prosecution two culprits. While their conviction was promptly followed by a presidential pardon, Washington drew a lesson for the people from the rebellion. He blamed the Democratic Societies, which were celebrating the virtues of the French Revolution, for fomenting the disorder.

The rebellion occurred during the elections of 1794 and inspired bitter party battles in Philadelphia, New York, and back-country Pennsylvania, where Federalists lost enough seats to weaken their influence in the House of Representatives. Some Republican victories represented general criticism of Hamilton's financial policies, especially the election of Gallatin, who had only a year earlier been ousted from the Senate because of his hostility to the administration. In the House, Gallatin provided the Republicans with expert knowledge of finance; eventually he was to assume Madison's position as party leader. In the meantime, he scrutinized appropriations and convinced the House that expenditures should be itemized. The contest for financial control was waged with a new Secretary of the Treasury, Oliver Wolcott; Hamilton had resigned in 1795 for personal reasons, and Jefferson had already retired in favor of Edmund Randolph. Leaving the administration did not remove Hamilton as a presidential advisor or lessen his power in the party, however, and he sought to influence the presidential elections of 1796.

By the time Jay's treaty with Britain had become an important political issue, Jay, in a spirit of friendship, had tried to convince the British that the United States intended no military reprisals for what were hostile, aggressive seizures of Americna property and citizens upon the high seas. He described the quarrel as a family matter, the sooner healed the better. The British, calculating American strength and alternatives (with some information indiscreetly given by Hamilton), decided that they could drive a hard bargain, and they did.

The treaty brought peace with Britain, trade with her West Indies, the evacuation of the western frontier posts, and a promise of settlement of prewar debts and claims arising from illegal seizures. It led indirectly to a settlement of outstanding difficulties with Spain, the right to navigate the lower Mississippi River and the right to deposit goods for three years at New Orleans. Though the Jay Treaty assured the nation of peace, it severely affected domestic politics. Many citizens denounced it for not clarifying neutral rights, for agreeing to arbitration of prewar debts, and for its submissive pro-British tone. It was plainly offensive, too, to France, and it was felt to sacrifice national honor and integrity for the sake of maintaining commerce. It was also, in the eyes of others, a sectional measure that would help business, insurance companies, and the aristocratic classes of the North. When the United States Senate approved the Jay Treaty by a narrow vote, the fight shifted to the House of Representatives, where its enemies demanded access to diplomatic correspondence and tried to block appropriations to put the treaty into effect. However, Washington's great prestige assured its enforcement, and Hamilton labored vigorously among Federalists to win support.

The treaty had greater emotional impact than almost any other issue of the day, and the Federalists realized that they would be severely tested in the coming elections. Washington's second term was nearing its end. Though most politicians predicted that he would retire, they were unable to choose candidates until he had announced his decision. This he did in September. The Federalist candidate was certain to be John Adams, the Vice President, who had managed to avoid the partisan emotion of the Jay Treaty and to keep on good terms with some Republicans. The Vice President and Jefferson were closer friends than were the Vice President and Hamilton, and Jefferson was reluctant both to be a candidate and to oppose his friend.

The Federalists divided in support of John Adams, who posed as a moderate and independent, and Thomas Pinckney, the negotiator of the boundary treaty with Spain, who had Hamilton's backing. The election contest began late but was heatedly waged. Newspapers and pamphleteers were often violent in their attacks, and the French minister blundered into the party warfare. Correspondence by the candidates and their friends mobilized support and heightened feeling. The election results were both close and scattered: close for the top-runners and scattered for second place. Adams received 71 electoral votes to Jefferson's 68, while Thomas Pinckney received 59 to Aaron Burr's 30. Other candidates, all minor favorites, split a total of 48 votes.

Washington's administrations had been highly productive, laying the foundations for national credit, departmental organization, and defense. Other policies had set the structure of the federal judiciary, the development of the West, and a republican pattern for politics. The Pinckney and Jay treaties assured the nation years of peace with Spain and Britain. The Pinckney treaty set the boundary with Florida on the thirty-first parallel to the Chattahoochee River, opening the Southwest to eventual settlement, and the Jay Treaty recognized the United States title to the Ohio Region. The Washington government responded to these developments by passing the Public Land Act of 1796. It provided for orderly division of frontier land into townships and sections, and offered land for sale in sections of 640 acres or by blocks of eight sections. The cost of these large purchases proved to be too dear for most Americans, and Congress in 1800 and 1804 gradually reduced the minimal purchase to 160 acres, though it retained the charge of two dollars an acre.

On leaving office, Washington issued a farewell address in which he denounced party spirit and factionalism and urged his countrymen to observe "good faith and justice towards all nations" but to hold a course outside of the European political system. While Washington retired to Mount Vernon, he was constantly in the thoughts of politicians like Hamilton, who would have recalled him to the nation's service and theirs. When he died unexpectedly in 1799, there was a national outpouring of grief. His deeds of valor in the Revolution were already celebrated in speeches and paintings, but his death brought tens of funeral sermons, plans for monuments, and exchanges of newspaper comments. But the most famous, perhaps the most influential, account of his deeds to appear was written by Mason L. Weems, whose *Life of Washington* (1800) so fictionalized his boyhood life that the episodes passed into American folk lore. The cherry tree story is the best remembered of the accounts: "I can't tell a lie, Pa; you know I can't tell a lie. I cut it with my hatchet."

President Adams and Hostilities with France

The first change of Presidents was smooth. John Adams was a member of Washington's party, and retained the old Cabinet. Though he did not weigh sufficiently his own political position in the Federalist party, he accepted his fellow Federalists as advisors and turned his mind to the grave international crisis at hand. France, embittered by the Jay Treaty, began retaliating against American shipping, seizing in a few months over three hundred merchant vessels. Her brazen contempt for international law was matched only by the treasonable disregard for national interest of some Republicans, who urged her to prey on Federalist shipping.

To combat French aggression, Adams called Congress into special session. Because he wanted to preserve peace, he urged negotiations in the spirit of friendship, and appointed Elbridge Gerry, John Marshall, and C. C. Pinckney as special envoys to Paris. But he had to recommend, too, enlargement of the navy, defense preparations, and increased taxes so that the nation could resist these threats. His address intensified party debate about the mobilization. Jefferson and the Republicans, refusing to think evil of France, accused Adams of being pro-British and unnecessarily belligerent, while the Federalists believed France to be a menace to liberty. No one knew that even then France was plotting an attack on Florida, Louisiana and Canada.

In October 1797 when the American envoys arrived in Paris, the French Directory was feeling the security of a treaty with Austria. Revealing contempt for Adams' administration, it refused to receive his envoys, humiliated them, and suggested a bribe and a loan as satisfaction for the Jay Treaty. Three lesser French officials, X, Y, and Z, carried out months of useless negotiations, which at last made unmistakably clear the fact that France had little respect for American friendship. The Federalists published the proceedings of the abortive negotiations, calculating that France would declare war as a protest. The immediate effect was widespread indignation in the United States, and the Federalist Secretary of State openly spoke of war.

During the spring and summer of 1798, Congress passed legislation against aliens, seditious publications, and political criticism. For those seeking citizenship the residence requirement was raised from five to fourteen years, and some House members, not at all satisfied, wanted to deny even the naturalized citizen the right to hold office. This was an obvious attack upon Swiss-born Albert Gallatin. A bill to deport aliens suspected of treasonable tendencies was passed, as was the Sedition Act, which attempted to suppress opposition in the newspapers. About a score of prosecutions were brought against men like Matthew Lyon of Vermont and James T. Callender of Virginia, who wrote violent pieces against the President. Jefferson accused the Federalists of conducting a reign of terror, but it was hardly that brutal. No hangings occurred, no whippings, no tar and featherings. With moderation and a sense of propriety, Adams restrained his followers from excesses and won strong national support, especially in New England where most Republicans were turned from office.

Though the Republicans chartered a cautious course in 1798, they attempted to spread their views. In the Virginia and Kentucky resolutions, written secretly by Madison and Jefferson, they stressed the dangers to liberty of excessive power in the hands of federal officials. The Constitution, they noted,

> was formed by the sanction of the States, given by each in its sovereign capacity. It adds to the stability and dignity, as well as to the authority of the Constitution, that it rests on this legitimate and solid foundation. The States then being the parties to the constitutional compact, and in their sovereign capacity, it follows of necessity, that there can be no tribunal above their authority.

This appeal to states' rights was to become a popular defensive position for minority groups in most serious disputes before the Civil War, although leaders would switch sides form states' rights to nationalism depending upon their fortunes. In 1798-99 the Republicans were careful to deny any intention to nullify federal laws while expressing their principles.

Adams was caught up in the war emotion. Like other Federalists, he allowed himself to be carried into the ranks of those favoring war against France. Although he did not declare war, he sent frigates and hundreds of smaller vessels and merchant privateers into battle against the French. They searched the Caribbean and Atlantic, even venturing into the Indian Ocean, for armed French vessels, capturing mostly small ships, perhaps eighty in all. Congress cooperated by voting funds, ordering additional frigates, and setting up the Navy Department; Adams selected Benjamin Stoddert of Maryland as the first secretary. While Adams conceived of the dispute primarily as defensive, he spoke vigorously of retaliatory measures and agreed to increase the United States army to fifty thousand men.

Adams disagreed with the war wing of his party, however, when it sought to use the army for offensive operations. He was irritated, too, when Washington as the commander-in-chief forced him to name Hamilton as second-in-command. Seeing the connection between Hamilton's leadership and the widening war, Adams realized that the New Yorker was using the crisis for political advancement and for glory as creator of an empire. Adams learned that Hamilton planned to lead American troops into Florida and Louisiana in a campaign of conquest and imperialism. The full plan included help for the self-styled liberator of Latin America, Francisco de Miranda, and an opening of new markets for American merchants. Hamilton, whose hero was Caesar, had visions of returning, laurel crowned, the first citizen of America.

His dreams of fame were shattered by Adams, who finally decided to check the movement toward war. By proposing to Congress a peace mission, he set off a bombshell and drove a wedge between himself and the Hamiltonians. While he could not be denied the peace mission, Cabinet members delayed the departure of the envoys, and Hamiltonians unleashed a fierce newspaper and pamphlet assault upon him. Eventually Adams was compelled to reorganize his Cabinet and enter the party lists. He was unable, however, to turn his desire for peace into a crusade that would unite the party. Factional animosities heightened as the war wing lost its issue, and many of his Federalist colleagues set out to punish Adams even at the risk of destroying the party.

Unfortunately for Adams, he was unable to benefit from the peace conference. Negotiations in Paris continued for seven months, into the election time of 1800, as Napoleon Bonaparte carried on war against the Austrians. Though the Convention of Môrtefontaine eventually resolved many commercial difficulties, including neutral rights, its major consequence was the restoration of peace. The special relationship for France in the Treaty of 1778, when she gained favored nation status, was now withdrawn. Like the Jay Treaty, the Convention removed the dangers of war and permitted the new nation to develop.

Meanwhile, the Federalists remained divided. Unless they reconciled their differences, their feuding meant certain defeat in 1800. A caucus of congressmen nominated Adams and C. C. Pinckney as the Federalist candidates. Unfortunately, Hamilton was unwilling to concede Adams the new party leadership, plotting to turn the electoral vote to Pinckney, and Adams, with less than presidential dignity, denounced Hamilton as a "bastard, and as much an alien as Gallatin." Adams had the party organization of New England on his side, and the important support of John Jay and Noah Webster in New York.

But he faced a well-organized Republican party. In May 1800 some forty-three national legislators attended a caucus in Philadelphia and chose as their candidates Jefferson and Burr, committing themselves to a bloc vote. Counting heavily on Burr's influence in New York City, Charles Pinckney's in South Carolina, and Thomas McKean's in Pennsylvania, the Republicans planned their strategy carefully, and Jefferson directed a campaign of correspondence and pamphleteering in which the aggressive war policies of the Federalists were denounced. He emphasized the moderation of Republicans, their liberalism, fear of centralized government, and devotion to agrarianism, and he won strong backing. Burr campaigned effectively in New York and carried the state for himself and Jefferson.

The Republicans in Power

The election of 1800 was one of those few decisive elections in American history. Jefferson called it revolutionary. Only when the final votes were counted did Jefferson and Burr realize how remarkable their victory had been. In the House of Representatives Republicans had won 66 of the 106 seats and in the Senate 18 of the 32 seats; only New England had voted heavily for the Federalists. The presidential contest, as they had planned, had resulted in a tie between Jefferson and Burr, and the decision was to be made in the House of Representatives.

The Federalists decided to embarrass the Republicans, perhaps even to sow seeds of discontent, by pitting Jefferson and Burr against each other. They hoped to upset Republican strategy by making Burr the next President. His reputation as a reprobate caused some to hesitate, but not until the House of Representatives had cast over thirty inconclusive ballots. Burr also increased the concern of Jefferson and some Republicans by daring to challenge the Virginian's preeminence and let the contest continue. With the thirty-sixth ballot, James Bayard of Maryland broke the tie in Jefferson's favor, and the immediate crisis passed.

To Jefferson fell the responsibility of making republicanism the creed of the people. On inauguration day, he invited all to join him and pledged a "wise and frugal government, which shall restrain men from injuring one another, shall leave them otherwise free to regulate their own pursuits of industry and improvement, and shall not take from the mouth of labor the bread it has earned." In private he promised to sink the Federalists "into an abyss from which there will be no resurrection," and he was determined to isolate Burr's influence in the party. The Twelfth Amendment to the Constitution, ratified in 1804, eliminated the chance of a tie between candidates on the same ticket. Perhaps the most memorable events of 1801 were the peaceful change of parties and the overwhelming success of Jefferson's policies. In 1804, the nation gave him and George Clinton, his new vice presidential running mate, a huge electoral vote, and the Federalist party sank into the abyss.

Jefferson's success reflected his unusual abilities as a politician. He was pragmatic, flexible, and nationalistic, possessing a complete devotion to the principles of 1776. But he was a party man and associated with the Republicans James Madison and Albert Gallatin, who settled day-to-day problems with imagination and liberality. Relying upon Virginians for guidance, he also drew on the talents of other southerners, Pennsylvanians, and the Clintonians of New York. He maintained party discipline and rewarded and punished party members; he was cautious, sober in his relations, and humorless. His democratic principles gave an impression of informality and equalitarianism, but he was a democrat in the philosophical sense that he

A Portrait of Thomas Jefferson by Rembrandt Peale
(*New-York Historical Society*)

believed the people should be allowed to live under minimal government, that public office should be open to educated men, and that education should be available to all according to their endowments.

On the surface, the republican spirit of politics set the Jefferson-
ians apart from their predecessors. This impression was heightened
by the pioneer life of Washington, the new capital city, where streets
were dusty or muddy and congressmen were crowded into boarding
houses; Jefferson used the opportunity to relax official etiquette, meeting
Congress informally and mingling with fellow citizens in the capital.
Beneath the surface, however, the Republicans retained the financial
policies of past administrations—the United States Bank, debt retirement, and the pattern of taxation. In foreign affairs, Secretary of State
Madison continued the Federalist policy of trade and neutrality.
Europe was again at peace, and the advantages of Federalist treaties,
through the appointment of joint commissions, were bringing solutions for most outstanding disputes with Great Britain and France.
When European war broke out again in 1803, Jefferson was to proclaim
American neutrality, and when foreign aggression on shipping became intolerable in 1807, to call for an embargo on all commerce. In
short, the Republicans employed federal power for worth-while
national ends.

The President liquidated the growing military establishment that
had sprung up during the quasi-war with France. With the resolution
of those difficulties in 1800, Congress reduced the army, and Jefferson's hands. Frigates were decommissioned and, if suitable for merchant vessels, were sold, and all new construction was suspended.
Obviously the navy drastically cut its personnel. The Republicans thus
did not take into serious consideration the perils of unsettled European
politics. Napoleon was consolidating his power in France, and the
lessening of tensions in 1801 was no guarantee of permanent peace
in Europe.

Nonetheless, Jefferson was soon forced to modify his position toward the navy when American commerce in the Mediterranean was
seriously threatened by pirates. Just two months after he took office,
the Moslem states of Tripoli declared war on the United States. The
Pasha felt that the United States was not paying him sufficient tribute
and began molesting American shipping in the Mediterranean. The
action immediately imperiled the flow of commerce, but Jefferson was
unwilling to apply military or diplomatic pressure to force the Pasha
to compromise, and for three or four years a naval squadron convoyed
ships off the North African coast while an American consul, William
Eaton, tried to persuade the Pasha to change his course. At last, though,
Eaton lost his temper. Employing a band of seamen and adventurers
and using American war vessels, he mounted an offensive and negotiated a treaty at cannon point. Though his operations were quickly
repudiated by the administration, this show of force had some effect

in securing a treaty. America continued to pay tribute to the Moslem states, however, until 1815.

Jefferson and the West

The Tripolian war was irritating to Jefferson because it diverted American energy from more vital issues and was a potential drain on the budget. Far more interested in the American West, he valued the political strength of the back country to his party, and was fascinated by the importance of the frontier to American development. At this time he learned that France was planning to take over Louisiana, which she had turned over to Spain in 1763, and was preparing a force to conquer Hispaniola as a stepping stone to Louisiana. The spectre of an aggressive European power like France occupying the West frightened him, because it would confine the United States to territory east of the Mississippi and involve the nation in European politics. His anxiety was increased when Spain terminated the American privilege of depositing goods in New Orleans. Her action, preliminary to handing over the colony to France, threatened the livelihood of frontiersmen, and they quickly sought Jefferson's sympathy and help.

The President reacted to this crisis in two ways. First, he considered it an opportunity to negotiate with France, and requested from Congress an appropriation of two million dollars. He planned to purchase New Orleans and the Floridas or, as a minimum, the right of deposit at New Orleans. Selecting as his personal emissary James Monroe, a fellow Virginian, Republican, and friend of France, he hoped to win a favorable reception. Second, Jefferson believed that vital American interests were at stake and advised Monroe and the resident minister at Paris, Robert Livingston, that in the event of failure they would have to seek an alliance with Great Britain.

Even before Monroe reached Paris, Livingston discovered that France was willing not only to sell New Orleans but to dispose of the whole of Louisiana for $12 million. The French expeditionary force in Hispaniola had been massacred by a native uprising led by Toussaint L'Ouverture, and Napoleon had shifted his plans from imperialism in America to the domination of Europe.

Fortune and French losses in Hispaniola gave Jefferson a great diplomatic opportunity. Embarrassed by this expansion of national authority, he was nonetheless flexible in political principles when he saw national advantages. By huge majorities his party approved the expenditure, and he was soon contemplating the purchase of West Florida to round out the Louisiana acquisition. He was satisfied that he had done the right thing, even though he suggested a constitutional amendment to give him the power and arranged before sovereignty was transferred to the United States to have the territory examined first hand.

Choosing Meriwether Lewis and William Clark, officers of the regular army, Jefferson instructed them to search for water routes into the back country. The famous expedition left St. Louis on May 14, 1804, went up the Missouri River into present-day Montana, and spent the winter in North Dakota. During most of 1805 Lewis and Clark tramped through Idaho, then moved down the Snake and Columbia rivers to the Pacific Ocean. Indians told them of trading vessels along the coast, but they saw none themselves. Reluctantly turning eastward, they returned to St. Louis in September 1806.

Lewis and Clark were not the first Americans to visit the Pacific coast. Robert Gray had explored the Oregon coast in the late 1780s while making a tour around the globe and had returned in 1792 to inspect the Columbia River. Other Boston seamen had visited Hawaii, then had turned east to search the coast for furs before they made the voyage to the Orient or returned to New England.

Even before Lewis and Clark could be rewarded by their grateful President, Zebulon Pike, under military orders, explored the upper Mississippi River as far as Sandy Lake. In 1806 he searched for the head-waters of the Red and Arkansas rivers, and while exploring in Colorado (and hiking on the mountain that bears his name), he was captured by a force of Spanish troops that had heard reports of his explorations. Pike was taken first to Santa Fe, then to Chihuahua, and finally escorted by way of San Antonio to Natchitoches and turned over to American offi-cials. Prisoner Pike, too, accomplished an important feat, as significant as that of Lewis and Clark, in giving American authorities first-hand information on the Southwest.

Closer to the East, and less dramatic, were developments in the Northwest territory. After the victories of Anthony Wayne in 1794 and 1795, population multiplied quickly; Ohio qualified for statehood in 1803. New Englanders and New Yorkers traveled across the Mohawk River valley to the Great Lakes, some founding Buffalo, Erie, and Cleve-land en route. Others moved into the southern part of Ohio, north from the Ohio River, as they spread across Pennsylvania and Kentucky. The Land Acts of 1796, 1800, and 1804 helped prospective settlers by making land available in smaller and smaller parcels.

The most notable man of the region was William Henry Harrison. Born in Virginia in 1773, he had been attracted to the West through military service, engaging in campaigns under Wilkinson and Wayne as he rose to the rank of captain. He was territorial delegate in the House of Representatives, helped Ohio win statehood, and worked for the creation of the Indiana territory, for which he was appointed the first governor. His policy of buying Indian lands slowly pushed the Indians westward and eventually created considerable tension between settler and native.

In the Southwest, Mississippi, the present-day state of Louisiana, and the larger purchase of Louisiana were given territorial government in the years after 1803. Some concessions to French law and customs

Henry Clay: A Leader of The War Hawks (*Chicago Historical Society*)

were made in the New Orleans territory, but Jefferson moved quickly
to extend American institutions and to prepare the people for statehood.
Territorial Governor William Claiborne, sometimes overcoming great
difficulties, piloted New Orleans territory through the dangers of
civil uprising to statehood in 1812 and as a tribute to his achievement
was elected the state of Louisiana's first governor.

Kentucky in the 1800s doubled its population (to 406,000 in
1810), and Lexington became an economic metropolis of the region.
Small manufacturing was developing as merchants found markets for
cordage, sail duck, and rigging materials, but the isolation of Lexington, which was thirty-five to forty days by wagon from Philadelphia,
limited industrial expansion. Enterprising politicians like the Virginian
Henry Clay, who moved into Kentucky in 1797 as a young man of
twenty, advocated roads, tariffs, banking legislation, and federal expenditures for internal improvements. Clay belonged to Jefferson's
party in the Kentucky assembly, practiced law state-wide, represented
new corporations, and in 1806 accepted a short-term appointment to
the United States Senate, where he supported projects for canal-building
and increased military expenditures.

The Burr Conspiracy

While such westeners as Clay were passionately loyal to the
nation, there were others who were adventurers, frontiersmen, and
army officers who filled their pockets with bribes. During these years
James Wilkinson was frequently involved in intrigues. A pensioner
of the Spanish government for over a decade, he also took bribes from
the British and was deep in plots to separate the Southwest from the
United States.

His plans coincided with those of Aaron Burr. Since the 1800
election contest in the House of Representatives Burr and Jefferson
had been alienated, and Burr was not only denied patronage but also
excluded from party councils in New York. His power was undermined
by the very people he had helped put into office. Bitter and vengeful,
he joined a Federalist conspiracy that planned to take the northern states
from the Union. Running as a candidate of the conspiracy, Burr had
wide Federalist support until Hamilton exposed the plot; then Burr's
popularity collapsed. He blamed Hamilton for the defeat, challenged
him to a duel, and shot him to death.

During this crisis in his career, Burr fell in with Wilkinson's
schemes. In search of adventure, he rode into the Southwest and visited
some important officials, especially a few discontented Louisianans.
He reached St. Louis in September 1805, where he and Wilkinson conferred. Burr then returned to the capital and further consultation with
a motley group of people, trimming or adjusting his plans, as he went,

to suit the prejudices of each person. Many welcomed the possibility of an expedition against Florida or Mexico; others wished to participate in an uprising against the United States.

Though Jefferson was aware that a plot was being prepared, he hesitated to act until he had hard evidence of treason. The President might have waited longer had not Burr's fellow conspirator, James Wilkinson, betrayed him. Wilkinson accused Burr of forming a plot to destroy the Union, and on the surface the evidence appeared to Jefferson to be serious: Burr was recruiting men in Kentucky and sending them to Natchez and was in correspondence with people throughout the Louisiana territory. As soon as Jefferson ordered Burr arrested, Wilkinson seized two conspirators, defying writs of habeas corpus, and sent them under military arrest to the East Coast. He had the cooperation of Jefferson, who asked Congress to suspend habeas corpus in all cases of treason and high crimes against the United States. The opposition in the House of Representatives was overwhelming. Both Federalists and Republicans branded the measure dangerous to popular liberty, and they welcomed the Supreme Court decision of John Marshall when he granted habeas corpus and freed the men for lack of evidence. However, some Republicans were outraged by the decision, even presenting constitutional amendments to deprive the Supreme Court of power to issue writs of habeas corpus.

In the meantime, Burr was brought before the circuit court in Richmond, indicted by a grand jury, and bound over for trial in August 1807. Presiding at the trial was Chief Justice Marshall, whose rivalry with the President in defense of the federal courts was well known. He was determined to provide the strictest standards of evidence in the face of a newspaper campaign against Burr and public denunciations from the President. The main issue of the trial, therefore, was the application of Marshall's definition of treason to the evidence collected against Burr. Was Burr present in the expedition and did two witnesses hear or see him conspire against the United States? The offense, measured by the definition, was not proved against Burr, to the anguish of the President and the anger of some congressmen. "The fact is," Jefferson wrote, "the Federalists make Burr's cause their own, and exert their whole influence to shield him."

Marshall was threatened with impeachment, the court with a constitutional amendment that would permit Congress to remove judges upon a two-thirds vote of the membership. Historians, however, have not yet proved conclusively what Burr was planning or plotting in the West, nor have they found Marshall's decision harmful to American liberties. Jefferson's image as the liberal President was damaged by his emotional outbursts against Burr, and Marshall's opinion, regardless of motivation, enhanced the cause of liberty. A public hanging of Burr was hardly necessary to arouse the instincts of patriotism and loyalty of people so easily rallied to the defense of the nation.

Jefferson and the Courts

The Burr trial ended a series of partisan disputes between the President and the courts. Since passage of the Sedition Act, Republicans had objected to the harsh prosecutions of newspaper editors for criticism of the government and to the use of the bench as a forum for political activity against their party. They had also been inflamed when the Federalist Congress in February 1801 had passed a judiciary act that created additional federal courts, judicial positions, and lesser offices, with the political spoils going to Federalists who had been turned from office by the election of 1800. They had been angry, too, at Marshall's appointment as Chief Justice. He was said to be "more distinguished as a rhetorician and sophist than as a lawyer and statesman." For years Jefferson had suspected Marshall's ideals, friends, and ability, and Marshall, reciprocating, believed his fellow Virginian was "totally . . . unfit . . . for the chief magistracy."

When Adams nominated Marshall to the chief justiceship in 1801, the Virginian was forty-five, a distinguished lawyer with no judicial experience, and a Federalist who had backed the ratification of the Constitution and held the general philosophical principles of that party without having voted for the Alien and Sedition Acts. Men of his party were divided on the appointment, but many noted his common sense and his "irresistible cogency." Beginning a tenure of office in 1801 that was to last until 1835, Marshall represented latter-day Federalism and a nationalist interpretation of the Constitution.

Almost the first act of the Jefferson administration was the repeal of the Judiciary Act of 1801. Proposed by John Breckinridge of Kentucky, the repeal legislation abolished the new offices and restored the Judiciary Act of 1789. Congress debated the revision heatedly, and ardent Republicans like John Randolph of Virginia asserted the right of judicial interpretation for all three departments of government. When the Congress passed the repeal bill, it took the precaution of delaying the next meeting of the Supreme Court until February 1803. It then set about organizing its own judiciary, creating six circuits with a supreme and district court judge in each.

The lines of battle were drawn. Marshall sensed the need for asserting judicial supremacy, and in writing the opinion in *Marbury v. Madison*, a case that was already pending, he decided to lecture the court's opponents. In doing so he exercised great caution and strategy. William Marbury, one of Adams' appointees, had not received his commission as justice of the peace before the Adams administration left office. Jefferson, believing the commission to be invalid, refused its delivery, and Marbury sought relief under the Judiciary Act of 1789, securing a writ of mandamus to force Madison as Secretary of State to show cause for delaying the commission. Madison ignored the court order.

From this minor issue Marshall drew his now-famous explanation of judicial supremacy. Disposing of the legal issues quickly, Marshall granted Marbury a right to the commission, noting that Madison had a moral obligation to deliver it, but denied the legality of the writ of mandamus as a proper means for compelling Madison to deliver it. In fact, he pointed out, the writ was an unconstitutional extension of the court's original jurisdiction. By raising the issue of unconstitutional use of power, Marshall gave himself the opportunity he wanted— to discuss the nature of constitutional authority. In general, he argued from principles like the following: (1) The constitution is the fundamental and paramount law of the land; (2) the judicial function is "to say what the law is"; (3) the Constitution is a written document, from which statutes draw their strength and authority; thus anything repugnant to the Constitution must be void. In conflicts between the Constitution and statutes, he noted, the courts must support the Constitution as the source of authority.

Since the decision required no action from the President or Congress, Marshall had protected himself from possible retaliation, but the decision actually caused little excitement. Most newspapers and letter-writers accepted it without great emotion, and the powerful Republican leader, Nathaniel Macon, believed the case was correctly decided, although he thought Marshall was pompous and confused in expressing his views. Nevertheless it was an important case. It offered officially the theory of judicial supremacy, and it was followed immediately by other decisions on a circuit level that put the theory into practice. It should be added that federal and state courts in the 1790s had already considered the constitutionality of legislation, and that Marbury v. Madison affirmed the idea.

Though Marshall's decision escaped serious Republican censure, federal judges were soon severely attacked. In part, the hostility was invited by Judge Samuel Chase, who made a practice of denouncing Republican legislation, when he let off a political blast before a federal grand jury. Judge Chase was hated already for his activities in favor of the Sedition Act, and his charge opened the way for retaliation by the Republicans, who wanted to impeach and remove him from the bench. They were not bent upon destroying the judiciary, but upon humbling some judges who were high Federalists. While their case against Chase was taking form, Jefferson presented evidence against Judge John Pickering of New Hampshire, who was apparently insane. The House of Representatives cooperated, charging him with inability to hold office, and convinced the Senate, which voted overwhelming to remove him. In Pennsylvania Judge Addison, also known for his outspoken opinions, was impeached by the Republican house of representatives and ousted by the Senate.

These were minor victories compared to the possibility of removing Chase from the Supreme Court. He was accused of misconduct, perversion of his position, and high-handed methods of procuring indictments. His trial during January 1805 was an exciting battle of Republican and Federalist attorneys bent on publicizing party philosophy. Representing the Republicans for the prosecution was John Randolph, the powerful, emotional Virginian. His ill health and differences with the President reduced the force of his attack and he was confronted by the skillful arguments of five eminent Federalist attorneys who exposed the inherent weakness in the case against Chase. In the end Randolph failed to carry the full Republican membership of the Senate, and Chase was acquitted.

Randolph immediately offered an amendment to the Constitution, proposing the removal of judges by a joint address of both houses of Congress. Like his colleagues, he was bitter over the political activities of judges and wanted an effective way to discipline them. Admitting that impeachment proceedings were cumbersome, he claimed that judges would continue to take advantage of their life tenure in office unless Congress had an easier way to remove them. Again he failed. The bitterness of the defeat was lessened, for Jefferson had the opportunity to appoint new Republican judges—William Johnson in 1804, Henry B. Livingston in 1806, and Thomas Todd in 1807. But Marshall remained on the bench to exalt judicial power and to influence the new judges.

European War and the Embargo Act

These battles with the courts continued to annoy the Republicans, but they did inspire popular support for the party. Other, more divisive issues, however, plagued Jefferson during his second administration. His arguments with John Randolph over the purity of Republican principles were very dangerous to party harmony. Randolph had been in the House of Representatives since 1799. Besides being chairman of the Ways and Means Committee for many years, he was also floor leader, perhaps because of his wit and ability as an orator. He clashed first with Jefferson over the purchase of Louisiana, then over plans to buy West Florida, and finally over the claims of speculators in the Mississippi territory. His vigorous opposition drew to him other party members, including Speaker of the House Nathaniel Macon. The President took the desperate step of having both men removed from their positions of House leadership. Most Republicans maintained their party loyalty, but many questioned Jefferson's policies and wanted a return to strict party principles.

The party was further divided by the renewal of the European war in 1803 and by Jefferson's neutrality policy. The war brought a return of British seizures of men and ships, and Britain tightened her rules on trans-shipment of French colonial products from the Untied States to Europe. By 1805 a crisis was threatening American commerce, and Jefferson, true to his Republican principles, decided to follow

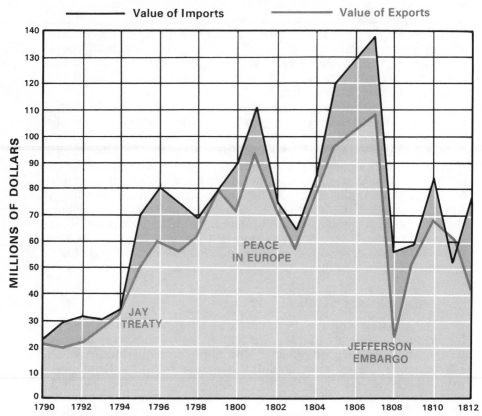

Foreign Trade, 1790-1812

——————— Value of Imports   ——————— Value of Exports

MILLIONS OF DOLLARS

PEACE
IN EUROPE

JAY
TREATY

JEFFERSON
EMBARGO

1790 1792 1794 1796 1798 1800 1802 1804 1806 1808 1810 1812

two methods for relieving the situation: (1) He would cut off all American trade with Europe, believing that farm products were essential to the European economy. (2) Before a nonintercourse act was imposed, he would negotiate a trade treaty to replace the expiring Jay Treaty. To facilitate these negotiations, he instructed James Monroe, the resident minister, to seek an indemnity for the ship seizures and impressments and a regularization of trade practices. Monroe found the British government friendly and cooperative, even willing to grant concessions. Unfortunately, just when something practical seemed possible, the British warship *Leander* accidentally killed an American citizen in a search operation within coastal waters. Americans reacted violently, and Congress responded to their feeling by passing a weak trade exclusion act. The administration appeared leaderless and confused in Congress, and British politicians labeled the act as bluff.

Jefferson still wanted to negotiate outstanding issues. To emphasize the importance of compromise, he searched for a distinguished envoy to assist Monroe. He chose eventually William Pinkney of Maryland, a Federalist lawyer who had considerable experience as a diplomat. Pinkney took detailed instructions with him to London, but he and Monroe followed Jay's precedent of securing the best agreement within the limits of the political situation—relief from impressment and seizure of products. They were able to win concessions on trade, but nothing substantial on impressment. Napoleon complicated the negotiations by establishing his so-called Continental System, which provided for a blockade of the British Isles and seizure of British trade: Britain learned of Napoleon's decree and asked for assurances from the United States that it would resist these restrictions. The American envoys believed a declaration to this effect would be a small price to pay for the trade concessions and urged Jefferson to accept their realistic position. But the President quickly rejected the treaty in 1807, because it had no provision against impressment, and noted that "we better have no treaty than a bad one." Both he and Madison, however, did not expect the rejection of the treaty to bring on war. In fact, Madison believed that Britain's Caribbean colonies needed American food, and Britain would soon adopt a conciliatory attitude.

The seizures continued. Both Britain and France molested American shipping and committed outrages against American crews. The worst was the *Chesapeake* Affair, in which the British man-of-war *Leopard* fired upon the *Chesapeake*, killed three seamen and wounded fourteen others, and impressed four crewmen. Americans reacted in anger; even Jefferson considered war; Congress finally passed in December 1807 an Embargo Act, which cut off American commerce with the outside world. Though patriotic citizens at first backed the President and Congress, the embargo was a severe test of loyalty. Smuggling occurred throughout New England and the Middle States, but still the loss of trade was great; unemployment, shortages, and rising prices brought bitterness. More important, the embargo did not force Britain to negotiate—Jefferson had overestimated Britain's dependence on American trade, and he had misjudged America's willingness to give up the flourishing war trade for national principle.

Before this crisis was resolved, the 1808 elections were held. The problem of succession was not difficult for Jefferson, for he had long considered James Madison, the Secretary of State, as his heir-apparent, although other members of his party like James Monroe, Vice President George Clinton, and John Randolph would have chosen another candidate. A caucus in January 1808 settled the matter; Madison and Clinton were nominated, and the party united reluctantly behind them. In a desperate move to challenge the Republicans the Feder-

alists finally nominated C. C. Pinckney and Rufus King, the unsuccessful candidates of the 1804 election. They did much better in 1808,
but Republicans, even without the magnetism of Jefferson, carried
twelve of the seventeen states and again won control of both houses
of Congress.

Madison and the War of 1812

The change in command was significant in 1809. Somehow Madison, a legislator of extraordinary skill, was inept as head of the party
and was unable to choose strong Cabinet officers, move decisively, or
inspire his associates. His small stature, negative personality, and lack
of a philosophy distinct from Jefferson's worked constantly to his dis-
advantage, especially at this moment of crisis in diplomatic affairs.

The Breakdown of Negotiations and the War Hawks

For a few months after his inauguration, Madison negotiated
through his Secretary of State Robert Smith with the British minister,
David M. Erskine, and reached a tentative understanding on impressment, reparations for the *Chesapeake* Affair, and the resumption of
trade. Most of its provisions were to be concessions by Britain, but
Erskine believed he adhered to the spirit of his instructions. He did
not calculate the harm that would be done when Foreign Minister
George Canning and the British Cabinet rejected the agreement.
Canning's instructions basically provided for American cooperation
with Britain in a plan of economic pressure upon France. For that
assistance he was willing to make concessions, but he was not ready
to offer America anything what would tie British hands in the war
against France or further American negotiations with France. In short,
Britain wanted the United States to be an ally.

The repudiation of the Erskine agreement by Britain found Madison
without an alternative policy. Trade under the Nonintercourse Act of
1809, which retained the embargo on British and French commerce
but relaxed restrictions on other nations' commerce, was still suffering
from British and French inspections and seizures. Almost everywhere,
American merchantmen were being harshly treated on the high seas
and were being given little or no protection. Congress, upon the demand
of shipowners and patriotic groups, again turned to trade regulation
and in the late spring of 1810 passed the Macon Act Number Two. The
Act, in restoring trade with France and Britain, provided that the first
power to recognize American neutral rights would have not only the
benefit of its trade but the reimposition of the Nonintercourse Act
on her enemy. It was curious legislation, even dangerous, because it
put the initiative into enemy hands and let these powers determine the
course of United States policy. Napoleon saw its advantage, pretended

to revoke France's harsh trade laws, and demanded that the United States impose the trade exclusion on Britain.

Though Madison had signed the Macon Act, he realized its dangers and thought he could use maneuvers by Napoleon as a means of coercing Britain. Somehow he fell into Napoleon's trap and refused to admit his error of judgment, even when his own advisors in Paris gave evidence of Napoleon's duplicity. Instead of investigating Napoleon's good faith, he gave Britain three months to comply or face nonimportation. On March 2, 1811, the Macon Act was enforced against Britain. Even then, Madison was neither clear about his policy objectives nor able to act upon advice. The nonimportation at this time had a serious impact upon Britain, for she was already suffering from a poor harvest and heavy unemployment. There were riots and disorder. In this crisis the Prime Minister was murdered, and the Foreign Secretary, Viscount Castlereagh, the most powerful man in the new cabinet, gave way to pressure from British friends of America who wanted peace and friendship. If Madison had calculated the effect of the trade policy upon British politics, he might then have wrung an agreement from a concilitary British ministry. But he had no resident minister to advise him, and he had allowed the Republican party to drift toward war.

Many of the new men of his party demanded war, and their belligerency, unlike the President's, did not include an understanding of the dangers of fighting the strongest nation in Europe. They were irritated with the hard policy of past British ministries, bitter over the loss of seamen and ships, aroused by the contempt shown to American sovereignty, and impressed by the possibility that they could retaliate by attacking Canada. Some imperialists among them saw an opportunity to strike a blow against monarchy and bring Canada republican institutions; others wanted to enlarge American territory at British expense. The party, nonetheless, had given the nation almost nothing with which to make this challenge: The army had only 7000 men until it was belatedly raised to 10,000 in 1812; the navy was made up chiefly of gunboats, almost worthless on the high seas, a few frigates, most of them in disrepair, and a few lesser ships of unknown value.

The 1810 Congress was vocal, energetic, and contemptuous of the older leadership. The House of Representatives chose as its leader Henry Clay, in place of Nathaniel Macon the Madison candidate, and he used his latent powers as Speaker to put friends into the committees, men like himself who favored war with Britain. On the Foreign Affairs Committee he placed John C. Calhoun, Felix Grundy, and John A. Harper, known War Hawks, who often spoke indiscreetly and were bent on vindicating the nation's honor. Though this Committee received little direction form Madison, it had the support of resolutions from fourteen of the seventeen state legislatures and the promise of Secretary of State Monroe, who succeeded Robert Smith in 1811, to back an aggressive policy if Britain did not renounce her orders in council.

Even as these young men tried to compel a solution to the nation's foreign problems, they were uncertain of their congressional support for war and failed to secure a tax program to finance the expected mobilization. When they argued for an embargo of American shipping in April 1812, their bill was weakly backed in the House and badly amended in the Senate. The congressional reaction reflected the state of the nation, which was reluctant to face the crisis. Many people regretted the dispute but promised cooperation to the administration; others regarded war as foolish or even insane. Plainly, the nation was distracted and unprepared for this test of strength with Britain. In the midst of the crisis Congress wanted to recess, and many members left for vacations, even as the committees anticipated Madison's request for a declaration of war by writing their own manifestoes.

The request for a declaration of war was presented early in June 1812. Most Republicans, hurrying back to the capital, gave their votes for war, but they were as divided as the general public about its significance. The Hartford *Connecticut Courant* said the war "was commenced in folly, it is proposed to be carried on with madness, and (unless speedily terminated) will end in ruin." In nearly every part of the nation men were divided on the war, its purpose, its support, and its outcome. Their attitude was reflected in the election of 1812 in which Madison was returned to office without much enthusiasm. The Federalist party, long considered to be dying, showed more vitality than it had since 1800. De Witt Clinton of New York, nephew of the late Vice President, was firmly supported in New York and New England, but Madison had the vote of the West and South to give him the margin of victory, 128 to 89.

If Madison had blundered into the war with the help of the War Hawks, he was permitted to blunder alone in conducting it. The nation's lack of preparedness was not quickly remedied by Congress, and there was no swell of popular support. Congress raised taxes reluctantly, and the revenue fell drastically short of expenditures. It issued bonds hesitantly, but purchases were disappointingly low because New England refused to back the sales. Gallatin raised $80 million from bonds, but he had to offer discounts and high interest to attract purchasers. He was handicapped, too, by the lack of institutional help and by hostility to his policies among bankers and congressmen. In the past he had the services of the United States Bank to handle treasury matters, and the relationship was beneficial to the nation. Republicans, however, harbored prejudices against federal banking, and even Madison himself would not give full support in 1811 to the bill to recharter the Bank. Responsibility for credit management then fell to local banks. Decentralization of financial services, without federal supervision, magnified the work of Gallatin's office, and he retired in disgust.

The confusion in finance occurred at a time when New York and New England, both areas of considerable wealth, were opposing the war. Their politicians and merchants, bitter over the war, refused to give Madison the wholehearted cooperation he needed, while they reaped the advantages of trade and shortages. Discouraging the purchase of war bonds, they openly resisted enlistments in the army and embarrassed Madison also in numerous petty ways. Finally, delegates from these northern states met at Hartford in 1814. Some leaders proposed a new national constitution, but the convention asked for seven constitutional amendments which would limit national power to tax and regulate commerce, and would require a two-thirds vote for the admission of new states. They were, in brief, a sectional response to the war—made not in the spirit of revolution but in the defense of their states rights.

Military Operations

The military phase of the war opened in the forests of Indiana with Governor William Henry Harrison's engagements against the western Indians. Peace in the territory had been uneasy because of defensive moves by the Indians, who feared the rush of population into their hunting grounds. The Shawnees were particularly fortunate to have Tecumseh as their leader. He had fought against American forces in the 1790s, was angry over the taking of Indian lands, and was ready to resist further aggression. With his brother, the Prophet, they mobilized Indian power and built a center of operations at the confluence of Tippecanoe Creek and the Wabash River. They developed also agricultural lands and herds of cattle, and imposed on their people social regulations that restored traditional Indian ways of life and prohibited liquor.

Tecumseh conveyed his thoughts concerning Indian welfare to Governor Harrison as early as 1808. He had promised then peaceful relations if the United States would halt its westward advance. If this assurance was not given, he threatened an alliance with Britain and war. These assurances were not given, and Tecumseh could not prevent local Indian groups from selling their birthrights from 1809 to 1811. The drift to war became a reality when the United States organized the Indiana territory in 1809 and moved troops into the area.

Harrison was committed to Indian removal and watched the ominous gathering of strength and alerted his men. Fortunately for him, in November 1811 the Indians, fired up by their own war hawks, attacked prematurely and then failed to press their advantages. His losses were serious, but the Indian withdrawal turned the Battle of Tippecanoe into an American victory. While the Indian uprising was blamed upon

British traders, whose ammunition and guns had reinforced the Indians, the British were wary of interfering. Only when their differences with the United States mounted into a war crisis in 1812 did they arouse the Indians, and their action was partly defensive, for the United States struck from the back country when it attacked Canada.

Instead of assaulting the strategic areas of Canada, American forces under William Hull crossed the frontier at Detroit. The old general moved slowly with his 1500 men, issued proclamations calling upon the settlers to rise up against British oppression, and awaited the result. The cool reaction of the settlers and a display of redcoats by British general Isaac Brock was enough to unnerve the commander and troops. In surrendering his army to Brock on August 16, 1812, he repeated what other American forces had done in July at Michilimack-inac, where they had fought a brief engagement with British troops and then had surrendered. For his timidity Hull was later court-martialed, convicted, and sentenced to be shot; a presidential pardon saved him.

On the Niagara front, John E. Wool attacked Queenston heights on October 13 and won a significant victory. Had the New York militia supported him then, he might have routed the British troops in another engagement, but instead the British were given time to bring in reinforcements. Their new strength overwhelmed the Americans, who were surrounded and compelled to surrender. The relief forces in New York, even when exhorted by Alexander Smith, firmly refused to cross the border, shot off their guns wildly, and searched for safety. In disgust General Smith left his command.

Near Lake Champlain, Henry Dearborn assembled troops for an attack on Montreal. His was the only strategically promising expedition, but he mobilized slowly, allowed cold weather to disrupt his plans, and ended his march at the border when his troops persuaded him to abandon the operation.

Poor generalship and weak discipline brought about these miserable actions on the land. On the sea, however, the bravery of Americans was exceptional. Victories were easily won over heavy odds; the *Constitution*, *United States*, and *President* gave the nation heroes. Congress quickly responded with appropriations, and Madison found a Secretary of the Navy, William Jones, who used the funds with great efficiency. However, the construction of new vessels took three years, and in the meantime Britain controlled the seas.

The American war record was no more decisive in 1813. Though American naval vessels moved easily on the Great Lakes, the futile seizing and burning of York brought retaliatory action against Washington in 1814. The American army in 1813 maneuvered, marched, and attacked frontier towns, but by December no American soldiers were left on Canadian territory. In the battles of Thames and Malden, Harrison won minor victories against the British and Indians. At Malden, Tecumseh lost his life on the battlefield while many of his fellow

Fall of Washington *(Library of Congress)*

warriors retreated in fright westward. The war had few real victories for either side, and the war record disgusted many people. Over the years most War Hawks, including Henry Clay, had become wiser men. Clay agreed to be a peace commissioner and set out for Ghent.

The British were willing to consider peace, but at the same time they planned a series of invasions of the United States in 1814, perhaps to strengthen the hands of their negotiators. They calculated without allowing for the unpredictable conduct of American forces. Before their reinforcements reached the Niagara front, Jacob Brown and Winfield Scott had crossed the river and seized Fort Erie. This battle was immediately followed by others at Chippewa and Lundy Lane, hard-fought, traditional engagements that took heavy casualties of both armies. The result bolstered American morale, because the battles prevented the British from moving into New York and revealed at long last the courage of Americans under fire.

Indecisive battles at Plattsburg convinced the British commander to delay his invasion of New York. In the Chesapeake area, the British navy moved easily against Washington, burned the public buildings, and frightened the Madison administration, which took flight when the militia failed to muster in defense. Symbolic of the nation's division were not only the burning of the government buildings but also the refusal of nearly eighty thousand militia to rise in defense of the capital.

One heroic act was Dolly Madison's rescue of the Gilbert Stuart painting of George Washington from the White House.

The British then moved their forces to Baltimore, but there the
defenders were prepared. The cannonading of Fort McHenry in September 1814 inspired Francis Scott Key to write the poem "The Star-
Spangled Banner" during the fateful night battle. The fury of battle
tested severely the militia who not only held their posts but drove back
a British landing party commanded by General Robert Ross, whom they
killed with many of his men. At New Orleans, too, the British tested
American defenses, and local forces turned back the enemy. The able
leader of American armies was Andrew Jackson, Scotch-Irish by descent
and frontiersman by experience and temperament. Trained as a lawyer
in North Carolina, he had moved to Tennessee in the 1780s, practiced
law, participated in politics, and served in high civil and military
positions in the state. At the head of volunteers in 1813, he had helped
in the seizure of West Florida and would have taken the rest of that
Spanish colony had Madison been willing to order its conquest. In
1813 and 1814 he fought the Creek Indians, and his success won him
the rank of major general in the American army.

When the British gathered to invade the gulf coast, Jackson displayed extraordinary energy in making preparations for its defense.
With a superior force, stern discipline, and firm decisions, he met the
British, took advantage of their mistakes, and threw them back in the
hardest fought battles of the war. The British general, Sir Edward
Parkenham, and two senior staff members lost their lives, as did
nearly two thousand of their troops. The rout in the mud and swamps
below New Orleans lasted ten days; then the hero Jackson, counting
only thirteen of his men dead and half a hundred wounded, journeyed
east for the congratulations of the nation. The Battle of New Orleans,
the greatest of the war, was won in January 1815, a few days after the
war was officially ended, but in that battle America had found a hero
and the celebration of his exploits would be reenacted many times in
coming years. A popular ballad of the 1820s, "The Hunters of Kentucky," well described Jackson's courage on that winter day of January 8:

> But Jackson he was wide awake,
>   And was not scar'd at trifles,
> For well he knew what aim we take
>   With our Kentucky rifles.
> So he led us down to Cypress swamp,
>   The ground was low and mucky,
> There stood John Bull in martial pomp
>   And here was old Kentucky.
> O Kentucky, the hunters of Kentucky!
> O Kentucky, the hunters of Kentucky!

Negotiations to end the war had begun in the summer of 1814 and proceeded at a leisurely pace, as the British awaited news of their counterattacks along the Canadian border. They anticipated victories from which they could demand territorial concessions, particularly in Maine, and the abandonment of American fishing claims in Newfoundland. The Americans hoped to secure a British declaration on impressment and neutral rights. Negotiations marked time until the fall of 1814, when the British ministry softened its attitude on advice of the Duke of Wellington, who was tired of fighting Napoleon and reluctant to fight in America. Albert Gallatin, one of the American commissioners, also favored compromise. The resulting discussions delayed major issues like boundaries and fishing claims until special commissions could study them, and ignored the issue of neutral rights, for the greater benefit of immediate peace. The Treaty of Ghent was signed on December 24.

Nearly thirty years had passed since the Constitution had become the supreme law of the land. During these years the United States had faced the menace of European conflict, with threats to shipping and the lives of seamen. Instead of war, Presidents Washington, Adams, Jefferson, and Madison until 1812 had depended upon negotiation to attain the national objectives of domestic peace, solvency, and republican experience in self-government. Though the Presidents had been confronted by crises, their successes can be measured in the reduction of the national debt, the lowering of taxes, the expansion of American territory and trade, the doubling of population, and in general the creation of a prosperous, successful republican government.

Though Americans fought the War of 1812 poorly, they took time to debate the objectives of the war, the rights of citizens, and the proper extent of federal control. Some citizens were unwilling to follow Madison's generals into battle, but few were disloyal to republican ideals. Almost no one wanted a return of British rule, a dictatorship, or an American king. If the war had any basic significance, it was that it revealed a breakdown of national leadership in a time of crisis and a weakening of national determination to avoid war.

American nationalism continued to mature. The celebrations of the Fourth of July each year, even in disaffected New England in 1814, magnified the heroic virtues of the Revolution, the sacrifices of Washington and his men, the glory of Lexington, Concord, and Bunker Hill, and the success of republican institutions. Historians were making of the past an almost religious experience, especially through Parson Weems's George Washington, Franklin's Autobiography and papers, and Noah Webster's spelling book and readers. The Revolution was for its survivors the event of their lives, an inspiration and a traumatic experience that they never tired of recounting.

Americans welcomed the peace in 1815 as an opportunity to renew their faith in republican ideals; they did not overthrow the party of Jefferson, but in the election of 1816 chose another Virginian,

James Monroe, to carry the Republican banner. In forming his Cabinet, President Monroe named the son of a former critic and Federalist, John Quincy Adams, as Secretary of State and a former War Hawk, John C. Calhoun, as Secretary of War. They depended upon the talented leadership of Henry Clay, again Speaker of the House of Representatives, to pilot necessary national reforms through the House.

SUGGESTIONS FOR FURTHER READING

Adams, Henry, *The United States in 1800*. Ithaca, New York, Great Seal Books, Cornell University Press, 1958.

Bemis, Samuel F., *Jay's Treaty: A Study in Commerce and Diplomacy*. New Haven, Conn., Yale University Press, 1962.

Billington, Ray Allen, *The Protestant Crusade, 1800-1860*. Chicago, Quandrangle Books, 1964.

Boorstin, Daniel J., *The Lost World of Thomas Jefferosn*. Boston, Beacon Press, 1960.

Chambers, William Nesbit, *Political Parties in a New Nation, 1776-1809*. New York, Oxford University Press, 1963.

Chinard, Gilbert, *Honest John Adams*. Boston, Little, Brown and Company, 1961.

Cunliffe, Marcus, *George Washington: Man and Monument*. New York, Mentor Books, New American Library, 1960.

Cunningham, Noble E., Jr. *The Jeffersonian Republicans, 1789-1801*. Chapel Hill, N.C., University of North Carolina Press, 1957.

DeConde, Alexander, *The Quasi-War: The Politics and Diplomacy of The Undeclared War with France, 1797-1801*. New York, Scribner Library, Charles Scribner's Sons, 1968.

Dewey, Donald, *Marshall Versus Jefferson: The Political Background of Marbury v. Madison*. New York, Alfred A. Knopf, 1970.

Foner, Eric, *Tom Paine and Revolutionary America*. New York, Oxford University Press, 1977.

Horsman, Reginald, *The War of 1812*. New York, Alfred A. Knopf, 1969.

Koch, Adrienne, *Jefferson and Madison: The Great Collaboration*. New York, Galaxy Books, Oxford University Press, 1964.

Kohn, Richard H., "The Washington Administration's Decision to Crush the Whiskey Rebellion." *The Journal of American History*, Lix, 567-584.

Kurtz, Stephen G., *The Presidency of John Adams*. New York, Perpetua Books, A. S. Barnes & Company, 1961.

Litwack, Leon F., *North of Slavery*. Chicago, Phoenix Books, University of Chicago Press, 1967.

Perkins, Bradford, *Prologue to War: England and the United States, 1805-1812.* Berkeley and Los Angeles, University of California Press, 1961.

Peterson, Merrill D., *Thomas Jefferson and the New Nation: A Biography.* New York, Oxford University Press, 1970.

Smelser, Marshall, *The Democratic Republic, 1801-1815.* New York, Harper & Row, 1968.

Stourzk, Gerald, *Alexander Hamilton and the Idea of Republican Government.* Stanford, California, Stanford University Press, 1970.

Watlington, Patricia, *The Partisan Spirit: Kentucky Politics, 1779-1792.* New York, Atheneum, 1972.

Wecter, Dixon, *The Hero in America: A Chronicle of Hero-Worship.* New York, Charles Scribner's Sons, 1972 (reprint).

7

The Common People in Office

WITH THE WAR OF 1812 ENDED, AMERICANS readily turned
their minds from Europe toward peace and reconstruction. The twenty-
five years after 1815 were decisive ones in the nation's history. European peace had also returned, and the United States could concentrate
on its own problems without the distraction of war trade and impressment. Population grew rapidly and spread west into the Mississippi
Valley, and almost a million European immigrants entered the United
States. Canals, roads, and railroads opened distant areas, bringing rich
agricultural products to eastern markets where the diversity of the
economy—in textiles, tools, pottery, and services—improved the
living conditions and gave more Americans time to assess their political institutions than at any previous time. In the South the growth
primarily of cotton, but also of sugar, rice, and tobacco, fashioned an
agricultural society in an area that used black slaves as its major
labor force. Fear of rebellion and sensitivity about slavery made southerners less willing than northerners to talk about political reform, but
they enjoyed prosperity and expansion that brought them and their
northern partners great wealth. Even though the future in 1815 looked
particularly bright, there remained many problems from the war, such

as national solvency, territorial boundaries, and political unity. The direction American progress should take was not clear, and many people, almost looking over their shoulders, sought instruction from Europe.

Change and the New National Spirit

Since 1790 the nation had gradually been changing. The northern cities were increasing in population. New York became the largest urban center when its population reached 96,000 and surpassed Philadelphia's, and its population continued to multiply decade upon decade. The concentration of people in the cities provided a variety and richness to life, with educational services, hospitals, societies for the promotion of worth-while projects, and diversions like theaters and museums. In Philadelphia and Boston, concerned people gathered to discuss history, philosophy, religion, and progress, often establishing societies to give form to their deliberations. The cities supported an active press with journalists, writers, and informed readers and an intelligensia that responded to national issues by social and political organization.

The North was changing from agriculture and commerce to manufacturing and commerce. Ample water power, population, and capital, as well as adventurous leaders, contributed to this transformation, and nearly every town had a mill or factory. A working class, dividing its time between farm and factory, grew in numbers as groups of promoters financed turnpikes, canals, and merchantmen in order to take advantage of new opportunities. Many immigrants from Ireland found jobs in these factories and businesses, and filled the places of men who left for the Middle West, California, and Hawaii. The business people of the north depended on credit services, stocks, bonds, and banking, and supported governmental policies that provided tariff protection and commercial regulations.

But the North was not the only region that was changing. In Pennsylvania capitalists were turning iron ore into manufactured goods and cotton, wool, and leather into saleable products. Farther south, diversified agriculture and cotton predominated. Though southerners explored the possibility of manufacturing textiles, many capitalists put their money instead into cotton production. After Eli Whitney's invention of the cotton gin in 1793, planters experimented with cotton seeds and soils and settled on a Mexican variety of cotton that resisted the frosts of early spring and throve in the piedmont country. Available black slaves provided a sturdy, dependable labor supply and were a major factor in the increased production. In less than a decade forty million pounds of cotton were grown, and by 1811 production had doubled. In 1850 more than a billion pounds of cotton went to market, an accomplishment made possible by the sweat of nearly three million slaves. Such astonishing crops were also a response to the development of a highly efficient textile industry in England, where the mechanization of production improved yearly in turning out finely printed and textured cloths in great quantity.

While cotton was the rising crop of the South, the annexation of Louisiana brought into the Union an area that could grow sugar extensively. After 1796 the inhabitants began to manufacture sugar, and acreage multiplied as French immigrants moved with their slaves from Santo Domingo. Some southerners migrated there too, but the difference in production methods and the advantages of rising cotton prices made most hesitate to exchange cotton for sugar. Sugar cane was widely planted, however, and by 1830 there were 691 plantations and 36,000 slaves engaged in the industry, whose gross profits that year were $50 million.

Changes in the economic life of the United States were rapid after 1815. Even those leaders of Congress familiar with the interests of their regions were often unaware of the character and direction of these changes. Most felt, however, the optimism, democratic spirit, equalitarianism, and pride in republican accomplishments that were spreading across the nation. Historians label these feelings "the new nationalism," but the immediate reaction to the return of peace was not so much something new as it was a blending of the Hamilton economic program with the Jefferson democratic outlook.

The tone of the era was set by President Madison in his annual message on December 5, 1815:

> Whilst other portions of mankind are laboring under the distresses of war or struggling with adversity in other forms, the United States are in the tranquil enjoyment of prosperous and honorable peace. . . . We can rejoice in the proofs given that our political institutions, founded in human rights and formed for their preservation, are equal to the severest trials of war.

Madison urged Congress to provide for a strong military establishment, a national currency, a protective tariff, a national system of roads and canals, and a "national seminary of learning," which would draw the youth and genius from every part of the country, infuse in them sentiments of enlightenment and patriotism, and send them home imbued with American ideals and liberties.

Congress quickly enacted most of Madison's proposals, save the national university, and in rapid order it set the total strength of the army at ten thousand men, authorized fifteen frigates, and reorganized West Point. Even more important was the establishment of a second United States Bank, with a capital stock of $35 million, the right to erect branch banks, and a monopoly of federal government business. The bank was chartered for twenty years. Madison hoped the bank would stablize credit and provide necessary supervision of banking practices in the states. In addition, Congress revised the modified basic tariff of 1789, raising rates high enough to protect the infant industries. While the tariff was intended as a temporary measure, spokesmen such as Daniel Webster for northern shipping interests and John Randolph for southern agriculturalists tried to change the mind of Congress. But the bill carried by overwhelming majorities in both houses.

Congress was also willing to follow Madison's recommendations for internal improvements by appropriating money for an extension of the Cumberland Road, eventually to spread from Cumberland on the upper Potomac to Wheeling, across Ohio and Indiana, and to Vandalia, Illinois. But Madison blocked a larger program of public works by presidential veto. His message of March 3, 1817, set limits on Congressional spending, and instead of letting John Marshall and the Supreme Court interpret the Constitution he chose to take upon himself the obligation of defining constitutional powers: "The legislative powers vested in Congress are specified and enumerated, . . . and it does not appear that the power proposed to be exercised by the bill is among the enumerated powers." Madison's successor, James Monroe, held similar views. Though he permitted the National Road to be completed, he stoutly resisted appropriations for its repair and the collection of tolls.

These presidential scruples effectively restrained Congress from enacting a program of public works. Men like Calhoun and Clay, who were committed to such a program, had to depend upon the states for the initiative. They discovered, however, that Congress could vote aid to the states and that Monroe's successor, John Quincy Adams, shared their enthusiasm. With Adams' cooperation, very large grants were made annually, but the planning and development of projects rested primarily in state hands. In New York, Governor De Witt Clinton put great strain on the state's financial resources when he backed the Erie Canal project in 1817. Costing more than seven million dollars and extending 360 miles, it opened in 1825 and succeeded almost immediately in tying the western grain to New York. While the people of other states gambled their financial resources on canals, everyone wanted to get a share of western trade. In 1850 over 3200 miles of canals operated with varying degrees of success.

The new canals opened fertile areas to food production, which had an important effect upon agricultural prices. Western grain replaced New Jersey and Georgia crops on the competitive market, even within those states, and in New England low prices made home production unprofitable. Farmers in desperation abandoned commercial production and sought full-time factory jobs, or left for western villages like Cleveland and Chicago that were taking on the appearance of boom towns as ports for the grain trade. Their prosperity, however was jealously regarded, and cities like Philadelphia pressed their state governments to develop a canal system. Transportation costs proved to be too great, and they had to await the perfection of the rail-road.

States' Rights versus the National Government

In their efforts to attract and control trade, the states often erected barriers against each other and sought to restrict the powers of the United States government. To hold them in check the Supreme Court accepted for adjudication some of the more controversial issues. In the case of *Gibbon v. Ogden* (1824) the Court held that Congress had complete control over commerce on navigable rivers and declared unconstitutional a state monopoly of steamboat traffic in New York. Three years later it extended federal supervision over land commerce by prohibiting state regulation of interstate commerce until a product's original box had been broken open and its contents passed into the general stream of commerce. Another case, *Willson v. Black Bird Creek Marsh Company* (1829), gave more flexibility to commercial regulation by letting the states legislate whenever Congress had not acted, but the decision had the effect of reserving for the Court the power to interfere with state regulation whenever important issues arose.

In another significant case, *McCulloch v. Maryland* (1819), the Court passed on the nagging question of broad versus strict construc-tion of the Constitution. Opponents of the second Bank of the United States had challenged congressional power to incorporate banks. In regulating credit, they argued, the United States had only the enumer-ated powers, and the Constitution did not give Congress the power to erect a bank. But Marshall, restating Hamiltonian doctrine, noted that the national government was "supreme within its sphere of action" and could use whatever was necessary and proper to carry out its will. The erection of a bank was described as an appropriate means to carry out its powers to regulate credit: "Let the end be legitimate, let it be within the scope of the Constitution, and all means which are appropriate, which are plainly adapted to that end, which are not prohibited, but consistent with the letter and spirit of the Constitution, are consti-tutional."

A most important issue in this case and in *Osborn v. The Bank of the United States* involved the right of the state to tax the bank. In 1818 and 1819 economic conditions were unsettled, and Ohio, wanting to assume control over credit, levied a tax of $50,000 on each branch of the United States Bank within the state. The tax was a direct violation of the *McCulloch* decision, and the bank sought relief by obtaining an injunction against Ralph Osborn, the state auditor. The Supreme Court finally decided the case in 1824 by holding that the state could not tax an agency of the federal government.

These decisions aroused many Republicans because the court pro-

tected the vested interests of propertied and business people, often at
the expense of the state legislatures and human rights. Both Jefferson
and Madison, from their retirements, criticized the *McCulloch* case,
and five state legislatures, with Virginia taking the lead, petitioned
Congress for a constitutional amendment limiting congressional power
to establish branch banking. Many newspapers and magazines, such
as the *Niles' Register,* attacked the decision in similar words: "A
deadly blow has been struck at the Sovereignty of the States, and
from a quarter so far removed from the people as to be hardly access-
ible to public opinion. . . . Nothing but the tongue of an angel can convince us of its compatibility with the Constitution."

The nationalistic decisions of the Court seemed out of harmony
with republican ideals. Many people accused Marshall of undermining
"the pillars of the Constitution itself" and destroying "the rights of the
state governments." The spirit of the country was changing, shifting
the emphasis from national power to states' rights and infusing certain
new democratic ideas into popular rule. One after another the states
were calling constitutional conventions, broadening the franchise,
making offices elective, printing election ballots, providing neighborhood voting booths, and democratizing party machinery. Many Americans wanted to broaden the basis of freedom, recalling the revolutionary ideology of 1776 when leaders hoped to pioneer new liberties
for mankind. The peaceful revolution of the 1820s, equalitarian in
sentiment, hoped to improve upon society by helping the insane,
the deaf, the blind, the ignorant, and the criminal, to work for lasting
peace and women's rights, and to abolish slavery. Many of these reformers were, like their philosopher John Taylor of Carolina, agricul-
turalists. They believed that farming was the true foundation of wealth,
that the town mechanic was a "blood brother" of the farmer, and that
virtue, the real and the true, sprang from close contact with the soil.
So the capitalist, the businessman, and the town dweller, who lived
off the farmers' wealth, were parasites, and their institutions such as
banks prevented a full development of the nation.

The agricultural commonwealth of equality, plenty, and independence was not completely opposed by the nationalists, but men like
Henry Clay recognized a different pattern of development. His American
System envisioned a self-sufficient economy of industry as well as of
commerce and agriculture that would reduce the dependence of the
United States upon European markets. He wished to use tariffs, banking,
and subsidies to create a powerful, diversified economy of plenty,
equality, and independence.

Nationalism and the West: The Monroe Doctrine

The national spirit persisted longest in America's conduct of
foreign affairs. Perhaps because the policy was concerned principally

with the West, its popularity endured. Between the close of the War of 1812 and 1821 six new states joined the Union—Indiana, Mississippi, Illinois, Alabama, Maine, and Missouri. These new states reflected the continuous western movement of the people. By 1820, nearly two million people of the nation's total 9.6 million lived in the trans-Appalachian area. The whole western region was arousing national interest. Traders were setting out from Westport on the Missouri River for Santa Fe; others were searching for furs in the Dakotas, Wyoming, Utah and Colorado; still others were rounding the Horn for trade with Hawaii and California. The West had its spokesmen, like Clay and Jackson, and two of the Presidents from the South and East, Monroe and John Quincy Adams, were equally determined to secure this land for the United States. There was also a new voice, that of Thomas Hart Benton of Missouri who was powerful, colorful and daring.

In 1815 the unfinished business with Great Britain consisted of another commercial treaty, an incomplete boundary with Canada, and provisions for the rule of Oregon. More and more American cotton and wheat found markets in England, while investors from London and Liverpool sought opportunities in American industry. Though Britain's mercantile laws disrupted trade, liberal Tories forced reforms in the 1820s, and trade increased steadily until regulations on commerce in the 1840s allowed a full exchange of products. The most important of the treaties was the Rush-Bagot Agreement of 1817, which limited armament on the Great Lakes. It laid the basis for decades of peace, and brought the growth of mutual respect between the parties. The Convention of 1818, like the Agreement of 1817, removed sources of argument and bitterness by extending the western boundary from the Lake of the Woods to the Rockies and by providing for joint occupation of Oregon. The willingness of Lord Castlereagh and President Monroe to find compromises when less understanding men urged harsher policies contributed to this series of successful treaties and laid the basis for a lasting friendship between the countries.

The administration was also interested in ending the Indian disturbances along the Florida boundary. Though the United States had twice annexed parts of western Florida, Indians moved across the border of Florida, using the swamps as asylum when they were chased by American troops, and runaway blacks also used Florida as a haven. Blacks erected a fort on the Apalachicola River and fired on Americans across the river. When the colorful hero of New Orleans, Andrew Jackson, assumed command of border troops in 1817, he sought administrative support for a campaign into Florida and received some assurances from a subordinate of the President. In a few weeks as he moved across the frontier, he pushed the Indians ahead of him and apprehended some smugglers whom he speedily executed. These measures were popular with the press and people but disturbed the government, which was weathering protests from Spain as it negotiated the purchase of Florida.

While the Cabinet debated policy, Henry Clay in the House urged Jackson's censure. The self-righteous general, infuriated by what he considered to be a personal assault, denounced his critics and rallied the people to his support. In the meantime, Secretary of State Adams placated Spain with a mixture of threats and assurances and made the best of an embarrassing situation.

In the end the United States and Spain signed the Adams-Onís Treaty (to be ratified in 1821), which provided for a settlement of outstanding issues between the nations. It transferred Florida to the United States for $5 million. It drew the boundary between Texas and the Louisiana Purchase along the Sabine, Red, and Arkansas rivers, thence northward to the 42nd parallel, and west along the parallel to the Pacific Ocean. Finally, the United States won whatever rights Spain had in the Oregon country. This agreement with Spain therefore expressed the national aspirations to assure itself of Florida, to set western boundaries, and to establish another claim to Oregon. In passing it should be noted that President Monroe then sent Albert Gallatin to London in order to arrange a division of the Oregon country. His years of negotiations, however, were unsuccessful, and the territory remained under the joint protection of Britain and the United States.

Preoccupation with Oregon also brought an exchange of notes with Russia in 1823. Russia had extended her Alaskan boundary southward into Oregon and had shown interest in San Francisco Bay. Her penetration into Spanish territory coincided with plans in Europe for a division of Spain's disintegrating American empire. With most of the empire in revolt, Spain was confronted with a task too formidable for her resources and was considering an offer of help from her European allies in exchange for spoils. This overture disturbed the United States, who had welcomed the destruction of colonialism and the rise of sister republics. For different reasons Britain, too, wanted the region to be independent. Therefore, her new foreign secretary, George Canning, suggested that the two countries issue a joint declaration against intervention in Spanish America.

The motives for Canning's proposal were complex, and a declaration may not have been his chief aim. His parliamentary backers were interested in trade and worried about higher duties imposed by the United States. He might have hoped that unified British and United States foreign policies would bring greater cooperation and, in turn, keep duties low. Canning was suspected of being an opportunist, especially by Secretary of State Adams, who valued a declaration against foreign occupation of Spanish America but who did not want the United States "to come in as a cockboat in the wake of the British man-of-war."

Adams looked upon these European maneuvers as an opportunity for the United States to make its own declaration of policy. Since he considered Great Britain America's chief rival, he urged President Monroe to reject Canning's suggestion outright. In place of a joint declaration he wanted Monroe to use the occasion of an address to Congress to lay down some basic principles of foreign policy. Monroe, Adams felt, should concern himself entirely with American affairs and warn Europeans against colonization and transference of colonies in the Western Hemisphere. Responding to this suggestion, Monroe permitted a lengthy statement on foreign policy to be included in his December 2, 1823, address to Congress. Both men wanted to leave open the possibility of American expansion across the continent and the eventual annexation of Cuba and Texas, but even more to give the United States a free hand to follow its own course. Both wanted the nation to confine itself to policies in the Western Hemisphere and maintain the natural separation from Europe that seemed to be indicated by geography and politics.

The Monroe Doctrine, therefore, was a political manifesto that emphasized American desires to republicanize the continent, to expand from coast to coast, and to control its own destiny. It reflects a childlike-bondness for the success that the Republic was achieving. Most Americans had come to regard the Constitution as a permanent, living document that would mold the nation's development; most thought the United States should expand westward. Most wanted a sea-to-sea country and a population equal to Europe's, and also an agricultural and commercial base which would give the people a high standard of living. While Americans generally shared these visions of a bright future, the kind of brightness was debated everywhere, particularly by leaders of the sections who had their own interpretations of the American promise.

The Changing Electorate

Since 1815 Americans reevaluated constantly their republican dogma. Many welcomed the new nationalism of Congress and the Supreme Court; they urged the development of a strong economy to prolong the prosperity that the nation had enjoyed since 1789. Many appreciated the vigorous foreign policy of John Quincy Adams, especially its emphasis upon westward expansion. But the changing electorate and the inclusion of new western states in the nation created a three-cornered sectional struggle over tariffs, banking, land policy, admission of new states, and the nature of American leadership.

Curiously, these changes were not reflected in the presidential elections of 1820. Monroe was reelected with almost no opposition, and the people were given no opportunity to choose between candidates or to participate in a debate of issues. Even though the nation had suffered economic crises in 1818 and 1819, partly because of credit policies of the United States Bank, the financial issue had little importance in the campaign. The same may be said of the antislavery agitation over the admission of Missouri, the use of federal money to

United States Capitol in the 1820s' *(University of Southern California)*

develop internal improvements, and the formation of a land policy. In short, the advantage of a national debate on issues was lost. The renewal of faith in the Republic and the sharpening of issues were delayed for four more years.

The Missouri Compromise

Of these issues, the most serious to escape national political debate was the Missouri Compromise. The dispute was caused by two rival interests. The South was spreading its cotton plantations through Alabama, Mississippi, and Louisiana, and was agitating for Missouri's admission as a cotton-and-slave state. If the trend were to continue, the whole of the Louisiana Purchase shortly would have cotton and slavery. Many in the North interpreted this expansion as a threat to their interests. They backed eventually the Land Law of 1820, which reduced the price of western land to $1.25 per acre and the minimum purchase to eighty acres. Settlers were thus helped to make their homes in the West. In the meantime, Congress authorized the establishment of the Arkansas territory and reported favorably for Missouri to become a state.

At this point, James Tallmadge of New York proposed that the extension of slavery be limited and that slavery in Missouri be extinguished gradually by freeing the children of slaves when they reached the age of twenty-five years. The proposal evoked an immediate, bitter debate, raising such questions as the permanence of slavery and slave states and the equality and rights of the states. Southerners questioned whether Congress could impose restrictions on the states and declared the Tallmadge amendment unconstitutional. Northerners countered by citing the Northwest Ordinance, which had restricted slavery, and by denouncing slavery itself as a moral evil. In a close vote the House put itself on record in favor of gradual emancipation.

In the meantime, the District of Maine, with the approval of Massachusetts, petitioned to become a state. Statehood for Maine immediately suggested a compromise, and with some negotiation among leaders, Maine and Missouri were paired, thus holding the balance of power between free and slave states. Congress set latitude, 36° 30', Missouri's southern boundary, to divide slave from free territory in the Louisiana Purchase. Here the dispute should have ended, except that Missouri, irritated by the debate over slavery, passed an obnoxiously proslavery constitution that denied entry of free blacks into the state. For a time Missouri's admission as a state hung in the balance; then a second compromise was arranged by Henry Clay, who proposed that Missouri's constitution be accepted without amendment if the state would pledge never to deny any citizen the right to enjoy his liberties. This compromise was finally accepted, and Missouri became a state in 1821.

While the Missouri Compromise again removed the issue of slavery and expansion from politics, John Quincy Adams revealed his opinion of this kind of legislation. In his eyes the Compromise changed the spirit of the Constitution and deprived blacks of the right of citizenship. He wrote:

> Already cursed by the mere color of their skin, already doomed by their complexion to drudge in the lowest offices of society, excluded by their color from all the refined enjoyments of life accessible to others, excluded from the benefits of a liberal education, from the bed, from the table, and from all the social comforts of domestic life, this barbarous article deprives them of the little remnant of right yet left them—their rights as citizens and as men.

In spite of this emotion, Adams and others could not push Congress into a consideration of black rights. Slavery as an institution was not widely debated in the election of 1822, nor was it a major issue in 1824.

The Unpopular Adams Administration

In 1824 the Republican party all but dissolved, as four Republicans vied for Monroe's place. On retiring, Monroe let it be known that he favored his Secretary of the Treasury, William H. Crawford, who was more representative of the plantation society than any other candidate. By birth a Virginian and by residence a Georgian, Crawford enjoyed a good reputation, was independent in his judgments, and had a blend of nationalism with southern sectionalism that won wide support. However, he had suffered in 1823 a brain hemorrhage that had left him partially paralyzed.

The other candidates—John Quincy Adams, Henry Clay, and Andrew Jackson—gained some of Crawford's support. Jackson, more than the others, was the popular candidate. His manners made him appear to be a new man in politics and thus he drew the favor of westerners, back-country people, workingmen, and the newly enfranchised. They were attracted by romanticized versions of his victory at New Orleans, his raids into Florida, and his fights with Indians and woodsmen. They admired his humble origins, moreover, which made him a true American, a practical and natural genius: "He alone of the three is gifted with genius—with those great powers of mind that can generalize with as much ease as a common intellect can go through detail." In spite of such tributes, though, the American people split their vote among the four candidates, and the final decision passed to the House of Representatives where the followers of Adams and Clay joined forces to make Adams the next President. The only major politician avoiding this bitterness was John C. Calhoun, who selected the vice presidency with the hope that it would lead to the highest office.

The decision was not made without bargaining and soliciting of votes, often by the candidates themselves, frequently by their followers. Henry Clay, whose ethics were politically determined, was deeply interested in the proceedings and ignored the instruction of the Kentucky legislature to back Jackson. Adams visited quietly with his supporters, who openly solicited votes or applied pressure on wavering leaders. Newspapers printed stories of deals, of Clay being appointed Secretary of State, of judgeships and ministerial posts being promised. When Adams was finally elected and chose Clay as his Secretary of State, the cry of corruption was widely heard, and it was repeated constantly for the next four years.

Adams was unable to counteract this hostility. Moreover, he was unwilling to remove Republicans who were disloyal to him, permitted opponents to dispense patronage, and refused, even when faced with evidence, to punish those plotting against him. By appointing some former Federalists, he alienated Republicans whom he had sought to befriend, and he made serious mistakes in the management of New York politics. With the party divided, Adams was unable to select issues that inspired support or rallied popular opinion. He proposed to increase the navy, build roads and canals, send American envoys into Latin America, and obtain commercial treaties. His policies were more national than Hamilton's and reflected Clay's American System.

They were not attractive to the new voters, who were more concerned with local issues and were searching for a political figure to embody their emotions and prejudices. Adams impressed them as cold, foreign, and aristocratic; his opposition seemed to be democratic.

There were issues, too, that inflamed public feeling against Adams. The President favored the western Indians in negotiations with the states and settlers. He was cautious in recommending changes in the tariff, when supporters in New York and the West expected vigorous proposals. He wanted to subsidize science and was ridiculed, instead, for proposing an astronomical observatory: "Those light-houses of the skies" became a national joke. Through the years Congress opposed him by withholding appropriations, charging corruption in government, and passing the famous Tariff of Abominations of 1828, whose unusually high duties were designed to arouse the nation against him.

Adams entered the election of 1828 without any attractive political program and was unable to build a nation-wide group of supporters. His opponent, Andrew Jackson, had been campaigning since the last election, and the rivalries and bitterness of the protracted contest made the campaign a personal feud. While politicians divided into factions, Adams and Clay versus Jackson and Calhoun, the election was decided by local men seeking national prestige. In every state outside of New England (with the exception of Maine), Jackson's friends had better organization than the President's. They blended their aspirations as rising politicians with their support for Jackson and used the prestige and dignity of the old order, personified by the candidate for Vice President, Calhoun, to offset criticism that the party was composed of the democratic rabble.

In New York, politics were in turmoil by the sudden death of De Witt Clinton. Three parties emerged in the 1828 elections, in which the contest over the governorship may have been more important than that for the Presidency. The tight discipline of the Bucktail Democrats, led by Martin Van Buren, won the election with a greater vote than was given to Jackson. In Pennsylvania, Adams was likewise unable to find an attractive, first-rate political figure to support him. Governor John A. Schulze remained neutral in the election, while Jackson men like James Buchanan organized a powerful party. The state's voters gave Jackson a two-to-one margin over Adams. Since the national elections had sectional overtones, most New Englanders voted for Adams, while southerners voted for Jackson. Split votes in New York and Maine and the enthusiastic support of the western citizens gave Jackson the electoral victory of 178 to 83.

The Jackson Era

The victory proved to be greater than the vote because the coalition which had backed Adams disintegrated soon after the election.

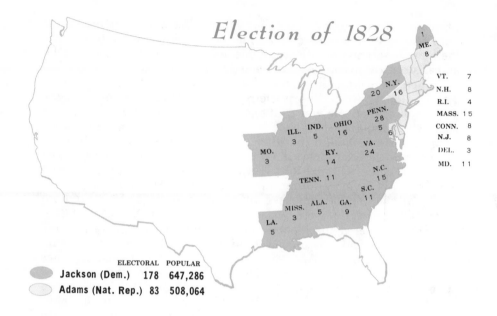

Election of 1828

	ELECTORAL	POPULAR
Jackson (Dem.)	178	647,286
Adams (Nat. Rep.)	83	508,064

Nearly everywhere new political alignments occurred so that the Jackson party, or Democratic party, gained in strength and politicians associated themselves with the President's policies. The opposition, in reforming itself, reflected hostility to Jackson's personality and policies.

Jackson symbolized the rise of the common people to political power. As the people's President his inauguration became an expression of emotion that brought a flood of well-wishers into the White House, and the turmoil so baffled the new President that he escaped from the disturbance by a window. A dignified gentleman himself, Jackson was no common man, much less one who would divide the wealth or free the slaves. He was a democrat, westerner, and loyal American, firmly believing that he was spokesman of these people and that no special qualifications were necessary for him or anyone to serve the people. Jackson had a practical education, including enough knowledge of the Bible, Shakespeare, and history to give him a feeling for language, and his day in power, but his knowledge of politics reflected prejudices against banks, professional politicians, and Indians. He acted often impulsively, or on suspicion, with incomplete knowledge, but he strove to protect his country's interests. He was a republican in the tradition of Jefferson, Madison, and Gallatin in that he accepted the great responsibility of purifying government, of restoring it and returning it to the people, and he felt, too, that government was limited in what it should do.

More than anything else, Jackson called upon the ordinary citizen to exert himself in behalf of justice, fair play, and equity, and he embodied in his own conduct the virtues of simplicity and honesty in handling public affairs. His administration reflected the reforming spirit of the day, but provided little guidance of a constructive kind. Reform was left to individuals, or to the states, and the Democratic party attracted, as a result, fewer leaders of movements than what might be expected. America, nonetheless, had never produced so many writers, historians, and philosophers dedicated to reform as it did in this era. The sense of destiny and satisfaction of Americans for their country was well reflected by the historian George Bancroft, who used words and phrases in his *History of the United States* to convey the uniqueness of the national experience. "Tyranny and injustice people America with men nurtured in suffering and adversity. The history of our colonization is the history of the crimes of Europe." Reformers like Horace Mann of Massachusetts agitated for public schools, free education, and practical subjects of study that would assist tradesmen and professional workers. He and his friends founded the first teacher's college in the United States and helped turn the classroom away from the paddle and birch rod. Other humanitarians like Dorothea Dix took up the causes of the convict and the insane, while some wanted to prohibit the sale of hard liquor. Women under the leadership of Elizabeth C. Stanton and Lucretia Mott launched a crusade for suffrage, but equality under the law was for some an even greater objective than the right to vote. They urged reform of dress, the marriage code, and inheritance laws. Religious reformers, reflecting the new democracy, denounced special clerical robes and ornate houses of worship, and called for simplicity and a revised code of social behavior. They proscribed card playing, dancing, and certain kinds of food; some of them would reconstruct society. Charles G. Finney, the great clerical voice of the day, held revivals and prayed for God's forgiveness in most population centers.

While Finney had a powerful spiritual impact, few people were interested in changing the pattern of American material development. They revered the Revolution and its leaders and counted off the years of successful republican rule; some patriotic citizens even worked to erect monuments. Jared Sparks, the greatest of the patriotic editors, published multivolume collections of Washington and Franklin letters. His literary efforts gave much publicity to the 40,000 Washington letters at Mount Vernon, letters which Sparks took to Boston for editing. The publicity eventually convinced the national government to purchase them for scholarly study and to deposit them in the Library of Congress. Sparks was most impressed with the insights he received from his editing: "I have got a passion for Revolutionary history and the more I look into it the more I am convinced that no complete history of the American Revolution has been written. The materials have never been collected; they are still in the archives of the states and in the hands of individuals."

Foreigners, too, studied national developments, and some on tours of the country noted the health and vitality of the Republic. The Frenchman, Alexis de Tocqueville, left one of the classic accounts of American society. His evaluation of Jacksonianism, though not so favorable as democrats might have wished, described the robust growth of equalitarianism and prosperity as well as the disappearance of great men, sophistication, and culture. In the place of the Revolutionary leaders were men of middling ability, crude manners, and practical learning. He worried, too, about the tyranny of the majority:

> When an individual or a party is wronged in the United States, to whom can he apply for redress? If to public opinion, public opinion constitutes the majority; if to the legislature, it represents the majority, and implicitly obeys its injunctions; if to the executive power, it is appointed by the majority and remains a passive tool in its hands.

Critics agreed that the new democracy unleashed an enormous amount of energy that affected society in various ways, making it generally unstable, inflammable, and intolerant. Waves of violence swept down upon secret clubs, the Masons, and Catholic convents. Bewildered foreigners were pelted in the streets and their homes searched. The antislavery publicist William L. Garrison was the target of so much bitterness in the North that he had to seek refuge. His fellow abolitionists were beaten and tarred and feathered, and a few murdered. Members of the Church of Jesus Christ of Latter Day Saints, Mormons, persecuted for their religious diversity, fled westward, finally to the hills of Utah.

Politics swirled around Jackson with the same force. In 1829 he drew new men to the capital, men who, in their hunger for office, pushed and plotted against the older leaders. The most notorious episode of the day was managed by the new Secretary of State, Martin Van Buren. Van Buren aspired to be President, but in his way stood Vice President John C. Calhoun. Calhoun expected to succeed Jackson, whose age and health made a second term doubtful. His prestige, experience, and campaign work gave him a strong claim to the succession. He calculated, however, without allowing for Van Buren. At this time Washington society was gossiping about the wife of Secretary of War John H. Eaton, a pretty ex-barmaid named Peggy who was said to have been intimate with Eaton even before her first husband had died. Some women of quality turned up their noses; the President's niece left the White House rather than entertain her, and Mrs. Calhoun followed the social pattern. Working cleverly upon Jackson's prejudices,

Andrew Jackson: Leader of the Common People
(*Yale University Art Gallery*)

Van Buren accused the Calhouns of ostracizing the "innocent" beauty. The President, motivated by the chivalrous feeling that Mrs. Eaton might have been wronged, gave her official recognition as a White House guest.

Sectional Issues

As Van Buren's stew boiled, other fires affected Jacksonian politics, and they burned Calhoun. His native state of South Carolina was suffering from declining cotton crops, as large planters sought better lands westward and lower prices critically cut profits. The state had hoped to make up the difference with a cotton textile industry, but was unable to attract capital and labor in spite of the proximity of raw material and water power. As the state settled deeper into depression, it became resentful and opposed such measures as the tariff that aided northern industrial society. The South marketed a large part of its cotton crop in Great Britain, and tariff duties lessened profits, which were returned in the form of British goods.

Tariff rates had been rising steadily since 1816. Adjustments, nearly always upward, failed to satisfy the North but intensified the bitterness of South Carolina. In 1828, politicians interested in creating support for Jackson sponsored a high tariff on raw as well as on manufactured items; they hoped to gather votes from all sections against the tariff and the Adams administration. But the bill passed. The Tariff of Abominations brought an instant protest from South Carolina, through Calhoun. Following the usual pattern of states at odds with national policy, he issued his famous South Carolina Exposition, asserting the right of a state to nullify a national law. The tariff, he wrote, was "unconstitutional, unequal, and oppressive, and calculated to corrupt the public virtue and destroy the liberty of the country"; the remedy for this evil was "interposition," a power reserved to the states, which could move by means of a state convention to declare national laws null and void. But Calhoun and his southern friends in reality counted upon Jackson's sense of states' rights and fairness to reform the tariff. To their sorrow, Jackson remained silent on the issues during the campaign and did not forcibly back a reform during his first years in office. The issue, however, was widely discussed among Democratic politicians, especially in 1830 when Daniel Webster and Robert Y. Hayne expounded on states' rights in a series of lengthy exchanges on the Senate floor. Party feeling was high in April, when leaders gathered to commemorate Jefferson's birthday and the room was full of nullifiers who hoped to draw Jackson to their side. But the President came with his toast prepared: "Our Federal Union. It must be preserved!" The toast stunned the audience, but Calhoun found words with which to answer: "The Union—next to our liberty, the most dear!"

Close friends of the President advised the elimination of Calhoun's supporters from the Cabinet and maneuvered the two men into other personal clashes. In May 1831 Van Buren and Eaton announced, as a tactical measure, their intention of resigning from the Cabinet so that Jackson could reconstruct the executive branch, thus forcing the Calhoun members also to resign their posts.

The new Cabinet apparently advised Jackson to request a revision of the 1828 tariff in his 1831 address to Congress. The announcement set off an immediate attack upon the tariff, and John Quincy Adams in the House and Henry Clay in the Senate successfully presented a new tariff. But the rates in the 1832 tariff were approximately as high as in the old tariff, and South Carolina erupted in anger, called a special convention to nullify the law and took measures to restrain federal officials. There was even talk of secession. The challenge to federal authority brought a quick response from Jackson, who asked Congress for power to employ force if the courts were obstructed. The new legislation was bitterly assailed by Calhoun, back in the Senate after the 1832 elections, and by John Tyler of Virginia. The debate continued for weeks, while Clay and Calhoun worked out a compromise tariff to lower duties over the ten years after 1833 to a base of twenty percent. The compromise did not satisfy all, but Calhoun did not want bloodshed, and the South Carolina secessionists hastily accepted his advice.

Democratic Politics

While the Jackson administrations can be described in terms of rivalries of subordinates, Jackson was the President and his eight years in office reflected his powerful personality. He was undoubtedly the least educated of the Presidents, but he appointed his own Cabinet and then kept it in its place by forming a special group of advisors (the Kitchen Cabinet) to inform him on the practical aspects of government. In many ways he used these men better as advisors than similar groups were used by John Adams and his son, both experienced politicians. From Jackson men received appointments for loyalty, and nearly a tenth of the rank and file of officeholders was replaced with partisans. In some cases, honest men replaced corrupt officials, but Jackson's record of appointing party workers undoubtedly received more adverse publicity than it did harm to the public service. This criticism did not worry Jackson. Though he insisted upon honesty and economy, he had great faith in the common people as public servants, and faith, too, in the Presidency as the representation of national feeling. He dared to speak out on national issues, lecture Congress, defy the Supreme Court, and use the latent powers of the Presidency. He used the presidential power to veto bills twelve times and used the pocket veto frequently, but as a follower of the Jeffersonian tradition he did not personally appear before Congress to deliver his messages.

As a Westerner, Jackson backed the states in their liquidation of Indian claims. Georgia had a long-standing quarrel with the Creeks and Cherokees. These tribes had treaty rights from the United States, but Georgia, asserting control over them, denied that they were foreign nations. The tribes appealed through a missionary friend to the Supreme Court, which finally ruled in their favor. They could not, however, get the decision enforced by the administration. Jackson in fact supported a policy of Indian removal, and in the Seminole War, in the Black Hawk War and in countless minor battles in areas outside of Georgia, Indians were forced to give up territory to whites. Nearly a hundred treaties were signed between 1829 and 1837 with Indian tribes who were removed as a consequence to land west of the Mississippi.

Like Madison and Monroe, Jackson opposed a general program of internal improvements. His Maysville Veto of 1830 put an end to such measures except for bills he approved for additions to the Cumberland Road and roads in the national territories. Jackson's land policy also revealed a western bias, and supporters like Thomas Hart Benton of Missouri backed lower prices for land and the right of preemption, which gave the squatter first chance to buy the land he had already settled on. The revenue from land sales was to be returned to the states. While these ideas encountered sometimes severe opposition, they were eventually written into legislation.

The Bank Fight and Panic of 1837

The most bitter issue of Jackson's day was the rechartering of the second United States Bank. Under the presidency of Nicholas Biddle since 1822, the Bank had used its vast powers to regulate credit, supervise state institutions, and act as a fiscal agent for the Treasury. Many people, suspicious of its size and power, disliked the Bank because it charged interest and seemed to make money out of nothing, or worse, to make money from government deposits of taxpayers' money. Its monopoly position, its policy of lending money to congressmen and newspaper editors, and its involvement with anti-administration politicians upset Jackson. When the Bank retained Daniel Webster, and Henry Clay decided to force the issue of its rechartering in Congress, Jackson denounced the bill as undemocratic and un-American and vetoed it.

The famous veto message touched the feelings of the vast majority of the people. In the election of 1832 Jackson and Van Buren, who returned from a short tour of duty as minister to Britain to be the vice-presidential candidate, faced Henry Clay and John Sergeant of Pennsylvania. While there were also an Anti-Mason party (William Wirt of Virginia) and a Nullification party (John Floyd of Virginia), the combined votes of the opposition candidates did not affect Jackson's commanding strength. The Democratic organization had taken form in most states, and the electoral victory of 216 to 49 probably was

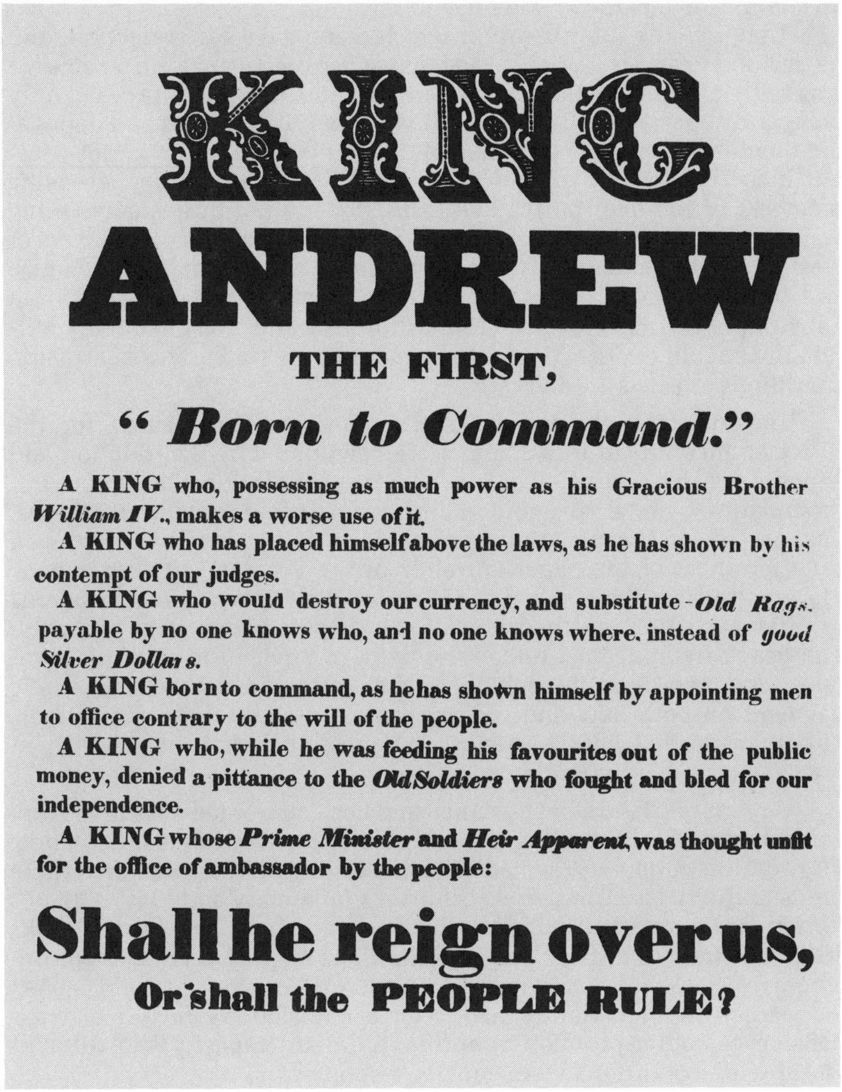

KING
ANDREW
THE FIRST,
"*Born to Command.*"

A KING who, possessing as much power as his Gracious Brother *William IV.*, makes a worse use of it.

A KING who has placed himself above the laws, as he has shown by his contempt of our judges.

A KING who would destroy our currency, and substitute *Old Rags*, payable by no one knows who, and no one knows where, instead of *good Silver Dollars*.

A KING born to command, as he has shown himself by appointing men to office contrary to the will of the people.

A KING who, while he was feeding his favourites out of the public money, denied a pittance to the *Old Soldiers* who fought and bled for our independence.

A KING whose *Prime Minister* and *Heir Apparent*, was thought unfit for the office of ambassador by the people:

Shall he reign over us,
Or shall the PEOPLE RULE?

Anti-Jackson Poster *(Library of Congress)*

an endorsement of the President's policy.

That was the interpretation that Jackson gave his reelection, and he decided to deal with the United States Bank as soon as the tariff issue was settled. Since the Bank had charter rights until 1837, he could only hamper its operations. By withholding United States funds and depositing them in state banks (Pet Banks), he struck a heavy blow, not without incurring the censure of the United States Senate and arousing members of his own party. The results of the political maneuvering were most unsettling: Government funds passed into the hands of western land speculators, in the form of easy loans from the Pet Banks, and the purchases of government land set off an inflationary spiral. Sales of public land rose from four million acres in 1834 to twenty million in 1836. In the East, in contrast, money was scarce, and near-panic conditions affected the market.

The events frightened Jackson's advisors. They feared for the safety of government funds, and were bewildered by the inflation and shocked by the vast sales of land. Jackson finally decided to control the inflation by requiring gold or silver as payment for land purchases, but this Specie Circular put a premium on hard money and reduced the usefulness of the paper currency of the Pet Banks. Other events, too, complicated the effect of the Circular. Americans were prosperous in 1834 and 1835 and had bought more abroad than they had sold. The heavy trade deficits forced the Bank of England to raise discount rates, and exporters, feeling the tight credit, demanded immediate payment on both new and old accounts. To settle these obligations, importers needed hard currency and pressed their banks, which in turn called in their commercial paper.

With public land sales curtailed and hard money held at a premium, banks had difficulty finding enough gold and silver to meet demands. The administration aggravated the situation by distributing its surplus funds to the states. The two distributions in January and May 1837 put further pressure on the banks and set off a business panic: Banks failed, businesses cut back on purchases, and many persons were unemployed. Jackson's harsh meddling with the economy had not caused the panic, but it certainly had been a contributing factor. Overexpansion of cotton production and textile plant capacity and difficult world-wide conditions were equally responsible.

As the depression deepened, Van Buren succeeded Jackson as President. His margin of victory was much less than Jackson's in 1832, partly because the opposition had organized itself into the national Whig party and partly because Van Buren was not as attractive as Jackson to Westerners. His opposition could not decide on a common candidate, however, and with William Henry Harrison and two other men splitting the vote, Van Buren won by 170 to 127. The split vote left him weak in Congress, and the anti-Jackson opposition, which was now generally known by the name of "Whig," became increasingly critical of Democratic policies, and were especially critical after they won both houses of Congress in the 1838 elections.

Van Buren was unable to solve the money crisis. Year after year he presented plans for an independent treasury system to take United States funds out of the banks, and year after year he was defeated. In 1840, Congress finally accepted the proposal. His party resisted Whig plans for a third United States Bank, however, and let the bankers of the northeast monopolize specie and set interest rates. In the end, the farmers and laborers who had believed Jackson to have slain the financial hydra of the second United States Bank found that it had grown new heads. Yet the heroic confrontation of Sir Galahad and the Bank, warmly applauded at the time, obscures other significant events.

Jacksonian America

The years of Jackson's presidency are difficult to characterize. But it is clear that the old leader's departure from office in 1837 had not ended the era, for Van Buren, Harrison, and Tyler in the coming eight years were to be guided by political conditions he had set in motion. During Jackson's "rule" the common people had achieved victory through an increase in educational advantages with the growth of public school systems, the multiplication of colleges, the spread of free libraries, and the popularization of community lectures. More secondary schools and four-year colleges were to be founded in the 1840s than in the 1830s, and women were admitted to the A.B. degree in many new institutions.

Though people debated the need of higher education for women, their debates extended to other social and political issues as well. Often arguments were carried on in such newspapers as the New York Tribune and the New York Herald, where the editors were depending upon circulation for their paper's success. Both presses used bright, sensational journalism to popularize social issues. This social ferment, in many ways, illustrates well the age. People felt deeply about the world about them, but were sometimes severely divided on the nature of the new society, were often narrow in their views of racial and religious questions, and were generally suspicious of government and politicians.

Some of these people were philosophers, writers, painters, clergymen, and scientists whose activities gave a rich dimension to national life. In his way, Ralph Waldo Emerson was a symbol of this age. His deep faith in humankind, in the democratic impulse, and in individualism was well stated in these lines; "Let man stand erect, go alone, and possess the universe." Other writers like Henry David Thoreau looked to nature and tried to capture for their readers some of the beauty that was being lost by the rising industrial society. The

Ralph Waldo Emerson

Hudson River School of painters, with Thomas Cole's idealization of landscape and space, exhibited in a visual way what was described in Thoreau's romantic essay on *Walden Pond*. More practical men like Benjamin Silliman and Joseph Henry, two distinguished scientists, were then exploring nature in their laboratories, while their counterparts, Oliver Wendell Holmes, Senior, and William Gerhardt, were establishing clinics and gathering data on disease through case studies. Their patients were often another kind of Jacksonian.

Into the United States came thousands of Irish Catholics in the 1830s. They settled in the seaboard cities, bringing with them their priests and religious institutions. Their poverty, strange habits of speech and dress, and, most distressing to some people, their religion set off waves of bigotry against convents, monasteries, and secret organizations. While the Irish survived, they were not very happy over being pushed down to the level of the impoverished blacks in

A Painting from the Hudson Valley School
(*University of Southern California*)

northern cities, as both groups vied for work on docks and in factories. Rivalry between them bred violence, repression, and suffering which added to the already existing poverty and misery of these Americans.

These uncertainties of northern life contrasted with southern conditions. In the South, farm and plantation, in a rural culture, depended upon cotton, sugar, or tobacco production and the help of several million black slaves. Jacksonianism left government to the states, and though there were some constitutional changes, banking and business reforms, and improvements in harbors and rivers during the 1830s, the South was very markedly different from the North in the variety of life and intensely sensitive about slavery.

For observers of both regions there was equal fascination. The South had much polish and gentility, but it had slavery, too. The North had much vigor and energy, but it had poverty and repression, too. Travelers from Europe were most often impressed by American customs. The people, food, hotels, river boats, and appearance of the land and cities inspired comparisons with experiences in Europe. Most travelers enjoyed what they saw, but some, like Charles Dickens, noted the raw cut in American life. For them, Jacksonian America was vigorous, unregimented, crude, and unpolished. Most admitted, nonetheless, that the experiment in democracy was succeeding.

SUGGESTIONS FOR FURTHER READING

Bartlett, Irving H., *The American Mind in the Mid-Nineteenth Century.* New York, Thomas Y. Crowell Company, 1967.

Bemis, Samuel Flagg, *John Quincy Adams and the Foundations of American Foreign Policy.* New York, Alfred A. Knopf, 1949.

Carstensen, Vernon, ed., *The Public Lands: Studies in the History of the Public Domain.* Madison, Wisconsin, University of Wisconsin Press, 1963.

Chase, James S., *Emergence of the Presidential Nominating Convention, 1789-1832.* Urbana, Illinois, University of Illinois Press, 1973.

Cooper, James F., *Deerslayer,* introduction by J. Grossman. New York, Washington Square Press, 1961.

Curtis, James C., *Andrew Jackson and the Search for Vindication.* Boston, Little, Brown and Company, 1976.

Dangerfield, George, *The Awakening of American Nationalism, 1815-1828.* New York, Harper Torchbooks, Harper & Row, 1965.

Dumond, Dwight Lowell, *Antislavery Origins of the Civil War in the United States.* Ann Arbor, Michigan, Ann Arbor Paperbacks, University of Michigan Press, 1968.

Eaton, Clement, *Henry Clay and the Art of American Politics.* Boston, Little, Brown and Company, 1975.

Liwack, Leon F., *North of Slavery.* Chicago, Phoenix Books, University of Chicago Press, 1967.

McCormick, Richard P., *Second American Party System: Party Formation in the Jacksonian Era.* Chapel Hill, N.C., University of North Carolina Press, 1968.

Morgan, Robert J., *A Whig Embattled: The Presidency Under John Tyler.* Lincoln, Nebraska, University of Nebraska Press, 1954.

Pattie, James O., *The Personal Narrative,* ed. William H. Goetzmann. Philadelphia, Keystone Western Americana, J. P. Lippincott Company, 1962.

Perkins, Edwin J., *Financing Anglo-American Trade: The House of Brown, 1700-1800.* Cambridge, Mass., Harvard University Press, 1975.

Pessen, Edward, *Jacksonian America: Society, Personality, and*

Politics. Homewood, Illinois, The Dorsey Press, 1978.

Remini, Paul V., *Andrew Jackson*. New York, Perennial Library, Harper & Row, 1969.

Smith, Henry Nash, *Virgin Land*. New York, Vintage Books, Random House, 1950.

Sydnor, Charles S., *The Development of Southern Sectionalism*. Baton Rouge, La., University of Louisiana Press, 1948.

Turner, Frederick Jackson, *Rise of the New West, 1819-1829*. New York, Collier Books, Crowell Collier and Macmillan, 1965.

Van Deusen, Glyndon G., *The Jackson Era, 1828-1848*. New York, Harper Torchbooks, Harper & Row, 1963.

Ward, John William, *Andrew Jackson: Symbol for an Age*. New York, Galaxy Books, Oxford University Press, 1962.

Weinberg, Albert K., *A Study of Nationalist Expansionism in American History*. Chicago, Quadrangle Books, 1963.

Welter, Rush, *The Mind of America, 1820-1860*. New York, Columbia University Press, 1975.

Wiltse, Charles M., *John C. Calhoun: Nullifier, 1829-1839*. Indianapolis and New York, Bobbs-Merrill Company, 1949.

8

The Western Destiny

IN THE 1830s AND 1840s THE UNITED STATES once again moved rapidly westward. This new growth rivaled the expansion of the Revolution and Jefferson's first administration in the acquisition of new territory. Also the push of people into Iowa, Wisconsin, Missouri, and California astonished men of the day, and some observers like J. L. O'Sullivan called the process "Manifest Destiny." "California," he wrote, "will ... next fall away from ... Mexico. ... The Anglo-Saxon foot is already on its borders. Already the advance guard of the irresistable army of Anglo-Saxon immigrants has begun to pour down upon it, armed with the plough and rifle, and making its trail with schools and colleges, courts and representative halls, mills and meetinghouses."

The Expansion West

The nation moved rapidly westward. The admission as states of Arkansas in 1836 and Michigan in 1837 officially recognized a fast growing population and reflected the relative safety of settlement and the availability of public land. The American settlers in Texas

Expansion of the United States, 1783-1853

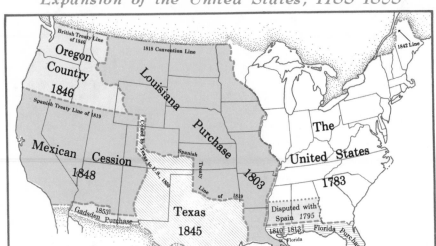

had revolted from Mexico in 1836 and had turned the territory into a republic. While thousands of Americans risked an uncertain future in settling in the republic, political leaders in Washington hoped for future annexation and statehood. Oregon remained undivided as a joint territory with Great Britain, but fur traders, missionaries, and settlers expected the territory to be joined to the United States within a decade.

Most politicians sensed this popular feeling and associated themselves with the West and expansion. Jackson's administration supported settlers by its Indian policy, showing its lack of sympathy for the Indians by waging war against them and defying court orders that might have guaranteed them legal rights. It released for settlement millions of acres of land in Georgia, Florida, and Alabama. It also favored settlers over speculators by allowing settlers to preempt land prior to the national survey and by sending the Corps of Army Engineers into the West to clear impediments to travel.

Their help made it possible to ship crops of corn, wheat, barley, and rye to markets in the North, and towns such as Cleveland, Cincinnati, Chicago, St. Louis, and Independence gained importance as trade centers. From the little town of Westport on the Missouri River trade in another direction took place—pack trains set out across Kansas in a southwesterly direction to Santa Fe where they conducted a brisk business with the frontiersmen of New Mexico. Adventurers like Sylvester and James Ohio Pattie pioneered trails from Santa Fe, and James Ohio survived to describe his adventures in California. When the Patties joined the caravans on the Santa Fe trail, trade already flourished. Over a hundred thousand dollars worth of merchandise was sold annually, products like cotton cloth, silks, and hardware. The realistic account of this trade by the former teacher Josiah Gregg, in his *Commerce of the Prairies*, gave great popularity to the trail, invited those seeking adventure to visit the plains of Kansas, its Indians, wild animals, and open spaces for a romantic experience.

As more and more Americans discovered this west of the Patties and Gregg, they idealized, or popularized, its habits of dress, drink, and life-style. City dwellers like Francis Parkman went West for adventure and observation, then to return to their homes and publish accounts. Parkman's *Oregon Trail* did not touch upon the territory of Oregon, but it describes his visits to parts of present-day Kansas, Wyoming, and Colorado, giving vivid views of forts, the countryside, and Indian ceremonies. Richard Henry Dana's *Two Years Before the Mast*, however, mixed adventure on the sea with land experiences along the California coast. His salty tales of a captain's brutality, of waves dashing against the ship, and of pastoral views of Mexican California were most attractive to readers who bought thousands of copies of his epic experience.

The West had a major impact upon the national politics in the 1840 Presidential campaign. Supporters popularized William Henry Harrison as an Indian fighter, hard drinker, and sturdy pioneer. Also they remembered his birth in a humble log cabin, his rugged independent life, and his battle with Tecumseh at Tippecanoe. Most of what people said of him reflects the virtues and vices of the West, but not necessarily of his life nor that of his runningmate John Tyler, a rich plantation owner and aristocrat. Harrison's easy victory (234 to 60) over Van Buren, the incumbent President, reveals the power of western imagery.

Not everyone, however, accepted expansion as an unqualified good for the nation. The presence of the Liberty Party in the 1840 campaign is evidence of discontent. Its small vote did not conceal the feelings of abolitionists who preferred to work within existing parties. Some reflective citizens questioned the advisibility of extending slavery into the West, raising the old emotion-laden issue. Since the Northwest Ordinance of 1787, statesmen had debated ways to contain slavery. In 1803, the addition of the Louisiana territory aroused some reformers, and in 1812 the admission of the state of Louisiana was not sufficiently important to bring national debate. Not until 1819, when Missouri applied for admission as a slave state, did the issue rise to critical levels, and by the compromise only the state of Louisiana, the territory of Arkansas, and part of present-day Oklahoma were to have slavery. The antislavery provisions of the Northwest Ordinance were, therefore, applied to the sweep of territory north of Missouri and westward to the Pacific. While the South could count on Florida's becoming a state, it had the short end of the compromise unless other lands could be found. Texas and the Southwest were possible areas in which to settle, but both were owned by Mexico.

Texas and the Slave Issue

The vast territory of Texas attracted the attention of Americans about the time they were making their first trade visits to Santa Fe in 1821. Moses Austin of Connecticut who was then a speculator, banker, and miner in St. Louis, Missouri, won the first grant of land from Mexico. Premature death prevented him from developing a colonization venture, but his son Stephen F. had the grant confirmed, coming off with a princely area of 60,000 acres and additional lands for prospective colonists. Five thousand colonists eventually accepted his offer of cheap land.

Within a decade more than twenty thousand other settlers entered Texas, broke land, and planted a variety of crops, sugar cane, corn, and cotton predominating. These energetic, restless people frightened the Mexican authorities by demanding local government and relief from cultural and political controls. As resistance mounted, they joined rival factions in Mexico's own disorders and in exchange for their help demanded concessions in Texas. When Mexican rule was not materially liberalized, the settlers declared their independence and expelled the Mexican authorities, but the challenge was immediately met. General Santa Anna hastened with 5000 troops to crush the rebellion, and in an encounter in San Antonio the Mexicans captured the frontier mission church, the Alamo, and put about 200 defenders to death. The troops then advanced toward other Texan settlements, which were frightened by the news of the Alamo. Fortunately, Texas General Sam Houston, reinforced by Americans, met Santa Anna near the San Jacinto River on April 21, 1936, and destroyed his army in a surprise frontal attack. The capture of Santa Anna halted Mexico's reconquest of Texas, and the settlers quickly moved to gain admission to the United States as a state.

While Americans contributed to rebel success, admitting Texas to statehood was another matter. Politics was too unsettled in both parties for any united effort. Jackson's second term neared its end in 1836; the national elections divided the nation; opposition among Democrats arose because of the possibility of a new slave state. Also the Whigs split into many groups and no single candidate unified the party. Martin Van Buren, as the Democrat standard bearer, thus won the election easily, but faced a divided, embittered party in the Congress.

Soon after his election he faced, too, the Panic which lingered during most of his term. Unlike Jackson, Van Buren did not inspire popular support and did not symbolize prevailing western emotions. Most enthusiasts went their own ways, and the ferment they created often deadlocked politics.

The Texas issue sharpened the agitation against slavery. An area as large as Texas could give renewed vitality to slavery, through further expansion of cotton and sugar crops which depended upon black labor. Many reformers had hoped to contain or eradicate slavery, and expected in a generation or two that it would decline of its own accord as the world became enlightened. Reformers were well aware of the importance of cotton and sugar in the Deep South, and the relation of these crops to expansion. By 1835, nearly three million blacks worked in the South, and the price of additional laborers rose almost yearly. While some new slaves were smuggled into the country, recruits for the work force depended chiefly upon the growing birth rate among native slaves and the movement of slaves into the cotton belt from states such as Virginia.

The life of a slave in the South was generally routine. He was busy in the fields year after year, doing his assigned tasks to the rhythm of the seasons. He usually worked well, though the whip and a system of incentives were sometimes needed. His health was looked after, his spiritual welfare recognized by Roman Catholic, Methodist, and Baptist clergy, his family guarded by a kind of marriage alliance. Of course, whatever may be said of his life, he was property, valuable and perishable, and his master was well aware of the profit motive in dealing with him. Not all slaves willingly accepted servitude. Some protested, fled when possible, and rose occasionally in rebellion. But the system provided harsh penalties for those rebels. Corporal punishment, mutilation, hanging, or separation from families often resulted. Even so, the number of riots was small. The Nat Turner rebellion in 1831 was the bloodiest affair and took the lives of fifty-five people. Afterward Southerners feared rebellion, took harsh measures to suppress opposition, and tried to enslave manumitted blacks.

To most Northerners the institution of slavery was intolerable, and they imagined the slave's life as one of constant suffering and submerged discontent. Slavery as an institution was attacked in the newspapers and outlawed in most northern states, but only a handful of whites there were willing to grant the black racial equality. In the South, white and black blood had mixed for centuries as the African lost his blackness and cultural heritage and found a place in the white community. There he was, nevertheless, doomed to slavery, concentrated in a few cotton-growing states, and made a tool of production. In the North, a few hundred thousand blacks lived as free laborers, but only a few hundred achieved wealth and professional distinction. Most lived in separate parts of town from the whites and held the

poorest jobs among the manual laborers. The overwhelming number
were denied by law full equality in the free society. Even those whites
who most abhorred slavery did little to raise the living standards of
northern blacks. Among blacks there were men like Frederick Douglass
who spoke for the cause of emancipation in the Lyceums and wrote
for magazines such as William Lloyd Garrison's *Liberator*, and blacks
in their churches and social clubs reflected on their place in society,
often agitating successfully to remove restrictions on freedom of movement in the North.

In the 1830s clergymen and publicists like William Lloyd Garrison
agitated against slavery, but their aim was more a protest against it
than an attack upon it. James G. Birney in 1835 denounced it as "a sin
against God and man" and asked for petitions to support his protest.
In the churches religious men divided over the interpretation of
slavery, and their petitions were often presented to the House of Representatives by John Quincy Adams. These petitions, however, drew
great opposition from Congress, and pro-slavery people often threatened bodily harm to the petitioners. A few lost their lives; more were
humiliated.

Texan annexation, as noted above, was part of the growing debate. The major issue involved extending slavery into the West. To
many agitators slavery seemed inappropriate for a democratic nation,
perhaps destructive of democratic society itself. They secured the
legislative backing of Michigan and Ohio, whose representatives declared the proposed annexation of Texas to be "unjust, inexpedient, and
destructive of the peace, safety, and well-being of the nation." Though
these legislatures were not ready to support abolition, many people in
those states joined political organizations that chose abolitionist candidates. In the 1838 elections some were chosen, but not enough to
please most antislavery people, who were becoming disenchanted with
the attitude of the major parties. In various third parties organized
throughout the Northwest, they backed James G. Birney as a presidential candidate in the 1840 election and attacked Van Buren's record.

The Whigs in Office

Antislavery agitation did not yet touch the major impulse of the
nation. The image of Jackson as hero, warrior, and nature's nobleman
still dominated the American mind. Though Van Buren's administration had experienced economic depression and opposition, he
was Jackson's successor, inheritor of the general's good will and favor,
and the party had to renominate him in spite of Whig propaganda that
had severely hurt his public image. To win votes, men such as Henry
Clay and Daniel Webster exploited issues of frauds in land sales and
blunders in Indian policy. They described the wars against the Semi-
noles of Florida as a move to help plantation owners catch runaway

Daniel Webster

slaves who had joined the Indians. They sought to neutralize the
Democratic advantage of having Jackson in the party by picking as
their candidate William Henry Harrison, who had spent almost a lifetime in the West. Though he had retired from active politics, he was
easily persuaded to run, and the Whig management developed a
political personality for him—a man from the West, born in a log cabin,
content with hard cider and simple pleasures, and a military hero in
the wars against the Indians and British. An exciting campaign followed
in which the glories of the West, the virtues of the common people,
and the idiosyncrasies of the candidates were exploited in arousing
public emotion.

Harrison's successful party expected Clay, Webster, and their friends to carry out a program of legislation that would remove some of Jackson's excesses. But on inauguration day the President contracted a severe cold. Within a month he was dead. His office passed to John Tyler, the Vice President and a Virginian of inflexible political opinions, who was less Whig and more anti-Jackson in philosophy than the party managers who had engineered Harrison's election.

As a southern Whig, Tyler did not favor proposals to charter another national bank or distribute to the states surpluses from land sales. Though he was persuaded that tariff rates should be adjusted, the 1842 tariff aroused much opposition in the South and became an issue in the next presidential campaign. The inability of the President and Congress to find compromises on major issues created a stalemate and, perhaps worse, bitterness in government which brought mass resignations from the Cabinet, Clay's retirement from the Senate, and Tyler's ouster from the Whig party. In foreign affairs, Tyler managed to retain the initiative, and with Webster remaining as Secretary of State until 1843, he secured a treaty with Great Britain that settled the boundary between Maine and New Brunswick and a boundary line west of Lake Superior to the Lake of the Woods. Other important matters were discussed with Great Britain, such as the slave trade and an extradition treaty, and some preliminary agreements were reached.

Manifest Destiny

Even though the diplomats did not settle the future of Oregon, they were aware of the emotion then sweeping the nation. The oratorical eruptions of Thomas Hart Benton, the persuasive senator from Missouri, were regularly heard in Congress: "Let the emigrants go on; and carry their rifles. We want thirty thousand rifles in the valley of the Oregon; they will make all quiet there. . . . Thirty thousand rifles in Oregon will annihilate the Hudson's Bay Company, drive them off our continent, quiet their Indians, and protect the American interests." Others predicted that "Our population is destined to roll its resistless waves to the icy barriers of the north, and to encounter Oriental civilization on the shores of the Pacific."

The feeling that God had intended Americans to go West motivated many potential settlers. They packed their belongings and prepared for the long trip over the Oregon trail to the Willamette Valley. Approximately five thousand pioneers had traveled over the trial by 1845. Hundreds more branched from that trail, or came by the Sante Fe or Old Spanish trails, into California. Men like John C. Frémont, the son-in-law of Thomas Hart Benton, publicized the West through their official activities and their adventures. Thomas O. Larkin at Monterey in California acted as an American consul and sent reports on the territory's resources and politics. In Oregon Americans established home rule, while in California United States forces off shore near Monterey,

A Critic's View of Manifest Destiny *(Library of Congress)*

believing that war had broken out with Mexico, temporarily took over the town. The United States soon apologized, but Larkin saw humor just the same in this serious *faux pas:* "The officers spent their time ashore hunting wild deer or dancing with tame Dears, both being plentiful in and around Monterey."

The President was affected by this national feeling for expansion, but he was primarily interested in Texas for the advantages it would give the South. When Webster left the cabinet in 1843, Tyler opened negotiations with the Republic of Texas, and in 1844, with the aid of Secretary of State John C. Calhoun he presented a treaty that would admit Texas as a United States territory. Mexico reacted immediately by notifying the United States that she would consider annexation a cause of war, and the threat caused the treaty to receive a cool reception in the Senate. Some Senators joined those who were already against the admission of slave territory in rejecting the treaty, and the overwhelming vote postponed annexation. Party leaders accepted the delay because they wanted to test popular reaction toward Texan annexation in the 1844 elections.

Clay tried to avoid taking a position on Texan admission and slavery, but he accepted annexation as inevitable. The Whig party, in nominating Clay for the Presidency, proved equally cautious. Texas should be admitted without war and without dishonoring the nation. Slavery was a transient institution and should not be involved in a discussion of the annexation, which was a permanent acquisition. The Democrats, too, had their difficulties reconciling divergent factions within the party. Theyc ast about for a candidate, passed over Martin Van Buren who had strong support, and turned to James Knox Polk, Speaker of the House of Representatives form 1835 to 1839, former governor of Tennessee, and favorite of President Jackson. The Democrats, in selecting a "dark horse" candidate for the Presidency, had the advantage of making expansion the issue. To win wide support, however, they tied the annexation of Texas with that of Oregon, promised a lower tariff and an independent treasury, and associated Polk with the Jacksonian tradition. Leaders of the Liberty Party again turned to James G. Birney, who waged a vigorous campaign against the spread of slavery. He directed his campaign chiefly against Clay and succeeded in drawing enough votes away from the Whigs in New York to give Polk an impressive election victory of 170 electoral votes to 105.

Tyler interpreted the vote as a popular mandate for expansion of the Union, and before he left office in March 1845 pressed to have Texas admitted as a state by joint resolution of Congress. The maneuver succeeded, and procedures were set up for annexation. By December 1845 the new state was formally admitted to the Union. This easier method, however, did not lessen the hostility of Mexico, which debated a declaration of war.

The War with Mexico

The threat of war did not deter Polk from completing the annexation of Texas. But the President hated violence, wanted to avoid it, and sent a special envoy, John Slidell, to Mexico to negotiate a settlement. As an expansionist Slidell used the opportunity of crisis to press Mexico for the sale of the Southwest and California to the United States. He was ready to pay claims of American citizens against Mexico in exchange for recognition of Texan boundaries. Unfortunately, because of unstable political conditions, Slidell was not officially received by the Mexican government. The delay permitted anxieties to intensify and Americans generally accepted war as the only solution to the mounting crisis.

In January 1846, Polk ordered Zachary Taylor to move his 3900 men into the disputed territory between the Nueces River and the Rio Grande. United States presence in this region was regarded as an act of war by Mexico, but no formal declaration was made because the legislature was not in session. Though Polk was restless, he waited and interviewed Slidell on his return to Washington. Polk recorded the tension in his diary:

> May 8, 1846.—Saw company until twelve o'clock today. Among others the Hon. John Slidell . . . called in company with the Secretary of State [James Buchanan]. . . . Mr. Slidell's opinion was that but one course toward Mexico was left to the United States, and that was to take the redress of the wrongs and injuries which we had so long borne from Mexico into our own hand, and to act with promptness and energy. In this I agreed. . . .

> May 9, 1846.—The Cabinet held a regular meeting today. . . . I brought up the Mexican question. . . . All agreed that if the Mexican forces at Matamoros committed an act of hostility, . . . I should immediately send a message to Congress recommending declaration of war. . . . I said that in my opinion we had ample cause of war, and that it was impossible that we could stand in *statu quo;* . . . that I thought it was my duty to send a message to Congress . . . by Tuesday next.

Before that message was sent, a clash of Mexican troops with Taylor's opened hostilities. There followed a declaration of war by the United States Congress, with votes of 40 to 2 in the Senate and 174 to 14 in the House, and an appropriation of $10 million. These votes, however, did not reflect the true feelings of many Americans who wished to deny the South the privilege of extending slavery into the Southwest. One of them, David Wilmot of Pennsylvania, offered a proviso to an appropriation bill in August 1846 to exclude slavery from territory to be acquired from Mexico. The amendment passed the House, but was rejected in the Senate.

Agitators were safe in their opposition, because the Polk administration had successfully concluded negotiations with Great Britain and won the greater part of the Oregon territory. Though the Democrats pledged to fight for the Oregon country to the line of latitude 54° 40', the British prime minister, Sir Robert Peel, graciously overlooked the brashness of campaign oratory and accepted a compromise line suggested by Polk himself. The Oregon treaty was signed as American troops swept across the Rio Grande into Mexico.

Taylor's troops easily captured Matamoros and then moved swiftly toward Monterey. The long desert march proved difficult because of transportation inadequacies and disease, but Taylor nonetheless rallied his men to the task of capturing the city. After three days of bitter fighting they occupied the city, permitting the Mexican forces to evacuate and retreat. Regrouping their forces under Santa Anna, the Mexican army, now in vastly superior numbers, met Taylor near Saltillo. In the hard battle that followed Taylor took advantage of a Mexican lack of military equipment, and not only did he repel the Mexican army in the decisive battle of Buena Vista but destroyed the remaining defenses in this northern region. The victories made Taylor a national hero in the United States.

In the meantime, Polk had decided on an attack directly upon Mexico City through the seaport of Vera Cruz. With Winfield Scott in charge, he ordered an expeditionary force from New Orleans and put ten thousand troops at Scott's disposal. Though the movement into the highlands west of Vera Cruz was almost unopposed, Santa Anna appeared near Jalapa and bitterly contested Scott's advance. Since the Mexican troops were poorly disciplined and their stragety was defective, Scott inflicted a severe defeat upon them (April 17-18, 1847). Then the Americans gathered supplies for the stiff climb over the mountains into the Valley of Mexico. They expected attacks in the mountains but were not opposed until they reached the floor of the valley. Then Santa Anna waged a series of unsuccessful battles that ended with Chapultepec on September 13. The next day Scott entered the capital.

While the campaigns of Taylor and Scott were decisive, other battles in the Southwest and California also had long-term importance. During the summer of 1846 Stephen W. Kearny took seventeen hundred men across the Kansas plains into New Mexico. Kearny captured Santa Fe without a battle and, declaring New Mexico conquered, split his forces. Sending Colonel A. W. Doniphan south to join Taylor, he set up a garrison in Santa Fe and then took three hundred men under his personal command into California.

Because of his great interest in that territory, Polk had already prepared for its conquest. A naval force was stationed off the coast, and Thomas O. Larkin, the American consul, reported regularly on politics. Months before war began, Polk sent Frémont into the area, ostensibly to explore the sources of some western rivers; the sixty-two members of his party, picked for their marksmanship, were ready for something more than squirrel hunting. So that they could be near to potential action, Frémont lingered in California during the winter of 1845-46. In the spring, the Mexican authorities, now suspicious of their presence, ordered them from the territory, and the party moved slowly toward Oregon.

At this point a special agent from Polk arrived in Monterey. After consulting Larkin and others in the capital, he rushed into the wilderness to speak with Frémont. The agent's message has remained a secret, but events began to move rapidly and Frémont was a part of the action. Some Americans in Sonoma revolted and declared their independence; news of the Mexican-American war brought a naval invasion of Monterey and military operations against Los Angeles. Most of these preliminary engagements were completed easily. Then the native Californians, resenting military rule, rebelled and compelled the conquerors to fight for the territory. Though these revolts were quickly put down, there arose a jurisdictional quarrel among military leaders in which Frémont was apparently the victim. Taken East, court-martialed, and convicted, he was pardoned later by the President. While his trial may have delayed his rise in national politics, he was soon a United States senator from California and an owner of vast lands in the state.

The politics surrounding Frémont seemed incidental to the war when Polk presented the Treaty of Guadalupe Hidalgo to the Senate for ratification in 1848. The Treaty would give the United States the Rio Grande as a Texan boundary and the Southwest and California as a western frontier. For this territory, however, the United States would pay $15 million to Mexico and assume obligations of more than $3 million in claims against Mexico. These terms, generous in spite of nearly total military victory, disturbed some United States senators, who scrutinized the treaty and gave Polk some uneasy hours as they debated its merits:

> From what I learn [writes Polk in his diary], about a dozen Demo-cratic Senators will oppose it, most of them because they wish to acquire more territory than the line of the Rio Grande and the provinces of New Mexico and Upper California will secure. What Mr. Benton's reason for opposing it may be no one can tell. He is apt to think that nothing is done properly that he is not previously consulted about. Mr. Webster's reason for opposing it is that it acquires too much territory. The result is extremely doubtful. If eight or ten Whig Senators vote with Mr. Webster against it, it will be rejected. Nineteen Senators will constitute one third of that body, and will reject it.

Ratification was finally assured when thirty-eight senators voted for the treaty. Five years later the United States completed its major acquisitions, except for Alaska and Hawaii, by completing the Gadsden Purchase, acquiring a large piece of western desert from Mexico enabl-ing a railroad to pass through the Southwest to the Pacific.

The Issue of Slavery in the Territories

During these war years, while the West dominated the minds of Americans, Polk secured the enactment of a new tariff and the Inde-pendent Treasury System. The Walker Tariff, named for his Secre-tary of the Treasury, generally lowered duties and procured sufficient revenue to pay the costs of the war. The Independent Treasury System separated the government from the banking business and permitted the growth of powerful investment houses which set their own condi-tions for expansion. They financed the new railroads, the textile fac-tories, and the shipping concerns. Their credit was available to the

Compromise of 1850

Free

Slave

Open to Slavery by Principle of Popular Sovereignty

South as well, as they moved to buy cotton and sugar and control market operations.

The vast development of business, however, was overshadowed by the issue of slavery. Almost everyone was interested in the spread of slavery into the new territories, and many leaders joined David Wilmot in seeking its prohibition. Attitudes toward slavery were decidedly sectional, and Southerners, in replying to antislavery advocates, denied that Congress had any right to interfere with the institution. But Northerners insisted that it did, and by 1848 nearly all of their state legislatures had urged the prohibition of slavery in the territories and the District of Columbia. While Congress admitted Texas and Florida as slave states in 1845, it restored the balance of free and slave states with the admission of Iowa and Wisconsin in 1846 and 1848. Further, it permitted Oregon to set up a territorial government in 1848 without reference to slavery.

The division of the nation over slavery in the territories was accelerated, too, when gold was discovered in California. Gold had been found earlier, but not in the quantities that James Marshall turned up in the millrace of the American River. Gold brought California into great prominence. Thousands of people rushed westward in 1848, so that this previously almost empty country had a sizable population by the end of the year. In 1849 California applied for statehood.

Politicians thus could not effectively avoid the issue of slavery and expansion. The Democrats, looking about for someone to replace the tired and infirm Polk, chose Lewis Cass of Michigan, Jackson's Secretary of War, who thought that the western territories should have the right to decide the issue. His proposed squatter sovereignty would put the decision into the hands of the settlers and free the national parties of the responsibility. This was begging the question; to many people, slavery was a moral evil and the opinions of settlers could not change the situation. In opposing Cass they invited the Whigs to take a firm position on slavery, but the Whigs also avoided the issue, selecting General Taylor as their candidate, who had no known views on expansion. Taylor, unlike Polk in 1844, was truly a dark horse candidate; his vice-presidential running mate, Millard Fillmore, was nearly as obscure. For those who wanted an affirmative statement on slavery the only choice was a third-party candidate. The leading abolitionists, John P. Hale of New Hampshire and Gerrit Smith of New York, were popular with reformers, but the choice of a moderate candidate who might draw Democratic votes to the party seemed more advisable.

When the Free Soil party met in convention, it adopted a platform which appealed to farmers, laborers, and reformers. Though the able Martin Van Buren and Charles Francis Adams were selected as candidates, not enough Democrats and Whigs were willing to change parties to give the new party victory. But it sent thirteen candidates to the House of Representatives and two to the Senate. The split vote in ten or more states may have given the election victory to the Whigs. One thing was certain: slavery had now become a major political issue.

President Taylor was a man of energy and courage who was proud of his election victory over Cass and Van Buren. He was admittedly inexperienced in public office, especially with the critical issues confronting the nation, but he was patriotic and firm in his attitudes. He had need of greater wisdom than he possessed, however, as 1849 unfolded. One after another the new territories showed their dislike for slavery and drew up constitutions that contained antislavery provisions. The settlers drew up free soil constitutions first in California, then in New Mexico, finally in Utah. The threat of so many free states entering the Union was too much for the South. Some leaders openly proposed secession; others believed that compromise was possible. In the nation's capital President Taylor reminded the United States Congress that more than a half century had passed since the Union had come into being. As slave owner, southerner, Virginian, general of the United States army, and the nation's President, he saluted the Union: "The patriots who formed it have long since descended to the grave; yet still it remains, the proudest monument to their memory. . . . I shall stand by it." Reconciling expansion and slavery in order to preserve the Union was the greatest task facing the President and the Thirty-first Congress.

An Important Link Between East and West *(Library of Congress)*

Since 1815 the United States had grown in population from 8.4 to 23.1 million and in territory from the Mississippi River to Oregon and California. The nation had achieved size and importance. Its people were realizing the republican ideals of 1776, were proud of that inheritance, and were discovering in the West the "true" image of the native American. Their idolization of Andrew Jackson and their elections of Harrison and Polk were recognition of the West's importance in molding opinions. With this constant expansion of the nation, the South and the East were changing also. The South had developed a plantation society, with almost half of its people enslaved blacks and with crops of cotton that fed the industries of Great Britain and New England. For even greater production Southerners looked to the West for new lands and supported the acquisition of Texas and the Southwest. The North since 1815 had received almost a million immigrants and had put them to work with native born Americans in factories and mills that provided a diversity of household items. They lived in cities that were growing and becoming centers of opinion, education, and research. Life was often hard, and Northerners rose in protest against low wages, debtor prisons, and social excess and turned their attention southward to the slavery that seemed to threaten their equalitarian society. Their reform movements in the East were not always effective, for many people chose to escape responsibilities and move west at this time rather than stay and do battle with vested interests. From their new homes in the Northwest, however, they soon recovered their zeal for reform and organized societies to battle the extension of slavery.

SUGGESTIONS FOR FURTHER READING

Bartlett, Irving H., *The American Mind in the Mid-Nineteenth Century.* New York, Thomas Y. Crowell Company, 1967.

Bemis, Samuel Flagg, *John Quincy Adams and the Foundations of American Foreign Policy.* New York, Alfred A. Knopf, 1949.

Carstensen, Vernon, ed., *The Public Lands: Studies in the History of the Public Domain.* Madison, Wisc., University of Wisconsin Press, 1963.

Cleland, Robert Glass, *This Reckless Breed of Men.* New York, Alfred A. Knopf, 1950.

Cooper, James F., *Deerslayer*, introduction by J. Grossman. New York, Washington Square Press, 1961.

Dana, Richard Henry, Jr., *Two Years Before the Mast.* Boston, 1840, many editions available.

DeVoto, Bernard, *The Year of Decision 1846.* Boston, Sentry Editions, Houghton Mifflin Company, 1960.

Dumond, Dwight Lowell, *Antislavery Origins of the Civil War in the United States.* Ann Arbor, Michigan, Ann Arbor Paperbacks, University of Michigan Press, 1968.

Eaton, Clement, *Henry Clay and the Art of American Politics.* Boston, Little, Brown and Company, 1957.

Gregg, Josiah, *Commerce of the Prairies*, ed. Milo M. Quaife. Lincoln, Nebraska, Bison Books, University of Nebraska Press, 1967.

Litwack, Leon F., *North of Slavery.* Chicago, Ill., Phoenix Books, University of Chicago Press, 1967.

McCormick, Richard P., *Second American Party System: Party Formation in the Jacksonian Era.* Chapel Hill, N.C., University of North Carolina Press, 1968.

Pattie, James O., *The Personal Narrative*, ed. William H. Goetzmann. Philadelphia, PA., Keystone Western Americana, J.P. Lippincott Company, 1962.

Polk: The Diary of a President, 1845-1849, ed. Allan Nevins. New York, Longmans, Green and Company, 1952.

Remini, Paul V., *Andrew Jackson.* New York, Perennial Library, Harper & Row, 1969.

Saum, Lewis O., *The Fur Trader and the Indian.* Seattle, Washington, University of Washington Press, 1966.

Sellers, Charles G., *James K. Polk, Continentalist, 1843-1846*. Princeton, N.J., Princeton University Press, 1966.

Smith, Henry Nash, *Virgin Land*. New York, Vintage Books, Random House, 1950.

Stampp, Kenneth M., *The Peculiar Institution: Slavery in the Anti-Bellum South*. New York, Vintage Books, Random House, 1956.

Stenberg, Richard R., "The Failure of Polk's Mexican War Intrigue of 1845," *Pacific Historical Review*, IV: 39-68.

Steward, George R., *The California Trail: An Epic with Many Heroes*. New York, McGraw-Hill Book Company, 1962.

Turner, Frederick Jackson, *Rise of the New West, 1819-1829*. New York, Collier Books, Crowell Collier and Macmillan, 1965.

Van Deusen, Glyndon G., *The Jackson Era, 1828-1848*. New York, Harper Torchbooks, Harper & Row, 1963.

Ward, John William, *Andrew Jackson: Symbol of an Age*. New York, Galaxy Books, Oxford University Press, 1962.

Weinberg, Albert K., *A Study of Nationalist Expansionism in American History*. Chicago, Quadrangle Books, 1963.

Woodward, Grace Steele, *The Cherokees*. Norman, Oklahoma, Oklahoma University Press, 1963.

Zollinger, James P., *Sutter: The Man and His Empire*. New York, Oxford University Press, 1939.

9

The Civil War

THE ACQUISITION OF THE SOUTHWEST from Mexico in 1849 aroused the free-soil members of Congress, who suspected a conspiracy to turn this territory into slave states. As they pressed for a declaration against the extension of slavery, they received strong opposition from the South, which realized that the discovery of gold in California in 1848 and the flocking there of more than 200,000 people in two years would surely make that state free-soil and that all the future states to be carved from the territory might follow California's example. The South interpreted the free-soil agitation as a threat, and prepared to fight the free-soil members of Congress.

The Widening North-South Split

Two battles were fought in the House of Representatives. The first lasted for three weeks (December 1849) as the House balloted for speaker. On the fifty-ninth roll call the regular Democrats assured themselves control, but control that could favor the South. Then a struggle over the clerkship of the House followed, and Southerners were victorious again in placing their candidate. These contests reflected President Taylor's inability to find effective floor leadership for the party, and his own political inexperience and naiveté portended serious problems for the administration.

With the organization of the House settled in this aggravated way, Congress turned to the issue of slavery in the territories, an issue put squarely before it by events in California. The area was rapidly being populated; it had drafted a constitution that provided for free institutions. Reaction to what was happening was spontaneous. Every state in the North except Iowa petitioned Congress to exclude slavery from the territories, while every legislature in the South opposed such interference. The rigidity of each position frightened some leaders, who hoped Whig President Zachary Taylor would be able to do something. His address that was read to Congress in December 1849, however, was unimaginative and disappointing. He proposed to let events determine policy: California was to be admitted immediately as a free state, while Utah and New Mexico were to make the judgment when they were organized as states. His "no action plan" appeared treasonable to the South and timid to the North. Members of his party were hostile to him; both houses of Congress opposed him; leaders of his party like Henry Clay and Daniel Webster avoided his company. As one observer noted, Taylor "is an honest, plain, unpretending old man, but about as fit to be President as any New England farmer."

Taylor had failed to grasp what was confronting the nation. The territorial problem he had defined in terms of the admission of states as free or slave, rather than in terms of sectional equilibrium. The Southwest, California, and Oregon held little hope of additional slave states, and the South rightly feared a loss of power and prestige, perhaps growing impotency in determining future national policy. Taylor was speaking, moreover, like a Jacksonian—the union must be preserved, but preservation would require force, and alternatives, and he was unable to exercise leadership even to organize Congress.

The Compromise of 1850

In this crisis Clay, who appreciated the adulation of admirers, decided that the only patriotic thing to do was to present a few ideas as the basis of a possible compromise. His plan was outlined in eight resolutions that were debated for a few weeks before they were considered by the legislative committees. They became, at least in spirit, the basis for the eventual Compromise of 1850, which provided for (1) the admission of California as a free state, (2) the territorial government of New Mexico without provision for slavery, (3) the redrawing of Texan boundaries in exchange for a national assumption of her debts, (4) the prohibition of the slave trade in the District of Columbia, and (5) a strong fugitive slave law.

Though Clay vigorously supported his own plan and inspired

warm public interest, he was denied the help of the administration. Taylor was bitter because his own suggestions had been brushed aside and in a fit of jealousy sent the constitution of California prematurely to Congress. His action heightened the angry debate, which was turning into a southern filibuster. Jefferson Davis spoke; Calhoun, in a speech whose extreme statements antagonized even his fellow Southerners, raised the issue of secession. No longer, he observed, was there a Federal Republic as in the days of Washington and Jefferson, but there was instead a consolidated government "as absolute as that of the Autocrat in Russia." More realistic was his assertion that disunion was already taking place not by a single blow but by gradual separation, "until the whole fabric falls asunder." In answering him, Webster pleaded for unity, moderation, and forbearance and denied that peaceful secession was possible:

> Secession! Peaceable secession! Sir, your eyes and mine are never destined to see that miracle. The dismemberment of this vast country without convulsion! The breaking up of the fountains of the great deep without ruffling the surface! Who is so foolish . . . as to expect to see any such thing? Sir, he who sees these States, now revolving in harmony round a common center, and expects to see them quit their places and fly off without convulsion, may look the next moment to see the heavenly bodies rush from their spheres and jostle against each other in the realms of space, without causing the wreck of the universe! There can be no such thing as a peaceable secession.

Webster's powerful voice strengthened the movement for conciliation, and tension was reduced. Other speakers like William H. Seward wanted no compromise with slavery and evoked the "higher law" of "the Creator of the Universe" to justify the exclusion of slavery from the territories. His speech drew wide support from free-soil radicals, the press, and northern clergymen. Horace Greeley of the New York *Tribune* gave the speech editorial prominence and proposed him privately as a future presidential candidate. Through these debates the administration used its resources to oppose compromise. The result was an open break with Clay, who denounced President Taylor in a public address. Clay rallied wide support as important Whigs joined him in demanding an end to the political crisis. The President's position was also weakened by a scandal in his Cabinet and some mistakes in judgment, which tended to alienate the public.

In a Fourth of July ceremony designed to win favor, the President taxed his weakened health. Doctors called when he began to feel ill, diagnosed his illness as cholera morbus, more likely typhoid fever. Five days later he was dead. His death left the country shocked and sorrowful, but those who had been fighting his recent policies looked to the moderation of Millard Fillmore in relief.

The new President, a lawyer by profession, was dignified and con-ciliatory in his relations with others. Though he was well regarded for his honesty, he was accepted as a rather dull, hesitant man who was a follower instead of a leader. Already committed to Clay's compromise, he appointed a strong Cabinet, with Webster as its most distinguished personage. The change of Presidents removed Seward and some aboli-tionists from places of influence and helped the forces of compromise. The new administration threw its weight behind the Clay plan, and Fillmore himself worked energetically to win votes, using messages, personal contacts, and patronage to soften the opposition. The victory in September 1850 was the combined endeavor of Webster, Clay, Stephen A. Douglas (the Senator from Illinois), and the President.

The Compromise brought a sense of relief, a feeling that revolution was averted, and some relaxation of tensions. Douglas told the Senate that he never expected "to make another speech on slavery. . . . Let us cease agitating, stop the debate, and drop the subject. If we do this, the Compromise will be recognized as a final settlement." Except in New York, New England, and parts of the Deep South, the Compromise was· accepted as Douglas had hoped. Still, party harmony had been severely tested by the crisis and the emotion of the past debate lingered in the November campaign. Probably the Whig party suffered the most. Discontent, strain, and frustration ran deep, especially in New York where Fillmore's enemies gained control and in Massachusetts where Webster's enemies abounded.

Much of the discontent arose from the Fugitive Slave Law. Mass meetings in northern cities denounced the law and offered platforms for Theodore Parker and Wendell Phillips, who demanded "immediate, unconditional emancipation on the soil." Their radical appeal for abolition aroused moderates, who did not want to disturb slavery where it existed. But the moderates felt conscience-stricken when they saw blacks hunted down by federal officials and hurried South without the protection of a jury trial. Incidents of brutality disturbed them because they hurt the cause of conciliation. While the number of runaway slaves was never large, slave-catching always aggravated the northern com-munity and threatened the lives of free blacks. Had the South been willing to accept a less severe fugitive slave law tension might have subsided. As it was, radical abolitionists succeeded in putting Charles Sumner and Benjamin Wade in the Senate, both powerful leaders often more devoted to the eradication of slavery than to the defense of the Union.

In the South the Compromise was debated for the better part of a year as politicians abandoned party affiliation to argue about the future of their section. Secession had, on the whole, little appeal for the people, who were proud of being Americans. During 1851 Southerners voted on issues involving secession, and unionists won almost everywhere. These victories, nevertheless, were for slavery under the American

A Scene from Stowe's Uncle Tom's Cabin *(Library of Congress)*

flag, and the elections in South Carolina left a feeling of uncertainty and uneasiness of future relations with the national government. The spirit of unionism undoubtedly predominated because of the prosperity and influence of the Whig party. There were still enough unionists in the party to unite with similar groups in the Democratic party and keep secessionists in a minority. But the Whigs were badly divided by the Compromise, and the deaths of Webster and Clay soon deprived the party of its national spokesmen.

The point where slavery touched the sentiments of both sections continued to be the enforcement of the Fugitive Slave Law. In most parts of the nation the strain was evident. In Cincinnati, Ohio, Harriet Beecher Stowe studied the slave society and was inspired to write *Uncle Tom's Cabin.* Her intimate descriptions of people caught up in the despotism of slavery deeply impressed her readers, who began to think of slaves as human beings to whom nature had given color. Her reproductions of southern life were those of a mild-mannered novelist; the story gained in impact when the readers saw frequent newspaper reports of atrocities committed against blacks. The New York *Tribune* often contained items of beatings and hangings and sometimes even of burnings at the stake. The *Southern Quarterly Review*, admitting cruelties, noted changes in work habits and discipline. Its editors pointed to slavery as a positive good, asserting that a few corrections in the system would remove most abuses. Few people in the North and South could forget the issue of slavery in spite of the Compromise of 1850, but the people of the North and West were occasionally distracted by the growing industrial development.

The Railroads, Commerce, and Expansion

With American attention directed toward other things, politicians chose two mediocre, neutral figures for the 1852 presidential contest, the Democrat Franklin Pierce and the Whig Winfield Scott, and avoided a confrontation of issues by ignoring prominent, controversial men such as Stephen A. Douglas and William H. Seward. The people chose Pierce by a landslide; he not only represented balance and peace but also was pleasant and uncommitted. With Pierce somewhere on the ship of state the nation allowed itself the luxury of a cruise into uncharted waters.

The great economic expansion of these years made possible an astonishing development of railroads. They were pushed ever westward and those already established were integrated into regional lines. Speculators and promoters enriched themselves by gaining land grants for their employers and playing cities and regions against each other as railroad centers. In the decade of the 1850s these companies received about twenty million acres of land, and political rewards and advantages were showered upon attorneys and agents who handled these matters. The total trackage had risen to 9021 miles in 1850, to 30,636 in 1860. Plans were under way for transcontinental lines on the eve of the Civil War.

The multiplication of speculators and their political spokesmen was not duplicated in other sections of the American economy, but there were expansion elsewhere and rewards for those who were willing to take risks. In water transport, shipping lines provided regular and swift schedules on most American rivers. Cargoes were moved easily and economically on a network of rivers and canals that tied the Mississippi and Ohio rivers together and made New Orleans, St. Louis, and Kansas City (on the Missouri River) important ports. Nearly eleven hundred steam vessels of various sizes, some costing as much as fifty thousand dollars, plied the rivers. On the high seas Americans developed the clipper ships, whose swift passages allowed their owners to bid successfully for world commerce. For a time in the 1850s American tonnage surpassed British and handled well over half of American foreign trade.

Manufacturing, too, expanded rapidly, though it supplied primarily the home market. Textile factories, flour mills, iron works, sawmills, and tool shops provided a vast quantity of items. During the decade of the 1850s the total value of manufacturing nearly doubled, to $1.8 billion. Aided by an expanding agricultural production that slightly surpassed its own total value, industry had a ready supply of raw material. Cotton production made impressive gains, and wheat, tobacco, and corn followed with increasing yields. In the Northwest, farms were mechanized, and a variety of tools like the reaper and the iron plow were expanding production units. Surpluses were moving off the farm, onto the canals and railroads to the urban centers of the Northeast and Europe. The farmer of the Northwest was losing his independence as he relied on distant markets and prices for the success of his crop.

This new industrial activity attracted great numbers of European immigrants. The dislocation in England, caused primarily by new inventions, had brought near revolution a few times after 1815, and many of these dissatisfied people sought opportunity in the United States. Famine in Ireland and political disturbances on the Continent also forced people to flee. For a few years in the 1850s more than three hundred thousand foreigners per year immigrated to America, and most settled, except for some Irish who went to New Orleans, in the North and Northwest. Cities like St. Louis and Milwaukee became centers of German culture, where schools and social organizations kept alive for generations the German heritage.

The coming of these millions of immigrants, whose religions and customs differed so markedly from the established Americans', aroused suspicion and hatred. Organizations like the American Protestant Association and the Order of the Star-Spangled Banner were formed to combat the "foreign menace," and politicians taking the name of Know-Nothings pledged themselves in secret to guard the nation from Roman Catholics. The foreign menace, however, never attained national prominence as an issue. Though huge votes in Massachusetts and New York reflected widespread bigotry, expansion of the nation had a greater, lasting importance, and these foreigners were soon employed in the factories and foundries, often at longer hours and lower wages than would have been tolerated by native-born Americans.

The interest of the nation again turned to expansion. Many people in the South desired the annexation of Cuba and parts of Central America; others were concerned about trade in California, Hawaii, and the Orient. To provide an easy route to the Pacific the United States and Great Britain negotiated in 1850 the Clayton-Bulwer Treaty, which promised the joint development of a canal across the Isthmus of Panama. The only tangible immediate result of the treaty was the building of a railroad by the United States. It expedited travel considerably for the goldseekers who were still flocking to California, but many people urged also a route across the western territory. Politicians in Illinois, Missouri, and Louisiana dreamed of the advantages to their states and sponsored governmental surveys of possible transcontinental routes.

The Kansas-Nebraska Dispute

Within every argument concerning the construction of railroads was the issue of slavery. However practical the route, or great the possibilities of profit, or attractive the advantages of a direct route to California, slavery became eventually a major consideration. In 1853 Congress authorized another survey of routes, and promoters interested various congressmen. Not the least of them was Senator Stephen A. Douglas of Illinois, chairman of the Committee on Territories. Douglas, already a successful land speculator, saw investment opportunities for four transcontinental lines and proposed governmental subsidies. The impracticality of building so many lines was realized by his colleagues, and the committee decided upon one line. In doing this, it opened the sectional issue of the route's location.

Douglas's committee was also at this time considering government for the Nebraska country. A bill was put aside in 1852 when objections from the South blocked its progress. The South wanted an extension of slavery into the territory, but was willing to compromise in exchange for a southern railway route. In 1854 Douglas tried to avoid the conflict by omitting from his bill any statement on slavery: the territory was to be organized and the people were eventually themselves to decide on the institution of slavery. Unfortunately, his opponents amended the bill, providing for outright repeal of the Missouri Compromise and the division of the area into two territories. In short, the amended bill would let Kansas and Nebraska, the two territories, decide the issue of slavery or freedom for themselves—and Kansas was expected to follow Missouri, becoming a slave state. These potentially controversial amendments were readily accepted by Douglas. He had no fixed views on slavery or free-soil, and was primarily interested in opening the territories for settlement and in the construction of a railway through them. In backing the bill, he stood squarely upon the position that the settler must decide his own institutions, and he won the support of President Pierce and the administration.

For the next four months Congress again debated slavery. With Douglas in the midst of controversy, the debates were deeply bitter, and reaction in the North mounted from indignation to anger. Many newspapers denounced the bill; old Jacksonians bolted the party;

popular emotion was often unrestrained. Almost everywhere in the North free-soil Democrats, conscience Whigs, and other angry people formed fusion parties. In Ohio and Wisconsin, dissidents objected to most recent governmental policies, but wanted particularly the repeal of the Fugitive Slave Law and an end to the extension of slavery. They called themselves Republicans and urged the organization of a national association. The name spread to similar groups in Massachusetts and New York.

The Republican party was only one of the new groups arising from the general disintegration of parties. For some reason the splinter parties had a natural affinity, even if they were backing such diverse reforms as temperance, antislavery, antiforeign legislation, reform of the tariff, homesteading in the West, and reform of the banks. While the Kansas-Nebraska bill became law, critics organized a party to oppose the law, Douglas, and the administration, and turned their bitterness against the Democrats in the 1854 elections. The Whigs suffered most from this; their free-soil supporters flocked into other, more dynamic expressions of protest, and in the South the Whig party was accused of being too weak in a time of national peril, unable to find the basis of a new national compromise as in 1850.

Hardly had the Kansas-Nebraska bill been signed when Douglas's theory of popular sovereignty was tested. The contest occurred in Kansas, which was more suitable than Nebraska for using slaves, and both North and South accepted the challenge of determining the issue. Free-soil people were encouraged to migrate West and proslave Missourians to move across the border; nearly two thousand adult male settlers were soon in the region. This large population permitted President Pierce to set up a territorial government in the late summer of 1854. As the first governor, he chose Andrew H. Reeder, an inexperienced spoilsman of Pennsylvania. Reeder proved to be a man of courage. He resisted proslave demands for an immediate election and waited instead until March 1855, when the population reached 8500. The elections then were not without irregularities, but he enforced the electoral laws and called upon Pierce for aid in throwing out fraudulent ballots, sometimes disregarding threats to his life. The proslave minority, with the help of Missourians across the border, won the election, and the President, taking a legalistic position, recognized the decision. His action not only angered the antislavery majority, who organized their own territorial government and appealed to Congress over his ruling, but also brought the governor's removal and bloodshed among the partisans.

The violence in "bleeding" Kansas infuriated some members of Congress and inspired personal acts of reprisal. Charles Sumner of Massachusetts, long known for his indiscreet remarks on slavery, was brutally beaten at his senatorial desk within view of another Senator. Southerners generally approved the attack as retaliation for

Sumner's slanderous remarks on slavery. Symbols of appreciation were awarded the assailant by various southern groups. Northerners were also inflamed, held rallies, and condemned southern brutality. Their reaction was even more explosive when proslave forces in Kansas burned Lawrence and imprisoned the governor. Worse still were the Pottawatami, Kansas, raids of John Brown, an abolitionist fanatic, who avenged the suffering of antislavery people by murdering five pro-slavery settlers. These murders led to other raids, and by the time order was restored hundreds of people were wounded or slain.

During the crisis the national elections of 1856 were held. The Democrats, faced with a collapse of leadership in the Presidency, should have nominated a vigorous man. Instead, they chose James Buchanan, then sixty-six, ripe with experience but cautious, pro-southern in sympathy, and in poor health. The new Republican party, in the Musical Fund Hall of Philadelphia, passed over well-known political leaders for John C. Frémont, whose reputation as pathfinder had the magic of Manifest Destiny. The Know-Nothings or American party and a group of Whigs held separate conventions, but backed Millard Fillmore as their candidate. The campaign reflected the conditions in Kansas, and violence sometimes erupted. National leaders like historian George Bancroft broke with the Democratic party over the issue of moral purpose and dedication. The campaign had the effect of making people choose new political alliances and defend their positions. Few leaders rose to such heights of patriotism as did Thomas Hart Benton when he spoke on national issues in every part of Missouri. Denouncing the hypocrisy of many spokesmen on the issue of slavery, he urged a compromise, union, and peace through the election of Buchanan in spite of a personal feud of many years.

When the sound and fury of the campaign ended on election day, Buchanan had won the Presidency as well as control of Congress. The Democrats boasted over their victory even to the point of arrogance, but some Southerners who had talked of secession if Frémont won were sorry that they had not insisted upon a more radical nominee than Buchanan. The new President was uneasy about the nation's future and was deferential of the South in an attempt to be conciliatory. The nation, too, should have been uneasy: the President was rigid, meek, hesitant, and devoid of fighting qualities, without any proven ability as a political manager.

Two days after Buchanan's inauguration the Supreme Court handed down its decision in the case of Dred Scott v. Sanford, an attempt to end the dispute over slavery in the territories. The Court, under the venerable Roger Taney, was badly divided. Taney, as spokesman for the majority, denied that Congress had power to limit slavery in the territories and asserted that the states had no authority to make blacks American citizens. His radical position was approved by the South, but it incensed Republicans and liberal-minded Northerners who

considered the decision little more than a manifesto of proslave interests. Anger quickly spread throughout the North and aroused a
sense of national shame, a feeling of despair and frustration. Many
thinking people accused Taney and Buchanan of conspiracy, and more
people branded the case an attack upon the Constitution. A writer
in the North American Review predicted that "the country will feel
the consequences of the decision more deeply and more permanently,
in the loss of confidence in the sound judicial integrity and strictly
legal character of their tribunals, than in anything beside."

The Dred Scott case did not solve the problem of slavery and freedom in Kansas. President Buchanan appointed another governor, the
able leader of Mississippi, Robert J. Walker, to find a compromise.
Though Walker called elections for a constitutional convention, he
could not rally the support of the free-soilers. The election for the
convention went by default to the proslave settlers, who drew up a
new constitution that gave the voters the choice of the free-soilers.
The election for the convention went by default to the proslave settlers, who drew up a new constitution that gave the voters the choice
of rejecting a further extension of slavery, but slavery, whatever the
vote, was guaranteed to Kansas slaveholders. By withholding their
vote in these elections, the free-soilers permitted their opponents to
win easily, but they used their power in the territorial elections to gain
control of the legislature. Then they resubmitted the proslave constitution to the people. The proslave groups withheld their votes in this
election, so that the constitution was overwhelmingly rejected. The
elections, however, clarified the issue. Kansas's free-soilers had mus-
tered nearly a third more votes in rejecting the constitution than the
proslave settlers had in ratifying it.

Unfortunately, Buchanan refused to accept this vote. He forced
Walker from office; determined to make Kansas a slave state, he submitted the proslave constitution to Congress. His surrender to the
slave interests irritated Democrats like Douglas, who used the President's action as an excuse for reaffirming their faith in the principles
of popular sovereignty. Douglas rallied support and in an interview
he and Buchanan exchanged bitter threats. They took the issue to
Congress where the split in the party widened as men fiercely debated
the merits of expanding slavery. Though administration Democrats
controlled both houses of Congress, they compromised sufficiently to
let Kansas vote again on the proslave constitution, promising immediate
statehood if the people accepted the constitution. But the free-soilers
of Kansas promptly rejected the compromise.

The prolonged debate in Congress discredited Buchanan, exhausted Douglas, and spread both the sectional and the party gap.
Throughout the North the President's friends lost heavily in the 1858
elections. Their majority in the Senate was reduced and control of the
House passed to a coalition of Douglas Democrats and Republicans.

These defeats reflected the bitterness over slavery that was affecting public attitudes toward most national issues.

The North was also disturbed by a declining industrial activity and by a loss of confidence in the market. For nearly ten years railroad expansion had proceeded rapidly, often into unprofitable areas, and expectations were proving to be unrealistic. So with manufacturing: Inventories were growing, prices falling, and foreign competition stiffening. The depression bankrupted some businesses, closed factories, and put millions of workers out of jobs. The hard times lasted a few years, and they revived political demands for a higher tariff, a new banking system, and liberalized land grants in the West. These demands served, as did the argument over Kansas statehood, to intensify sectional rivalry, and undoubtedly contributed to the defeat of administration Democrats in 1858.

At this time a spectacular series of debates occurred between the President's critic Stephen A. Douglas and an Illinois corporation lawyer, Abraham Lincoln. Douglas's great prominence in the debates on Kansas had made popular sovereignty known everywhere in the nation and had won him the praise and cooperation of eastern Republicans. Lincoln's reputation was state-wide, mostly as a Whig politician and lawyer, for his successful record in handling corporate litigation. The prize the two men sought was the senatorship of Illinois, held by Douglas since 1847 but to be filled in 1858 by the legislature that was being packed with hostile administration Democrats.

Lincoln, attacking Douglas's popular sovereignty, put himself on record against slavery and its spread into the territories. He raised the serious question of the permanence of the national union if slavery continued to be a legal institution. While he refined his position during the debates, he denied that the Republican party was an abolitionist party but affirmed his belief that the black had a right to life, liberty, and property—"a right to eat the bread, without leave of anyone else, which his own hand earns." In those rights, he said, the black "is my equal, and the equal of Judge Douglas, and the equal of every living man." Lincoln was conservative toward the black, nonetheless, and had little interest in improving his social position as a freed person, and was ready to return him to Africa. But Lincoln's moral position on slavery separated him from Douglas, who refused to accept slavery as immoral. Lincoln took their argument a step further by showing that popular sovereignty conflicted with the Dred Scott decision. "Can the people of a United States territory," he pressed Douglas at the Freeport, Illinois, debate, "exclude slavery from its limits prior to the formation of a state constitution?" Douglas immediately agreed that, in spite of the Court decision, the people had the power to exclude slavery.

For this reason border state and southern politicians denounced Douglas, and though he won the Illinois election, they insisted that his position on slavery was unacceptable. No settlers, they said, could deny them the use of slaves in the territories: The Freeport doctrine was plainly dishonest and unconstitutional. Northern abolitionists were also unhappy with Douglas's position and felt that Lincoln had the stronger argument. They agreed with Lincoln that slavery was a devisive force that would disrupt the nation, that slavery was now accepted as a permanent institution, that plans for its restriction and eventual eradication were necessary, and that it was morally wrong as an institution. For many Northerners, however, the Freeport doctrine was accepted as a realistic view of what was happening in the territories—the settlers were choosing free over slave institutions.

A few weeks after the Illinois elections the debate over slavery moved to Congress. For most of the first session Congress was deadlocked over issues, and the President and national leaders were unable to find compromises to get machinery moving again. Debates raged again on the proposed Pacific railroad, on a homestead bill, on a revision of the tariff. Oregon and Minnesota were admitted as states, but almost nothing else of significance took place in the Thirty-fifth Congress. Opinions had hardened, and nothing promising was expected of the next Congress.

In the meantime, John Brown of the Pottawatami murders in Kansas was touring the Northeast, soliciting arms and money for abolitionists in Kansas. Secretly, he laid plans to attack some part of the Appalachians, call for a slave revolt, and create a new nation. He gathered support from abolitionists and encouraged a large group of conspirators to back his scheme. On Sunday evening, October 16, 1859, he led an eighteen-man army against Harpers Ferry in western Virginia, a United States arsenal. The few sentries were easily overpowered and several million dollars worth of arms captured. By morning his men had killed a railroad employee and one or two local inhabitants; the word of the insurrection had spread. Soon militia from the surrounding towns was converging on the Ferry, and Buchanan ordered federal troops under Robert E. Lee to recapture the arsenal. Within a few hours Brown and four of his men were taken. Brown was quickly tried for treason, found guilty, and sentenced to hang. His co-conspirators hastily burned their papers and silently let him die for the crime they had encouraged.

Brown faced sentence of death with dignity, and his parting letters and courtroom oration at sentencing rose to a kind of moral grandeur:

> I did no wrong, but right. Now, if it is deemed necessary that I should forfeit my life for the furtherance of the ends of justice, and mingle my blood further with the blood of my children and with the blood of millions in this slave country whose rights are disregarded by wicked, cruel, and unjust enactments, I say, let it be done.

Emotion ran so high in the nation that this madman's dream of insurrection exerted a strange power. Somehow Brown came to symbolize the desperation of many people who longed for action. Bells rang in many villages at the time of his execution and his letters and speeches were quoted and remembered. Responsible Republicans separated themselves from this radicalism, but the incident seriously unsettled most Southerners, who took stern measures to insure the docility of their slaves.

The 1860 Elections

The Thirty-sixth Congress organized in 1860 during this emotional crisis. Its members reflected the growing tension, and, particularly in the House of Representatives, sectional feeling kept them from selecting their officers. For weeks the House balloted on a speaker and finally, in late January, found a compromise candidate. But Congress could not get down to work. The homestead bill, the tariff, and a score of measures that would have remedied economic ills were either stopped in the Senate or vetoed by the President. Everyone in the Democratic party seemed bent on dividing it, raising issues of slavery in the territories, challenging Douglas's Freeport doctrine, or embarrassing the President. Congress was not in the mood to legislate in this election year.

The Democrats were divided. The southern part wanted slavery protected in the territories and demanded that Douglas abandon his theory of popular sovereignty before the party nominated him for the Presidency. Though Douglas had a majority of the delegates to the Charleston convention, he lacked a two-thirds vote to win nomination, and needed southern support. The threat of a schism did not disturb party leaders, even when delegates from four states left their seats and a deadlock of ten days broke up the convention. Six weeks later in Baltimore, however, the deadlock divided the party into hostile factions. One nominated Douglas and the other John C. Breckinridge of Kentucky.

In Chicago, the Republicans gathered in the "Wigwam," an auditorium especially built and decorated for the occasion. The symbolic wigwam, the western city, the planked streets and walks surrounded the hall provided a rustic atmosphere that was later reflected in the nationalistic platform. In a party rich with leaders, the delegates were particularly impressed with the campaigning of Lincoln's followers, who brought into the hall rails that Lincoln could have split as a young man. His humble origins and kinship with the laboring man gave him a magic in the convention that eventually permitted him to win victory on the third ballot.

A fourth party, the Whigs-Know-Nothings, met in Baltimore and organized the Constitutional-Union party. Standing foursquare on the Constitution, the party chose John Bell of Tennessee and Edward Everett of Massachusetts as their standard-bearers. The party presented a powerful appeal to the conservatives who put union and peace ahead

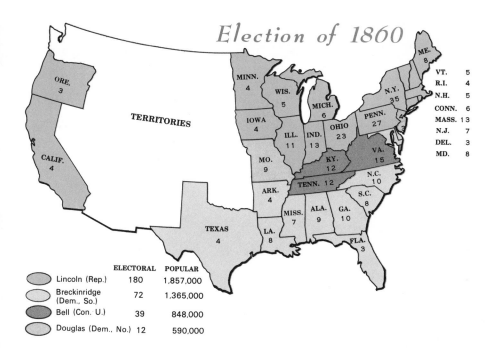

Election of 1860

	ELECTORAL	POPULAR
Lincoln (Rep.)	180	1,857,000
Breckinridge (Dem., So.)	72	1,365,000
Bell (Con. U.)	39	848,000
Douglas (Dem., No.)	12	590,000

of all other issues. They campaigned on the basis that a vote for their party might throw the election into the House of Representatives, where a compromise might be worked out between the North and South. It was a party of desperation and fear.

The campaign emphasized what the people already felt—that the nation was deeply split, and that the election would undoubtedly signal its breakup. The Republican and Democratic candidates represented the separate sections. The Democrats seemed shaken by the threat to the Union, but the Republicans were not concerned by the danger of their sectional appeal and explained how their platform would benefit the North. Their concentration upon its major planks of a homestead law, tariff and banking reform, no slavery in the territories, the building of a railroad to the Pacific, and the admission of Kansas as a free state won them strong support in every northern state. In November Lincoln obtained 180 electoral votes, his opponents 123. The popular vote reflected the deep cleavage between the sections:

Lincoln	1,866,452	Breckinridge	849,781
Douglas	1,376,957	Bell	588,879

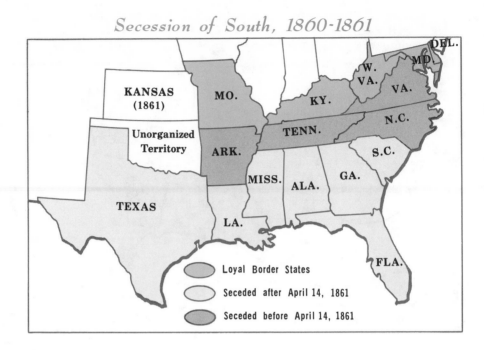

Secession of South, 1860-1861

Loyal Border States

Seceded after April 14, 1861

Seceded before April 14, 1861

The Civil War

Even before Lincoln's election was official, South Carolina did what states had been threatening to do since the founding of the Union: It appealed to the right of revolution (the ultimate recourse), called a special convention, and voted 169 to 0 for secession. Impressive votes followed in Mississippi, Florida, Alabama, Georgia, Louisiana, and Texas. In early February 1860 a congress met at Montgomery, Alabama, adopted a provincial constitution, chose Jefferson Davis as president and Alexander H. Stephens as vice president, and drew up a permanent constitution that the seven states ratified by May. That month North Carolina, Tennessee, and Arkansas seceded, and Robert E. Lee, after weeks of trauma, left the Union for military service in the Virginia forces. This startling progression of events stunned most Northerners.

Of those events the election of Davis had a major impact upon the North. He was well known in national affairs, better known than Lincoln, who was one year younger than his fellow Kentuckian. A West Pointer, the son of a Revolutionary veteran, and a plantation owner, Davis was a man of dignity, learning, and experience, being a one time Secretary of War for Pierce and United States Senator for Mississippi.

He was energetic, but slow and deliberate, and he lacked a capacity to sort out the important from the unimportant in using his energy. For this moment of crisis, however, he appeared to be well prepared for the duties awaiting him.

As Buchanan's term of office approached its end, he lectured Congress on the crisis, but those around him despaired of the future: "The Union is passing away like a bank of fog before the wind." Buchanan was in poor health, sometimes unable to leave the second floor of the White House, and indecisive; his Cabinet divided; his party splintered. He let the crisis mount without using his vast prestige in the South to rally the unionists. Instead, he blamed the North for the crisis and recommended northern capitulation on the basis of the Dred Scott decision. He refused to strengthen or support federal forts in the South, denying Fort Sumter in Charleston Harbor reinforcements until its defenses had become critical. Even then, when South Carolina refused to let a relief party enter the harbor, Buchanan retreated from a confrontation.

Men close to the heart of public affairs, however, galvanized by the rapid disintegration of the Union, acted to find a compromise. Both houses of Congress offered the South protection for its slave institutions by means of an unamendable constitutional amendment, and their committees sat for weeks arguing over provisions of a general peace proposal. Virginia asked for a peace convention, and twenty-one states responded to the invitation. With Former President John Tyler presiding, the delegates recommended a constitutional amendment that would allow slavery south of the line of latitude 36°31′ and guarantee the slave states equality in approving the acquisition of any new territory. All these compromises eventually failed. For later generations, aware of what the Civil War cost America in loss of life, suffering, and waste, the failure of peace negotiations at this time seems unnecessary and even unconscionable. The men of the time, however, were reckless and incensed, even dared their opponents to make war, even obstructed peace negotiations. The sad fact is the unwillingness of many leaders to believe, their inability to understand, that civil war was upon them, that the struggle could drag on for years, that the American Union was shattered. At the heart of their problem was the continuation of slavery: The many proposed compromises guaranteed slavery in the South. In an age when most European nations had abandoned it, to allow its existence in the United States was an anomaly that was apparent to many people. Unfortunately, the problem of finding a new role for the black person was not thought out.

Even Lincoln was ready to compromise the issue of slavery for union and thought in terms of gradual emancipation. He was not clear in his own mind, however, about the future of blacks in America, and spoke of their return to Africa as a solution for social position in society. But he was "for no compromise which asserts or permits the extension

Abraham Lincoln in 1860 *(Chicago Historical Society)*

of the institution on soil owned by the nation." The President-elect was finding a middle path as he made his appointments, studied current and past courses of action, and readied himself for the move to Washington. As a native of Kentucky and a long-time resident of Illinois, he had served in the state legislature and the House of Representatives, but he had spent the preceding twelve years mostly practicing as a lawyer in Illinois. He was not familiar with eastern politics and society and moved uneasily within them. His reputation and connections were painfully local, and as he entered into Washington affairs, he made tactical errors, or said the wrong things, or relied upon politicians whose judgment was not as good as his own.

His inaugural address was awaited with great anxiety, for nearly everyone sensed the imminent breakup of the nation and wanted to hear what course of action he planned. Lincoln pledged himself to be conciliatory with the South, but he was firm in holding that states could not secede from the Union:

> I therefore consider that, in view of the Constitution and the laws, the Union is unbroken, and, to the extent of my ability, I shall take care, as the Constitution itself expressly enjoins me, that the law of the Union be faithfully executed in all the States. . . . In doing this there needs to be no bloodshed or violence; and there shall be none, unless it be forced upon the national authority.

During his first month in office, he arranged for the reinforcement of Fort Sumter at Charleston, evaluated the popular support his administration was receiving, and watched the news from Virginia, where the Union cause was precarious.

Before he could replenish supplies in the fort, southern batteries opened fire on it. Crowds from Charleston gathered at the waterfront on April 12 to see the fort's flag shot away and fires break out among the buildings, and cheered the declaration that day of formal war. Virginia left the Union on April 17. The forty-six counties of northwest Virginia, however, broke away from the state, and two years later formed the free state of West Virginia.

On April 15 Lincoln called for 75,000 volunteers for a three-month enlistment and issued various presidential decrees intended to bring a quick end to hostilities. On May 3 he called for 42,000 more men, this time for three years service, and raised the strength of the regular army to 18,000 men. Hardly anyone tried to predict the results of these measures, but many felt that a few solid engagements would crush the insurrection. Men joined state regiments in great numbers—frequently accepting the invitations of local politicians who recruited them in exchange for commissions. Patriotic zeal in both North and South added strength at first, but palled, and the forces lacked the steel of discipline and experience. After the initial battle of Bull Run on July 21, Lincoln realized that the Union needed to organize its manpower. To

George McClellan, a thirty-four-year-old veteran of the Mexican War, he gave full authority to turn recruits into an effective army. McClellan, however, lacked the military capacity to judge the advantages of speed. With infinite care he drilled his volunteers into a well-disciplined force, but he hesitated to employ it. He planned for the day of the great battle and victory, not realizing that the war could drag on for years or that he should be putting constant pressure on the south in order to hasten that day of victory. In the meantime, he left the President to explain the inaction on the Virginia front, to worry about mounting costs of battle and problems of morale, and to maintain discipline within the Republican party.

Strategy and Politics in the War

With the war proving longer and costlier than anyone had expected, Lincoln had to develop new strategy. He chose to emphasize reunion of the states instead of abolition as the essential term for peace. There were more than 800,000 slaves in the border states, and he did not want to antagonize those states. However, he supported recruitment of blacks into the army, organized various black regiments and service forces. More than 186,000 blacks eventually served in the army, participating in most battles of the war, and some 38,000 lost their lives. Still Lincoln avoided making liberation of the blacks the issue of the war. Partly because of prejudices in the North, his cautious attitude became a policy matter, and his party thus lost an issue that might have rallied popular support or at least have separated it from the War Democrats. In relations with Europe, the North could not present its cause in the strongest terms by making the principles of liberalism its own. The war deeply divided England; in confusion she sent to the South significant military aid and constructed Confederate raiders in her shipyards. Even such liberal statesmen as William E. Gladstone purchased Confederate bonds.

Parenthetically, it should be noted that President Jefferson Davis of the Confederacy and his colleagues also misjudged the length of the war. They expected victories over the North, or aid from Europe when cotton supplies diminished, but they miscalculated. Scarcities of food and arms became a constant problem, and the allocation of manpower was a nightmare. The South's population of six million whites and three million blacks was no match for the twenty-two million whites and blacks in the North. While the South could count on the excellent generalship of Robert E. Lee and Stonewall Jackson and thousands of spirited soldiers, interior lines, and a wide popular support, the long war put an insuperable strain on its resources.

Early in the war Lincoln proclaimed a blockade of southern ports. He had to wait for years while the shipyards constructed sufficient numbers of vessels, but gradually the blockade became tighter and

General Robert E. Lee *(Library of Congress)*

tighter. Under the direction of Secretary of the Navy Gideon Welles, naval vessels struck at southern ports, capturing New Orleans, Mobile, and islands and ports along the Atlantic coast and opening the Chesapeake waterway. These actions reduced southern trade and gave the administration significant victories while the land campaigns were being organized.

Waging war on the land was extremely difficult because of the long frontier, the rough terrain, the location of the capital near the battlefront, and the scarcity of military leadership. Complicating these problems were home-front morale and unity. For most of the war years the North seemed divided. Some people objected to the war, rioted, blocked enlistments, and spread discontent. Others protested the employment of blacks as longshoremen when white workers struck for higher wages. They burned black homes and businesses and rioted against government attempts to protect blacks. Pacifists urged negotiations, denouncing Lincoln as a warmonger. Southern sympathizers carried out subversive campaigns of violence against anyone supporting the government. Politicians often ignored the sacrifices of men at the battlefront as they inspired dissension and declaimed against the President. Countless numbers used the opportunities of war to turn profits from shortages and to gamble otherwise on the market. Peacetime pursuits also distracted many from the national crisis.

The North, however, was fortunate to have Lincoln at the head of its government. His spirit of moderation and good sense kept radicals in his party from invoking severe laws against dissent and thereby dividing the nation still more. While the government rounded up hundreds of troublemakers and refused to honor writs of habeas corpus for some of those imprisoned, there were no blood purges or public executions and no widespread suspensions of public liberties. Moderation was also evidenced in other measures. Conscription was imposed only when a manpower emergency required it; taxes were levied in many forms, perhaps too lightly on those taking excessive war profits; the states were permitted to run their ordinary affairs without undue federal interference. The administration, moreover, redeemed some of its election promises. It passed the Homestead Act, which gave 160 acres of free land to each prospective western settler, and the Morrell Land Grant Act, which assisted in the establishment of agricultural colleges to promote scientific farming. It backed tariff measures and set up a federally chartered banking system.

Some of these measures were passed before the 1862 elections and reveal the shift in national power that was occurring in federal-state relations. The Republicans were restoring national power in the manner of Hamilton and Marshall. Their reversal of the trend toward states' rights that had continued since Madison's veto of internal improvements in 1817 was dramatic. They provided for national military recruiting, a national income tax, and a national excise tax system, and they were thinking of national citizenship. Their program for changing the federal republic into an American nation was rapidly taking conscious form as they waged war and dealt with disloyalty.

They were not able to solve either problem satisfactorily before the 1862 elections, and the election results reflected public discontent. If not for the votes of border states, New England, and the Far West, they would have lost control of the House of Representatives. Even so, their majorities shrank almost everywhere. They were fortunate that the Democrats had no leader of the stature of Stephen A. Douglas, who had died in 1861, or their losses might have been greater than they were. The friendly New York Times described the election reaction to Lincoln's administration in this manner:

> The very qualities which have made Abraham Lincoln so well liked in private life . . . his kindheartedness, his concern for fair play, his placidity of temper . . . unfit him for the stern requirements of deadly war. . . . He is all the while haunted with the fear of doing some injustice, and is ever easy to accept explanations. The very first necessity of war is extreme rigor, and yet every impulse of our constitutional Commander-in-Chief has been to get rid of it.

The Operational War

The Times was reacting to the military situation. Lincoln had been able neither to present the nation with a first-class military victory nor to hold out the promise of an early end to the war. McClellan moved slowly and allowed the advantage of his superiority of troops to be lost by unnecessary caution. Opposing master strategists like Lee and Jackson, he overestimated Confederate strength and permitted himself to be outmaneuvered. Moreover, he had to contend with civilian interference. Lincoln and his advisors feared an attack on the capital while McClellan was fighting on the Virginia peninsula and withheld substantial forces for the defense of Washington. The intereference unsettled the wary McClellan, who delayed his advance on Richmond even though he was within five miles of the town. A possible Union victory was turned by brilliant strategy of Lee and heroic efforts of J. E. B. Stuart into the Seven Days' Battles (June 25-July 1, 1862), a retreat of the Union forces to the James River, and their withdrawal from the peninsula. Lee was free to push northward and threaten Washington.

Lincoln attempted to satisfy his critics by reorganizing the army command. Making Henry W. Halleck the general-in-chief and John Pope the commander of the Potomac army, he ordered a drive against Confederates that would push them deep into Virginia—as Pope had boasted he could do easily. At Bull Run Pope met Lee coming up from Richmond, and during the battle committed errors of judgment that allowed his troops to be thrown back in confusion. The defeat forced

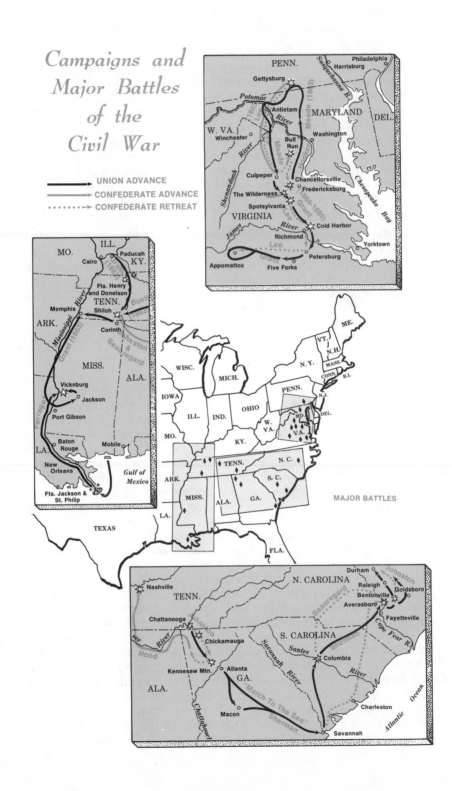

Campaigns and Major Battles of the Civil War

→ UNION ADVANCE
→ CONFEDERATE ADVANCE
······→ CONFEDERATE RETREAT

PENN.
Philadelphia
Harrisburg
Gettysburg
Potomac
Lee (1863)
Meade (1863)
Susquehanna R.
Antietam
River
MARYLAND
DEL.
W. VA.
Winchester
Washington
Shenandoah
Bull Run
Hooker-Meade
River
Chesapeake Bay
Culpeper
Chancellorsville
The Wilderness
Fredericksburg
Grant (1864-1865)
Spotsylvania
VIRGINIA
Lee
James
River
Cold Harbor
Richmond
Yorktown
Grant
Lee
Petersburg
Appomattox
Five Forks

ILL.
MO.
Paducah
KY.
Cairo
Grant (1862)
Fts. Henry and Donelson
Ohio River
Buell (1862)
TENN.
Memphis
Shiloh
Mississippi River
Corinth
Johnston
Beauregard (1862)
ARK.
Grant (1863)
MISS.
ALA.
Vicksburg
Jackson
Farragut
Port Gibson
Baton Rouge
Mobile
LA.
New Orleans
Gulf of Mexico
Fts. Jackson & St. Philip

WISC.
MICH.
N.Y.
ME.
VT.
N.H.
MASS.
IOWA
PENN.
CONN. **R.I.**
N.J.
ILL. **IND.** **OHIO**
MD. **DEL.**
MO. **W. VA.**
KY.
TENN.
N.C.
ARK.
S.C.
MISS. **ALA.** **GA.**
LA.
TEXAS
FLA.

MAJOR BATTLES

Durham
Johnston
N. CAROLINA
Raleigh
Goldsboro
Nashville
Bentonville
TENN.
Averasboro
Beauregard
Fayetteville
Chattanooga
Cape Fear R.
Johnston
Chickamauga
S. CAROLINA
see Hood
River
Savannah River
Santee
Columbia
Sherman
River
Kennesaw Mtn.
Atlanta
GA.
ALA.
Chattahoochee
"March To The Sea"
Sherman
Macon
Charleston
Atlantic Ocean
Savannah

Lincoln to restore McClellan to command of the army and to adopt emergency measures. There followed tense days of marching as McClellan tried to reorganize Union forces and halt Lee's advance northward. In the mountains of Maryland the armies finally met in a series of inconclusive battles. Lee had divided his forces in attacks on communications at Harpers Ferry and Hagerstown; if McClellan, during these hours of division, had acted on his intelligence reports, he might have won a great victory. Instead he permitted Lee to take a position at Antietam, regroup his men, and in September fight to a draw. Weeks of inaction followed, with Lee moving into the safety of Virginia and Jeb Stuart's cavalry riding around McClellan's army with daring and heroic raids into Pennsylvania.

In October Lincoln lost patience and replaced McClellan with Ambrose E. Burnside. At Fredericksburg, where he had forces of 114,000 men to Lee's 72,000, Burnside lost twice as many men as did Lee, without accomplishing anything worth-while. In January 1863 he was succeeded by "Fighting Joe" Hooker, a likable and outspoken soldier of vigor and courage. Hooker's qualities of leadership did not match Lee's either; the battle of Chancellorsville left him confused. Again Lee moved northward as Union forces regrouped and rushed to stem his advance. He was finally stopped in July 1863 at Gettysburg by George G. Meade, the new Union commander. The two-day battle, July 1 to 3, one of the bloodiest of the entire war, was a turning point in the conflict. Even more significant, Gettysburg was fought at the same time as Vicksburg in the West. That battle was the culmination of a series of bitter engagements in 1861 and 1862 that pushed Confederate forces southward and discovered for the North a general of extraordinary ability, Ulysses S. Grant.

The son of an Ohio tradesman, Grant won his appointment to West Point in 1839. The Academy gave him a good education but little inspiration for a military career. When the Mexican War broke out, he served his country as a first lieutenant and later accepted garrison duty in the West. To relieve the monotony and loneliness there, he took to liquor; in 1854, rather than stand court-martial on a charge of drunkenness, he left the army. Seven years of poverty followed in which he passed from job to job. In 1861, by an unusual set of circumstances, his military training brought him to the attention of the governor of Illinois and of the President. He was successively commissioned a colonel and a brigadier general and put in charge of troops at Cairo, Illinois. His energy and initiative in attacks at Belmont, Missouri and on the border forts at Donelson and Henry marked him as an exceptional leader. With the help of John A. Rawlins, a member of his staff, he overcame his weakness for liquor and exploited opportunities to win the rank of major general. In 1862 he cleared Confederates from the Tennessee River to a point near the Mississippi border, where his raw recruits suffered a setback at Shiloh meeting house. His superior,

General Ulysses S. Grant (*Library of Congress*)

Henry Halleck, jealous of Grant's successes, assumed personal direction of the army, doubled the number of troops, and pushed on to Corinth. The reinforced army compelled the Confederates to withdraw southward and the "great victory" gave Halleck national recognition and promotion to Washington.

Northern naval forces meanwhile had cleared the Mississippi River to Vicksburg, making this town the last military objective in dividing the South. Grant, freed of Halleck's interference, turned to its siege. The heavy concentration of Confederate troops at Raymond and Jackson forced battles before he could surround the town, but successes in mid-May 1863 enabled him to begin a siege that lasted until July 4.

The fall of Vicksburg permitted Grant to turn to even greater objectives. The strategy was clear. Western forces had driven the Confederates from Kentucky and western Tennessee, divided the South by controlling the Mississippi River, and occupied New Orleans. General William S. Rosecrans was advancing on Chattanooga and General Burnside on Knoxville. Momentary reverses halted Rosecrans's attack in late September, but Grant moved his army into the area and put William T. Sherman in charge. In the battle of Chattanooga of November 23 to 25, Union forces won a decisive victory that opened the way to Atlanta and the lower South.

During these impressive land operations the navy was tightening the southern blockade. Though blockade runners from the Bahamas crept in and out of Confederate ports, everywhere in the South shortages were causing anxiety, affecting the efficiency of railroads, and undermining morale. The hope of foreign intervention was also fading. European countries, particularly Great Britain, found substitutes for cotton, and the expected economic crisis did not develop, at least not one severe enough to force Britain into the war. Offsetting some trade irritations for Britain was Lincoln's Emancipation Proclamation in 1863, which gave a humanitarian character to the war and delighted European reformers. Military reverses, too, hurt the southern cause.

Grant's promotion to commander of all northern armies was symbolic of the changed military conditions. With headquarters in the East, he coordinated northern attacks. He applied pressure directly on Lee on the Potomac front while Sherman cut the lower South apart with a march into Georgia and South Carolina. Grant finally cornered Lee in an area close to Richmond and Petersburg, severed his supply lines, and hit him again and again until Lee surrendered at Appomattox Court House in April 1865.

These last months of war were costly in men and materiel, in wasting the energy of millions of people, in sowing bitterness and suspicion. The North and South had lost approximately 610,000 men in battle and from contributing causes since 1861. From four to five million men had given days, months, years, or their lives to the conflict. Many returned home with intense feelings of hatred that lingered for decades to come. The cost of the war in supplies and in energy may never be estimated. Lincoln tried to find significance in this price of blood and treasure when he spoke at the dedication of Gettysburg cemetery on November 19, 1863:

> Now we are engaged in a great civil war, testing whether that nation, or any nation so conceived and so dedicated, can long endure. We are met on a great battle field of that war. We have come to dedicate a portion of that field, as a final resting-place for those

who here gave their lives that that nation might live. It is altogether fitting and proper that we should do this.

But, in a larger sense, we can not dedicate—we can not consecrate—we can not hallow—this ground. The brave men, living and dead, who struggled here, have consecrated it, far above our poor power to add or detract. . . . It is rather for us to be here dedicated to the great task remaining before us—that from these honored dead we take increased devotion to that cause for which they gave the last full measure of devotion—that we here highly resolve that these dead shall not have died in vain—that this nation, under God, shall have a new birth of freedom—and that government of the people, by the people, for the people, shall not perish from the earth.

Reunion Under Lincoln

Looking thus to freedom and peace, Lincoln planned carefully for the future reunion of the country. From his first days in office he had sought every opportunity to invite the South to return. His conditions were not exacting; these Americans must renounce their violent ways and return to the fold as citizens. In 1862 the military governments he erected in Louisiana, Arkansas, and Tennessee were mild and temporary ones. Lincoln hoped the experience in these areas would become the basis for a plan of union.

At the opening of Congress in December 1863 he asked approval of a general plan for reconciliation. As if to underscore his good will, he granted full pardon to most rebels, except major offenders. Pardon required an oath of loyalty to the Constitution, and an assurance of support for the Emancipation Proclamation. Lincoln's policy of mildness and generosity was based upon the Amnesty Act of 1862. It displeased some congressmen, who thought the South should suffer for rebelling and the black should be assured of his newly won freedom. They were dissatisfied with Lincoln's definition of war aims and were anxious to replace him with Secretary of the Treasury Salmon P. Chase or another man of determination and "clear thinking." However, Lincoln's prestige had grown consistently. His good nature, his humor, his honesty, his dedication—all qualities that blended well with his unusual physical characteristics of height, homeliness, facial expressions that reflected his intense feelings—raised him above the politicians of his day.

Lincoln nevertheless faced the 1864 elections with fear of defeat. His party was divided over the war as well as split by personal ambition. Some leaders who wished to punish Southerners by confiscating their property and imposing long imprisonments met at Cleveland and nominated John C. Frémont as their presidential candidate. Little popular support developed for Frémont, however, and the regular convention in Baltimore easily nominated Lincoln. In gratitude, he left the choice of Vice President to the convention, which, as in 1860, searched for a candidate who could bring loyal Democrats into the party. From a wide selection of men, including Vice President Hannibal Hamlin, the leadership threw its support to Andrew Johnson, formerly the senator from Tennessee, and Johnson won easily on the second ballot. The Democrats chose General McClellan, who advocated a vigorous prosecution of the war and denounced those who would sue for peace at any cost. While the campaign was marred by smears, both Lincoln and McClellan refrained from formal addresses. Lincoln took advantage of opportunities to speak with visiting groups at the White House and was benefited by favorable war reports. The elections gave him a 400,000-vote plurality, an electoral margin of 212 to 21, and victory in every state except Kentucky, Delaware, and New Jersey.

His election, however, did not unite the party. For him these closing days of the war brought out all the tragedy of a divided nation. The best policy he could espouse was one of conciliation: "With malice towards none; with charity for all; with firmness in the right, as God gives us to see the right, let us strive on to finish the work we are in; to bind up the nation's wounds." This spirit of forgiveness he incorporated into a plan for national reconstruction that would permit the disobedient states to return to full membership in the Union when as few as one-tenth of their citizens pledged their loyalty. He promised, further, pardons, civilian government, and help in restoring peace to their territories. Louisiana was among the first of the rebel states to accept his invitation.

The presence of Louisiana's representatives in Washington set off arguments in Congress. Lincoln's party debated the kind of reconstruction that was appropriate, and like him, too, it searched for a constitutional approach that would keep power in federal hands while the task of finishing the war was carried out. Lincoln's veto of a congressional plan, the Wade-Davis bill, to impose conditions for readmission upon the disobedient states, had raised the issue of constitutional amendments to guarantee the black his freedom, and Republicans generally backed the need for amendments. Where Lincoln and some members of his party differed most was in the spirit of the reconstruction. Lincoln seemed less vindictive, more forgiving than congressional leaders who wanted to exclude the disloyal, traitors, and fellow travelers, and to demand an oath from the people before Southerners could resume their privileges of citizenship.

Death of Lincoln

The political argument was serious and crowded out other issues before Congress. But the people were in a festive mood as they celebrated the end of the war and repeatedly called upon the President to appear in public to acknowledge their serenades. Lincoln obliged, joked with the groups, and enjoyed the informality. He promised to say something about the end of the war, but observed that he wanted to make no mistakes because "everything I say, you know, goes into print."

As part of the festivities Lincoln and his wife went to Ford's Theater on April 14, 1865 to witness a performance of *Our American Cousin.* The play was in the third act when a southern sympathizer, John Wilkes Booth, shot the President; Lincoln died the next morning. His sudden death changed the political situation drastically.

Lincoln's death occurred at the worst of times in this crisis of national unity. The hostilities on the battlefields had ended, but the process of bringing loyal and rebel Americans together was only beginning. Lincoln had, in the spirit of forgiveness, offered an immediate opportunity to Southerners to join in planning the future. Some Northerners reacted in bitterness to his policy, but Lincoln put his prestige on the line when he invited Louisiana to rejoin the Union. Conciliation through union had been his objective; his death now challenged that objective, and the new President, Andrew Johnson, had to meet the arguments and criticisms of Congress.

Long after the Civil War had ended its critics have argued over the causes—the Compromise of 1850, "bleeding" Kansas, weak national leadership, and the lack of national responsibility. The Civil War was admittedly a complex bundle of prejudices, misunderstandings, and calculations of profit. Men by the thousands gave their lives or bled in the cause; men by the thousands, too, enjoyed the opportunity to make easy profits. Most critics of the war agree, however, that the nation received a new set of heroes, some pageantry, some folklore, some patriotic songs, but they point to Abraham Lincoln as the founding father of the new national republic.

SUGGESTIONS FOR FURTHER READING

Barney, William L., *The Road to Secession: A New Perspective on the South.* New York, Praeger Publishers, 1972.

Berwanger, Eugene H., *The Frontier Against Slavery.* Urbana, Illinois, University of Illinois Press, 1967.

Blassingame, John W., *The Slave Community: Plantation Life in the Ante-bellum South.* New York, Oxford University Press, 1972.

Cash, W. J., *The Mind of the South.* New York, Vintage Books, Random House, 1961.

Davis, David Brion, *The Slave Power Conspiracy and the Paranoid Style.* Baton Rouge, LA, Louisiana State University Press, 1969.

Donald, David, *The Politics of Reconstruction, 1863-1867*. Baton Rouge, LA, Louisiana State University Press, 1965.

Douglass, Frederick, *Narrative of the Life of Frederick Douglass*. Garden City, New York, Dolphin Books, Doubleday and Company, 1967.

Eaton, Clement, *A History of Southern Confederacy*. New York, Macmillan Company, 1954.

_____, *The Mind of the Old South*. Baton Rouge, LA, Louisiana State University Press, 1967.

Eckenrode, H. J., *Jefferson Davis: President of the Old South*. New York, The Macmillan Company, 1930.

Johannsen, Robert W., *Frontier Politics on the Eve of the Civil War*. Seattle, Washington, University of Washington Press, 1966.

_____, ed., *The Union Crisis, 1850-1865*. New York, The Macmillan Company, 1965.

Nevins, Allan, *The Emergence of Lincoln*, 2 vols. New York, Charles Scribner's Sons, 1950.

_____, *Ordeal of the Union*, 2 vols. New York, Charles Scribner's Sons, 1947.

Nichols, Roy Franklin, *The Disruption of American Democracy*. New York, The Macmillan Company, 1948.

Potter, David M., *The Impending Crisis: 1848-1861*. New York, Harper & Row, 1976.

Pressly, Thomas J., *Americans Interpret Their Civil War*. New York, The Macmillan Company, 1965.

Randall, James G., *Lincoln: The Liberal Statesman*. New York, Dodd, Mead & Company, 1947.

Stampp, Kenneth M., *The Peculiar Institution: Slavery in the Anti-Bellum South*. New York, Random House, 1956.

Stowe, Harriet Beecher, *Uncle Tom's Cabin: or, Life Among the Lowly*. New York, Collier Books, Crowell Collier and Macmillan, 1962.

Tate, Allen, *Stonewall Jackson: The Good Soldier*. Ann Arbor, Michigan, Ann Arbor Paperbacks, University of Michigan Press, 1965.

Thomas, Benjamin P., *Abraham Lincoln*. New York, Modern Library, Random House, 1969.

Van Alstyne, Richard W., "British Diplomacy and the Clayton-Bulwer Treaty, 1850-1860." *Journal of Modern History*, II, 37-47.

Woodward, C. Vann, *Reunion and Reaction*. Garden City, New York, Anchor Books, Doubleday and Company, 1956.

Reconstruction and Rebirth of the South

THE TASK OF 1865, IN LINCOLN'S WORDS, was "to bind up the nation's wounds" and "to do all which may achieve and cherish a just and lasting peace." From the beginning of the war Lincoln had affirmed his belief in the Union, which he felt was older than the states, and the Union was perpetual regardless of the wishes of any state. Since the Constitution said nothing about secession and nothing about disobedient states, he had used force in 1861 to compel obedience. In his eyes, Southerners were rebels and liable to penalties for disobedience and treason. He hoped in 1865, to soften the punishment by returning them quickly to "that proper practical relation" which they had enjoyed before secession. They would be required, however, to ratify the Thirteenth Amendment of the Constitution, which outlawed slavery throughout the United States.

Lincoln had thought of himself as the architect of a restored Union, in the sense that he would guide the rebel states back to full partnership in the government. As commander-in-chief he claimed the power to impose martial law, to grant pardons, and to set tests for loyalty. As his reconstruction program unfolded, he was cautious in his explanations, but firm in his actions. In 1863, he offered the "ten-percent plan" to any group of voters who equalled one-tenth of the 1860 voting population and who took an oath of allegiance, the privilege of organizing a new state government. It would then abolish slavery as a condition for recognition of readmission. He was aware, nonetheless, that Congress considered the return of the South as a proper matter for legislation and wanted to assume responsibility for setting the standards of readmission for the rebel states.

Congressmen were sensitive, and Lincoln, as a political realist and leader, was careful to keep rivalry over policies with Congress within bounds. Like Congress he was well aware of the danger of a unified southern vote, but he counted upon the South to return to Congress as many former Whigs as Democrats. His reconstruction policy, therefore, reflected the sensibilities of Republicans regarding the control of Congress. He was intent, too, to restore peace and prosperity to the old South, to repair the damage of war, and to adopt a reasonable policy toward the black as a free partner in southern life. He was careful in his instructions to southern leaders, but he would let them decide upon the degree of black involvement in the restored governments. Lincoln felt, even in 1865, that the blacks should be persuaded to migrate to Africa.

Lincoln risked much in developing these policies because some Republicans in Congress wished to impose severe punishment upon the South. They accused Lincoln of being "soft," foolish, and wrong-headed, and a few believed in April 1865 that his assassination was a "godsend to the country." Republicans were worried about the political consequences in Congress of southern votes and reflected northern bitterness over the death of 360,200 soldiers in the war. The victory won on the battlefield they did not want lost on the floors of Congress. A rejuvenated Democratic party, however, might easily overturn Republican control of Congress. Since Lincoln's policy might let southern leaders return easily to office, the threat was immediately raised, and Republicans questioned Lincoln's wisdom.

Andrew Johnson's Reconstruction

Lincoln's death brought his Vice President, Andrew Johnson, into office. A war Democrat and a self-made man, the new President rose out of poverty in the South to become a member of Congress, wartime governor of Tennessee, and Vice President of the United States in 1865. He was outspoken in his hatred for southern aristocracy and secessionists and his frequent, violent speeches had embarrassed Lincoln. Most people agreed that he lacked Lincoln's finesse, nobility of language, and sense of destiny, but in office he surprised friend and foe alike by showing a willingness to bind up the nation's wounds. Johnson was above everything else a Democrat, and he looked to Andrew Jackson and Thomas Jefferson for inspiration. He idealized the self-sufficient farmer, liked the rural environment, and favored the states over the national government. He wanted the new South to reflect his interests in agrarianism. Though he admired Lincoln, he did not appreciate the changes occurring in the North, the railroads, manufacturing, and urbanization. The new business classes that were emerging with Republican help frightened him. These people violated his preconceptions of an ideal society.

Johnson's democratic ideas, however, had not made him an emancipationist. Slavery he had defended before the war, and freedom for the black he reluctantly accepted at its end. Johnson had been less concerned with the black than with the power of the old southern aristocracy. Slave ownership widely spread among the yeomen, he had thought, would be a blessing for everyone in the South.

Johnson's reconstruction policy, therefore, had old-time Democratic ideas in it. The states would decide upon policy; the common folk would rise to power; the blacks would be guided to freedom. He formulated his ideas, unfortunately, in the face of known hostility of Congress, which insisted on federal supervision of the South. Instead of calling Congress into session during the mourning period following Lincoln's death in April, he went his own way until the next December. He allowed the southern states to elect officials and reestablish civilian governments, to plan their own reconstruction, and to handle the problems of the freed black. Wanting the South back in the Union as quickly as possible, he overlooked southern policies that were certain to irritate northern opinion, especially that of the abolitionists, who were agitating to make the ex-slave an equal member of American society. He failed to weigh public reaction to southern treatment of the black. How could he justify the fact that not one southern state granted the franchise to the black—not even to educated blacks? That most states formed special black codes to regulate black affairs, codes that appeared to reimpose servitude? Perhaps even more shocking to the sensibilities of the North was the election of many Confederate officers and leaders to public office; some tried to resume their prewar offices in Washington!

Johnson was obviously embarrassed by this southern arrogance. The black codes, in particular, tied blacks to the land, imposed heavy penalties for disobedience, and laid down rules to separate the races. The southern legislatures, furthermore, refused to accept the consequences of defeat. Some voted pensions to Confederate veterans; others refused to repudiate Confederate debts. Johnson's plans for a yeoman-controlled South were ignored. The President had failed when Congress convened in December 1865 and took matters into its own hands.

Congressional Opposition

Seven months after Johnson took office, the Thirty-Ninth Congress assembled. It was divided into four or five uneven groups, the largest of which was the moderate Republicans. Johnson could not count on any warm support because he was a War Democrat, but he had usual support, nonetheless, from those who honored the Presidency and accepted him as head of the party. Believing that once he realized how badly he had missed the mark in his reconstruction policy, Congressmen hoped he would join the Congress in developing another policy. Some Congressmen were willing to wait for presidential direction, long after Congress had organized. As the months passed, however, the moderates became increasingly bewildered by Johnson's uncompromising attitude, and drifted toward the radical group who insisted upon stern measures for southern reconstruction.

These Radicals, often lead by Thaddeus Stevens and Charles Sumner, were a diverse group, but many favored giving blacks economic equality. Stevens wanted to confiscate large landholdings in the South and distribute the land to those without property, blacks and whites alike. He would, likewise, assure suffrage to blacks and equality to all others before the law. A bitter man, his bark and bite often disguised his true opinions, but he was genuinely interested in the welfare of freedmen. His Radical colleagues wanted to preserve the war tariff, retain legislation that favored the North, such as banking and taxes and which promoted the development of railroads. Stevens favored high tariffs too. The Radicals wanted, like Stevens, congressional control of the South, and in various degrees they disliked Johnson for his racism and hostility to business.

By the summer of 1866 these Radicals had a working majority in Congress. They had already prepared for this time of power by joining moderates in an investigation of the South. A committee of fifteen members, formed in December 1865, had formulated a series of policies that were then put into bills. One after another Congress passed, as it developed its own plan of reconstruction, only to have most of them vetoed. It rewrote some bills and passed others over the veto. It strengthened the Freedman's Bureau, then under the direction of Oliver O. Howard, and invested it with multiple duties—to distribute food, help the black find employment, and protect him during the transition period to full citizenship. The Bureau also provided other enormously worthwhile services, like hospital care, educational support (247,333 pupils in 4329 schools), and the distribution of land. To be sure that the black enjoyed these advantages of citizenship, Congress passed over the President's veto a civil rights act and later incorporated many of its major provisions into the proposed Fourteenth Amendment. It defined citizenship and empowered the federal government to guarantee it. The reaction in the South was severely hostile, and ten of the eleven states rejected the amendment (with Johnson's encouragement). Their action undoubtedly alienated both the South and Johnson from moderate opinion in the North.

Reconstruction of South, 1866-1877

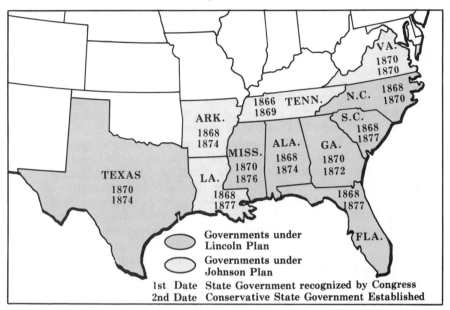

In defending his vetoes, Johnson spoke courageously, but foolishly and incautiously, indulging in name-calling that only drew further fire from Congress. On an election tour in 1866 he blistered his opponents, frequently using inappropriate language and exposing himself to undignified opposition. Newspapers burlesqued his remarks; cartoonists exaggerated his foibles; congressional speakers ridiculed his ideas. These election antics awakened—or more properly created—hatred of the South, associated Johnson with the South, and inspired all sorts of people to spread propaganda. Released northern prisoners told accounts of southern brutality; people who had traveled in the South gave impressions that the people were barbarians, undeserving of compassion, and only the black was worth saving from the poverty of war; publicists asserted that Democrats were in league with ex-Confederates. In facing the assault, Johnson left the impression that he was a madman and drunkard, favored Southerners and Democrats, and was a dissembler and traitor. Many honest and well-meaning people read him out of the Republican party and some even would have liked to remove him from the Presidency.

While congressional elections are often difficult to interpret, the results of those in 1866 were obvious. The Radicals and their friends

won a two-thirds majority in the Congress and swept the elective offices
in most states. Radical leadership now was able to impose federal
standards of citizenship upon the South and, in its arguments with
the President, put the direction of the program in the hands of a small
group of Congressmen, including such luminaries as Stevens of
Pennsylvania and Sumner of Massachusetts.

To put salt into Johnson's election wounds, they urged the "Lame
Duck" Thirty-ninth Congress to move the meeting time of its December
session back to March 1867, in the hope of keeping Johnson from taking
the reins of government. The majority agreed to this illegal maneuver,
and also restricted the President's power as commander-in-chief by
making Ulysses S. Grant the responsible military leader. It passed, too,
the Tenure of Office Act which limited the power of the President over
appointments and removals from office. In effect, the Senate had the last
word on the fate of men whom the President would remove from office.
Congress was especially protecting Edwin Stanton, the Secretary of War,
who had opposed Johnson and whose help was essential in reconstructing the South. Finally, the House of Representatives resolved to inquire
into the conduct of the President, with the intent of impeachment.
The Judiciary Committee launched an investigation of Johnson's
policies that lasted three months, but concluded, in June 1867, that
there were no legitimate charges.

The session ended with the passage of the First Reconstruction
Act. It divided the South into five military districts, imposed martial
law upon the citizens, and ordered the former states to hold constitutional conventions. Most Confederate officeholders were excluded from
participation in the new governments. Before the states could apply
for admission to the Union, they were compelled to extend the franchise to all eligible males who now included blacks and ratify the Fourteenth Amendment. Each district was placed in charge of a military
governor who had at his disposal units of the national army. Congress
thus wiped away what Johnson had done since 1865 and challenged in
addition any lingering ideas of states rights.

Congressional Reconstruction

When the Fortieth Congress met on March 4, 1867, in its extra-
legal session called by the previous Congress, it proceeded to carry
out the work of its predecessor. Supplementary reconstruction acts
were passed one after another. The purpose of these acts, like the
original one, was intended to impose the congressional will upon the
South. In Congress discipline was maintained by unseating several
Democrats. The Senate used its power to confirm presidential appointees by rejecting men whose loyalty was doubtful to the Radical
cause. With these rough measures (as well as others), Congress exercised considerable power inspite of the repeated vetoes of the Presi-

dent, and it moved even against him with new plans for impeachment.

In the South, meantime, the military governors were frequently arbitrary, but they imposed peace on the states, took steps to hold conventions by enrolling the electorate, and ordered some changes in the economies. The new constitutions represented advances over the older ones. Suffrage was broader, the criminal laws more humane, and property laws more protective of debtors.

The new legislatures were dominated by outsiders, carpetbaggers who came South to assist the blacks and take advantage of political opportunities. Thousands of these people directed various organizations, companies, and governmental bureaus. In Republican party politics they were charged with the job of turning blacks into Republicans, separating them from their former masters, and seeing that they were registered as voters. While Republican rule was occasionally corrupt in the states, as legislators deflected funds into public display or into personal luxuries, much progress also was achieved in financing railroad construction, improving roads, rivers, and harbors, and extending public education and social services.

This corruption, wherever it existed, should be measured against the boss rule in New York, the management of western railroads, and the conduct of Indian affairs. It should be measured, too, against the experience of the people serving in the southern legislatures. Most of the men, white and black, were unfamiliar with their tasks; in South Carolina the majority for one session were freed blacks anxious to learn; elsewhere carpetbaggers who had only recently come to the South shared control with blacks and scalawags. Their record was nonetheless comparable to those of other legislatures outside the South, at least in the promotion of progressive reforms.

Congress stood behind the southern legislatures by passing protective laws. It insisted that Amendments 14 and 15 to the Constitution be ratified, guaranteeing civil rights and prohibiting race as a bar to citizenship. It passed enforcement acts beginning in 1870 protecting citizens from such organizations as the Ku Klux Klan. The Klan, a southern subversive organization, had spread widely over the South in answer to the Reconstruction. It used methods of terror and intimidation against blacks and other Republicans and forced the Radicals to employ the army and courts to beat down resistance through the use of prosecutions and fines. The Force Law of 1871 imprisoned and fined hundreds of Klan members and, by 1872, crushed the organization for the time being.

The Impeachment of Johnson and the Election of 1868

As the power of the Radicals mounted, they gained courage to assault directly the President who had been unable to stop Radical legislation with his vetoes. Though his influence with the people had declined sufficiently to encourage the Radicals to make the fight, they awaited an occasion that would give them reasonable grounds. The opportunity to impeach him occurred in February 1868 when he removed Edwin Stanton from the cabinet. Challenged thus, Congress moved to enforce the Tenure of Office Act by removing the President.

In its statement of charges to the Senate, the House listed nothing specific, as would be proper, but made a bold demand for impeachment against Johnson, accusing him of "high crimes and misdemeanors." The House then instructed its committee to press the Senate for a vote of impeachment, promising that charges would be provided as soon as possible. It also instructed the committee to ask the Senate to summon Johnson to answer the charges!

The House managers had some difficulty refining the charges against Johnson. But the charges were incidental to the purpose of the trial, as Sumner described the motivation of Congress: "this proceeding . . . is political in character—before a political body—and with a political object. . . . I have . . . called it one of the last great battles with slavery."

The trial began on March 5 and dragged on until May 26. One by one the charges were presented, and the managers of the impeachment and the defenders of the President spoke long and convincingly in supporting their positions. The President's chief defense attorney, William M. Evarts, presented powerful rebuttals of the charges, accusing the House of attempting to upset the balance of power by removing the President. Evarts regarded the President's removal of Stanton as a constitutional test of the Tenure of Office Act, a test and not a crime. Evarts' appeals surely had impact, for all the final votes, taken from May 16 to 26, were decided by votes of 35 to 16, one fewer than the required number for conviction. Many of those voting for conviction emphasized that the impeachment proceedings should not be considered a trial in the judicial sense. They believed, quite rightly, that Johnson had lost the confidence of his adopted party and should be removed from office. Others, with greater hesitation, wondered if impeachment were the best method for ridding the nation of a poor leader.

Since the President could not be ousted, members of the Republican party turned to the alternative method for getting rid of a President. As their presidential candidate for 1868, they selected the popular military leader Ulysses S. Grant, who had carefully avoided involvement in the impeachment proceedings so that he could remain acceptable to most members of the party. For Vice President they chose Schuyler Colfax, Speaker of the House, a firm supporter of national reconstruction and a widely known former newspaper editor well connected with industry. While the Democrats sympathized with Johnson, they nominated, after much argument, the distinguished Horatio Seymour of New York, a critic of the reconstruction. The campaign was a vigorous affair, and the popular choice was closer than the electoral results (214 to 80) would indicate, but the Republicans reaped the advantages of backing the blacks and having control of the South.

The Grant Administrations

The coming of Grant to office closed the painful contest between Congress and Andrew Johnson, but opened under Grant two terms of unusual corruption in the Presidency. Historians agree that he was an honest man who was abused by his friends. They feel, moreover, that he did not have the fortitude to face up to national problems and dipped at times into partisan politics that "became a national scandal." His administration, they believe, spread corruption to politics on all levels.

For a time after his election Grant's officials exercised firm control of the South. The process of reconstructing governments continued, and state after state qualified for readmission to the Union. In these states some military forces remained, but the occupation was limited to troubled areas. The Klan officers were rounded up and prosecuted, and surveillance was provided for a few ex-Confederate officers. Grant's government, however, also began its withdrawal from the South at this time. It discontinued the supervisory services of the Freedmen's Bureau and returned to the states initiative to guard the liberties of all citizens. Elections were not supervised, and more and more conservatives replaced Republicans in local government. The state courts, also filling with conservative southerners, adopted new attitudes toward the black, and the decisions were backed by the Supreme Court, which sought to reestablish the traditional pattern of federal-state relations.

The attention of Congress to the South became less intense as Sumner, Stevens, and men of their opinion died or retired, and there was a change of ideology and political goals even by those old Radicals who remained in Congress. The new leaders, facing new issues and new crises, were less concerned with the welfare of blacks than with the possibility of personal profit. The Civil War remained in the background, however, and was used for emotional purposes during a campaign or to humble Southerners or to exploit blacks.

The New Spoils System

In the 1870s the spoils of office dominated the minds of many leaders, but political corruption had been evident in a serious form since the 1850s. Political morals seem to be lower in this decade as leaders filled their pockets with bribes. The spread of corruption from the Vice President to congressmen, from state to local officials, amazes modern eyes. Almost everywhere, it seems, politicians found ways of collecting fees. The public became aroused when Congress voted salary increases and two years' back salary, but nearly everyone

A Thomas Nast's Cartoon of Grant's Troubled Presidency
(*University of Southern California*)

in the President's Cabinet, save Secretary of State Hamilton Fish, was exploiting his office for personal gain. The larger scandals surfaced after Grant was reelected in 1872.

Election results showed that the people retained admiration for the President, but he was totally unfit to meet the challenges of office. Bewildered and inexperienced in politics, he hardly knew what he was doing and was badly advised by his Cabinet and friends. He was loyal to his subordinates but blind to their weaknesses. He was willing to hear advice, but unable to select the appropriate course of action. He had little feeling for what the country needed, and events had little significance for him.

Politics reflected the rise of a new order. Since the 1850s railroad construction, textile manufacture, and steel production had made great strides. In 1869 the Union Pacific joined the Central Pacific in Utah to complete the first continental railroad linkage of the East with the Far West. Changes in the northern economy were apparent in the demand for products, the need for investment funds, the marketing of merchandise, and the enlargement of the work force. The South, too, was falling under the domination of new financial and industrial combinations. Its cotton crops went North over railroads rebuilt and controlled by Northerners, and its politicians, accepting gifts of stock and money, resembled their opposite number in the North. The need for agricultural workers rose dramatically, and the black, who was mostly unskilled, drifted into manual labor. Soon he found himself bound by a caste system and kept from schools, professions, and social institutions that would have enabled him to rise.

Such issues as the tariff, the civil service, and the scarcity of money dominated politics. The tariff had often been raised during the war, principally for revenue purposes, but it had remained nearly unchanged since 1865. The prices of commodities were held at unnatural levels, providing high margins of profit and monopoly control of the market at a time when costs of production and wages were falling. Even when tariff reduction was agitated before Congress, only minor adjustments were made. Many politicians, corrupted by bribes, seemed insensitive to the public welfare.

A code of ethics was absolutely necessary to establish standards of public responsibility. Providing a civil service was obviously not enough, when the Senate was full of corporation executives and the House was packed with clients of manufacturers. Favoritism in legislation was detrimental to the public interest, but frequently that interest was not easily understood by the citizen. So it was with the money supply which was inflexible and controlled by those who possessed gold. With the economy expanding, the demand for investment funds increased yearly. Credit resources, however, were inadequate, and the government refused to free the currency from the limitations of a gold support system. Those who had gold could charge premium

Thomas Nast's View of the Democratic Party in 1872.

interest rates and exercise monopoly controls of the market.

These issues introduced into politics new men, who usually publicized their war records yet drew their inspiration and support, as did James G. Blaine and Roscoe Conkling, from corporate and spoils connections. Their attention was absorbed by distribution of offices and contracts and the establishment of a patronage system in their states. Conkling, the son of a well-to-do judge, never accepted bribes himself, but he managed the spoils of the New York custom house with extraordinary skill. As leader of the machine, he bought and sold offices in the market for personal and party power. He regarded reformers as rivals for "office and plunder."

With Conkling as an example, many politicians tried to imitate his success; others reacted with much hostility as they joined a small group of leaders known as the Liberal Republicans who preached reform. They attacked the tariff and exposed corruption in high places and were frightened by what they saw happening to democracy. They wanted the federal government to restore full citizenship to all Southerners. Hoping to separate the government from business and industry, they backed the unusual candidacy of Horace Greeley, the editor of the New York *Tribune*, who was nominated as Democratic standard bearer in 1872. These Republicans for the most part were men of good will, devoted to separate reforms, and willing to sacrifice peace of mind to work for their objectives. But they were not united as a group except in their demand for a democratic and responsible government and were frequently incapable of assessing political realities.

The Election of 1876

Their publicity nonetheless exposed the worse excesses of the Grant administration and made honesty in government a campaign issue in the 1876 elections. The contest between Rutherford B. Hayes of Ohio, who had served three terms as Republican governor, and Samuel J. Tilden of New York, who had prosecuted the Tweed Ring and served as governor of his state, occurred in depression times of heavy unemployment and numerous busines failures which had persisted since the Panic of 1873. The Democrats had won control of the House of Representatives in 1874 and the swing of popular support seemed to be to them. Reform of government became an issue, but both candidates were careful to refrain from attacking the major issues of the day—currency reform, the tariff, and a code of government ethics.

Between the candidates the public had little to choose. Since the tide was favoring the Democrats, the election of Tilden seemed imminent, but this prediction did not allow for the machinations of the parties. Nineteen electoral votes in three southern states and one vote in Oregon created much uncertainty. The Republican party, however, exercised some control in three southern states. Its men brought in electoral votes favoring Hayes, making the total electoral vote 185 to 184. The Democrats, not to be outdone, conducted their own canvass and discovered results favorable to Tilden. The confusing votes, of course, required an arbitrator, and Congress finally set up an electoral commission of fifteen men. It was agreed that there would be equal party representation from the Congress and courts and that the fifteenth member would be David Davis of Illinois, who was not firmly connected with any party. Further complicating these proceedings were disputed ballots from Oregon where the Democratic governor ousted one of the presidential electors, because he was a federal official and chose a Democratic elector who was the next highest in the popular

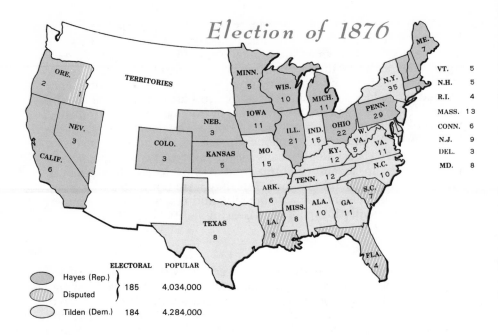

Election of 1876

VT.	5
N.H.	5
R.I.	4
MASS.	13
CONN.	6
N.J.	9
DEL.	3
MD.	8

	ELECTORAL	POPULAR
Hayes (Rep.) }	185	4,034,000
Disputed		
Tilden (Dem.)	184	4,284,000

vote. The election of David Davis to the United States Senate apparently disqualified him as a commissioner.

Although the plurality of 250,000 popular votes for Tilden seemed to indicate that the Commission should select him as the next President, Davis's replacement broke the deadlock in favor of the Republicans, and in the Commission's report Hayes was given the Presidency by a margin of one electoral vote. Northern Democrats threatened a filibuster, thus a delay in acceptance of the Commission's report, and some leaders even talked of a renewal of the Civil War. To avoid this serious probability, Northern Republicans and Southern Democrats arranged a secret conference, in which their leaders bartered and compromised. Apparently the Democrats went along with Hayes's election, while the Republicans agreed to permit the South to manage its own relations with the blacks.

The Reconstruction Southern Style

Some historians have made this compromise of 1877 the equal of those in 1820 and 1850. It is difficult to prove, however, what was actually compromised, except that troops were to be withdrawn from South Carolina and Louisiana when Hayes became President. Undoubtedly, too, the Republicans were expected to moderate attacks on the Democrats as the bloody plotters of civil conflict and to lessen their support of blacks in the South. Hayes complied by naming Southerners to posts in his government and asking help of Congress in providing funds for internal improvements. Other understandings may have been reached, but they are not readily apparent.

What is certain about the years after 1877 is the gradual return of white rule to the South. Blacks were not only pushed out of office, but were forced into an inferior position. Imposed upon them was a peculiar system of servitude, a caste system, that was not slavery but similar in spirit. Formed by racial bias it depended upon prejudicial laws and bigoted social customs. The guiding principle was to establish and maintain white supremacy.

Servitude of this new kind developed fast, and laws followed giving solid reality to what was informally happening. Segregation of churches, schools, and public services became the rule by 1890 and the political parties invented various kinds of devices to keep blacks from participation. Literacy requirements determined voters; gerrymandering divided black power; and the appointments to office were placed in the hands of the governor or legislature so as to by-pass local interests. Even so, no southern state had a uniform code regulating black behavior. The only common device used among the states, and basic to the enforcement of inferiority, was the poll tax. The financial burden it imposed was too heavy for most blacks to bear. Moreover, literacy tests were employed, as were registration technicalities, which limited black participation in politics.

The economic side of southern life contributed to the caste system. Since fertile land was owned by the white population, blacks (and poor whites) were used as day laborers and sharecroppers, or in tenancy. With labor and land abundant, the owners of land set their rate of profit from cotton and sugar crops, and left the blacks often very little return, at times not even enough for subsistence. The blacks fell, as a result, into deep poverty as debtors. Sometimes, in seeking relief, they turned to theft, but the states reacted with harsh measures; not the least brutal was the convict-lease system. Convict services were purchased from the state, and the owners of service used convict labor for rail construction, mining, and field agriculture. Contractors provided the convicts with clothing, housing, and food, and in exchange for these necessities blacks were exploited with little governmental protection. The whip came into common use, and recalcitrant convicts were also "softened up" by being thrown into pits and chained, given bread and water diets, and shackled into work gangs.

The impact of black bondage upon the South was visible in the creation of a two-class society, in the development of the Democratic party as the voice of the dominant white, and in the persistence of an uneasy relationship between the races. The equilibrium was main-

Black Population, 1790-1880

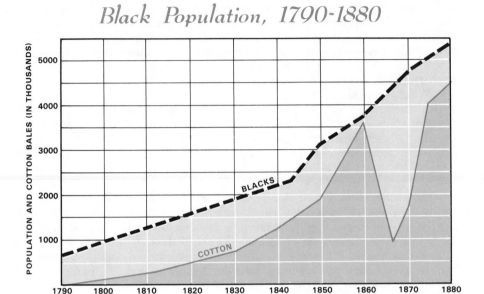

tained, unfortunately, with beatings, convict labor, and racial bias.

The New South: Industry

The decades after 1865 brought great changes in southern life. The devastation of war was quickly removed, and railroads were put into operation, then expanded and modernized. Nearly 30,000 miles of new lines were added by 1890, and rail lines in Texas and Arkansas opened new routes as transcontinental links. Southern railroads carried primarily agricultural products—cotton, tobacco, and sugar —but in the late 1870s their loads included also the raw materials from a broad range of extractive industries and finished products of textile mills that were being built in Tennessee, Georgia, and South Carolina. By 1900 the South had over four million spindles in operation, with expansion planned for millions more.

This new economic effort gradually changed the face of the land. Cities were rising, attracting immigrants as laborers, and providing urban institutions like schools and colleges, banks and insurance companies, small shops and handicraft industries. The new textile mills, often located in these cities, used indigent white laborers who had left the farm for town and city jobs. These mills were attractive to business people because of cheap labor and favorable laws—sometimes no laws at all regulated the hours of the employment of women and children. Laborers lived often in the mill towns, paying high rents for miserable housing and receiving wages barely sufficient to provide subsistence.

The New South: The Literature of Reconciliation

These harsh conditions of life, however, should not hide the beauty and charm of the South. The quiet tempo of life was reflected in the relaxed, rural atmosphere that permeated folk ways. The prevailing chivalry was captured by authors of the day in their tales of the post- and ante-bellum South. Men such as Thomas Nelson Page wove some reality into their stories, but their magnolia-scented plots lifted the commonplace into a charming, imaginative way of life. Whites were often gentle folk, while blacks were usually childlike adults, smiling and happy as they went about their daily chores. Page's use of black dialect in *Marse Chan* added realism to his dialogues, and his daring depiction of northern soldiers falling in love with southern belles helped foster reconciliation between sections.

The work of Henry W. Grady, moreover, hailed the coming of a new South of industry and progress. In his editorials in the Atlanta *Constitution,* he labeled himself the pensman of the reformed South, advocating diversity of industry and agriculture. He proclaimed the death of the old South in these words: "There is a South of union and freedom . . . thank God, [it] is living, breathing, growing every hour."

Grady was popular with Northerners who applauded his efforts to bring union and stability to the nation. They were ready to accept his solution for the black problem—a paternalism of whites over blacks —and the Democratic party leadership welcomed anything that minimized black rights as an issue. The United States Supreme Court, too, had given its support to the southern caste system and state interpretation of citizenship. In the Slaughter-House cases (1873) it had placed the protection of citizenship in the hands of the states. Years later, in 1896, it accepted the southern practice of separate but equal to the use of accommodations on trains. The rule spread to most forms of southern race relations in the coming fifty years.

Some voices were raised against southern (and northern) bias toward the blacks. Henry Cabot Lodge of Massachusetts introduced a bill in the House of Representatives setting up federal inspection of voting registration. His efforts failed, even though he won Republican endorsement of his ideas in the 1892 platform of the party. Senator Henry W. Blair of New Hampshire, in the 1880s, introduced legislation to assist schools in meeting the problems of illiteracy, but he, too, was unsuccessful. Another spokesman for justice was Booker T. Washington, the black leader who was named head of Tuskegee Institute in 1881. He spent a generation developing industrial training for blacks, and a lifetime trying to determine the future direction of blacks in American society. His fame eventually gave him platforms on which to voice the needs of blacks in the South. His gentle language and cautious program for black improvement was deceptive to racists, because he preached peace and patience. Looking into the future, however, he offered blacks the longterm objective of full integration into American society.

"Reconstruction" is a poor word to describe what happened to the South between 1865 and 1900. Lincoln planned to return the defeated South to full partnership to the union with as little punishment as possible. Johnson had a similar plan. Both Presidents would have permitted the South to devise schemes for black education and governmental participation without much federal interference. Congress, however, wanted an assurance of black involvement in the South, and it compelled the southern states to write constitutions, broaden the franchise, and accept blacks in the new governments. Much reorganization of the southern governments occurred, but Congress, in the 1870s, lost interest in following through on its program. In the breach the South developed a caste system for blacks that ground them into poverty and inferiority.

SUGGESTIONS FOR FURTHER READING

Abbott, Martin, *The Freedmen's Bureau in South Carolina, 1865-1872.* Chapel Hill, N.C., University of North Carolina Press, 1967.

Berry, Mary Frances, *Military Necessity and Civil Rights Policy: Black Citizenship and the Constitution, 1861-1868.* Port Washington, N.Y., Kennikat Press, 1977.

Belz, Herman, *Reconstructing the Union: Theory and Policy During the Civil War.* Ithaca, New York, Cornell University Press, 1969.

Brock, W. R., *An American Crisis: Congress and Reconstruction, 1865-1867.* New York, St. Martin's Press, 1963.

Cash, W. J., *The Mind of the South.* New York, Vintage Books, Random House, 1961.

Donald, David, *The Politics of Reconstruction, 1863-1867.* Baton Rouge, La., Louisiana State University Press, 1965.

Franklin, John Hope, *Reconstruction After the Civil War.* Chicago, Ill., University of Chicago Press, 1961.

McKitrick, Eric L., *Andrew Johnson and Reconstruction.* Chicago, Illinois, University of Chicago Press, 1960.

Patrick, Rembert W., *The Reconstruction of the Nation.* New York, Oxford University Press, 1967.

Perham, Michael, *Reunion Without Compromise: The South and*

Reconstruction, 1865-1868. Cambridge, England, Cambridge University Press, 1973.

Pike, James Sheperd, *Republicanism and the American Negro, 1850-1882*. Durham, N.C., Duke University Press, 1976.

Pressly, Thomas J., *Americans Interpret Their Civil War*. New York, The Macmillan Company, 1965.

Silby, Joel H., *A Respectable Minority: The Democratic Party in the Civil War, 1860-1868*. New York, W. W. Norton & Company, 1974.

Stampp, Kenneth M., *The Era of Reconstruction: 1865-1877*. New York, Random House, 1967.

Tindall, George Brown, *The Persistent Tradition in New South Politics*. Baton Rouge, La., Louisiana State University Press, 1975.

Trefouse, Hans L., *Impeachment of a President: Andrew Jackson, the Blacks, and Reconstruction*. Knoxville, Tenn., University of Tennessee Press, 1975.

————, *The Radical Republicans: Lincoln's Vanguard for Racial Justice*. New York, Alfred A. Knopf, 1969.

Woodward, C. Vann, *Reunion and Reaction*. Garden City, New York, Anchor Books, Doubleday & Company, 1956.

————, *Origins of the New South, 1877-1913*: Vol. 9, *A History of the South*. Baton Rouge, La., Louisiana State University Press, 1951.

The American Republic

Appendix

When, in the Course of human events, it becomes necessary for one people to dissolve the political bands which have connected them with another, and to assume, among the Powers of the earth, the separate and equal station to which the Laws of Nature and of Nature's God entitle them, a decent respect to the opinions of mankind requires that they should declare the causes which impel them to the separation.

We hold these truths to be self-evident, that all men are created equal, that they are endowed by their Creator with certain unalienable Rights, that among these, are Life, Liberty, and the pursuit of Happiness. That, to secure these rights, Governments are instituted among Men, deriving their just Powers from the consent of the governed. That, whenever any form of Government becomes destructive of these ends, it is the Right of the People to alter or to abolish it, and to institute new Government, laying its foundation on such Principles, and organizing its Powers in such form, as to them shall seem most likely to effect their Safety and Happiness. Prudence, indeed, will dictate that Governments long established should not be changed for light and transient causes; and, accordingly, all experience hath shewn, that mankind are more disposed to suffer, while evils are sufferable, than to right themselves by abolishing the forms to which they are accustomed. But, when a long train of abuses and usurpations, pursuing invariably the same Object, evinces a design to reduce them under absolute Despotism, it is their right, it is their duty, to throw off such Government, and to provide new Guards for their future Security. Such has been the patient sufferance of these Colonies; and such is now the necessity which constrains them to alter their former Systems of Government. The history of the present King of Great Britain is a history of repeated injuries and usurpations, all having in direct object the es-tablishment of an absolute Tyranny over these States. To prove this, let Facts be submitted to a candid world.

He has refused his Assent to Laws the most wholesome and necessary for the public good.

He has forbidden his Governors to pass Laws of immediate and pressing importance, unless suspended in their operation till his Assent should be obtained; and when so suspended, he has utterly neglected to attend to them.

He has refused to pass other Laws for the accommodation of large districts of People, unless those People would relinquish the right of Representation in the legislature; a right inestimable to them and formidable to tyrants only.

He has called together legislative bodies at places unusual, un-comfortable, and distant from the depository of their Public Records, for the sole Purpose of fatiguing them into compliance with his measures.

He has dissolved Representative Houses repeatedly, for opposing, with manly firmness, his invasions on the rights of the People.

He has refused for a long time, after such dissolutions, to cause others to be elected; whereby the Legislative Powers, incapable of Annihilation, have returned to the People at large for their exercise; the State remaining in the mean time exposed to all the dangers of invasion from without, and convulsions within.

He has endeavoured to prevent the Population of these States; for that purpose obstructing the Laws for Naturalization of Foreigners; refusing to pass others to encourage their migrations hither, and raising the conditions of new Appropriations of Lands.

He has obstructed the Administration of Justice, by refusing his Assent to Laws for establishing Judiciary Powers.

He has made Judges dependent on his Will alone, for the tenure of their offices, and the amount and payment of their salaries.

He has erected a multitude of New Officers, and sent hither swarms of Officers to harrass our People, and eat out their substance.

He has kept among us, in times of Peace, Standing Armies, without the Consent of our legislatures.

He has affected to render the Military independent of and superior to the Civil Power.

He has combined with others to subject us to a jurisdiction foreign to our constitution, and unacknowledged by our laws; giving his Assent to their Acts of pretended Legislation:

For quartering large bodies of armed troops among us:

For protecting them, by a mock Trial, from Punishment for any Murders which they should commit on the Inhabitants of these States:

For cutting off our Trade with all parts of the world:

For imposing Taxes on us without our Consent:

For depriving us, in many cases, of the benefits of Trial by Jury:

For transporting us beyond Seas to be tried for pretended offences:

For abolishing the free System of English Laws in a neighbouring province, establishing therein an Arbitrary government, and enlarging its Boundaries, so as to render it at once an example and fit instrument for introducing the same absolute rule into these Colonies:

For taking away our Charters, abolishing our most valuable Laws, and altering fundamentally the Forms of our Governments:

For suspending our own Legislatures, and declaring themselves invested with Power to legislate for us in all cases whatsoever.

He has abdicated Government here, by declaring us out of his protection, and waging War against us.

He has plundered our seas, ravaged our Coasts, burnt our towns, and destroyed the Lives of our People.

He is at this time transporting large Armies of foreign Mercenaries to compleat the works of death, desolation and tyranny, already begun with circumstances of Cruelty and perfidy scarcely paralleled in the most barbarous ages, and totally unworthy the Head of a civilized nation.

He has constrained our fellow Citizens, taken Captive on the high Seas, to bear Arms against their Country, to become the executioners of their friends and Brethren, or to fall themselves by their Hands.

He has excited domestic insurrections amongst us, and has endeavoured to bring on the inhabitants of our frontiers, the merciless Indian Savages, whose known rule of warfare, is an undistinguished destruction of all ages, sexes and conditions.

In every stage of these Oppressions, We have Petitioned for Redress, in the most humble terms: Our repeated Petitions, have been answered only by repeated injury. A Prince, whose character is thus marked by every act which may define a Tyrant, is unfit to be the ruler of a free People.

Nor have We been wanting in attentions to our British brethren. We have warned them from time to time of attempts by their legislature to extend an unwarrantable jurisdiction over us. We have reminded them of the circumstances of our emigration and settlement here. We have appealed to their native justice and magnanimity, and we have conjured them by the ties of our common kindred, to disavow these usurpations, which, would inevitably interrupt our connexions and correspondence. They too have been deaf to the voice of justice and consanguinity. We must, therefore, acquiesce in the necessity, which denounces our Separation, and hold them, as we hold the rest of mankind, Enemies in war, in Peace Friends.

WE, THEREFORE, the Representatives of the UNITED STATES OF AMERICA, in GENERAL CONGRESS assembled, appealing to the Supreme Judge of the World for the rectitude of our intentions, DO, in the Name, and by Authority of the good People of these Colonies, solemnly PUBLISH and DECLARE, That these United Colonies are, and of Right, ought to be FREE AND INDEPENDENT STATES; that they are Absolved from all Allegiance to the British Crown, and that all political connexion between them and the State of Great Britain, is and ought to be totally dissolved; and that, as FREE and INDEPENDENT STATES, they have full Power to levy War, conclude Peace, contract Alliances, establish Commerce, and to do all other Acts and Things which INDEPENDENT STATES may of right do. AND for the support of this Declaration, with a firm reliance on the protection of divine Providence, we mutually pledge to each other our Lives, our Fortunes, and our sacred Honour.

The Constitution of the United States of America

We the people of the United States, in Order to form a more perfect Union, establish Justice, insure domestic Tranquility, provide for the common defence, promote the general Welfare, and secure the Blessings of Liberty to ourselves and our Posterity, do ordain and establish this Constitution for the United States of America.

Article I

Section 1. All legislative Powers herein granted shall be vested in a Congress of the United States, which shall consist of a Senate and House of Representatives.

Section 2. The House of Representatives shall be composed of Members chosen every second Year by the People of the several States, and the Electors in each State shall have the Qualifications requisite for Electors of the most numerous Branch of the State Legislature.

No Person shall be a Representative who shall not have attained to the Age of twenty-five Years, and been seven Years a Citizen of the United States, and who shall not, when elected, be an Inhabitant of that state in which he shall be chosen.

[Representatives and direct Taxes shall be apportioned among the several States which may be included within this Union, according to their respective Numbers, which shall be determined by adding to the whole Number of free Persons, including those bound to Service for a Term of Years, and excluding Indians not taxed, three fifths of all other Persons.][1] The actual Enumeration shall be made within three Years after the first Meeting of the Congress of the United States, and within every subsequent Term of ten Years, in such Manner as they shall by Law direct. The Number of Representatives shall not exceed one for every thirty Thousand, but each State shall have at Least one Representative; and until such enumeration shall be made, the State of New Hampshire shall be entitled to chuse three, Massachusetts eight, Rhode-Island and Providence Plantations one, Connecticut five, New-York six, New Jersey four, Pennsylvania eight, Delaware one, Maryland six, Virginia ten, North Carolina five, South Carolina five, and Georgia three.

When vacancies happen in the Representation from any State, the Executive Authority thereof shall issue Writs of Election to fill such Vacancies.

The House of Representatives shall chuse their Speaker and other Officers; and shall have

the sole Power of Impeachment.

Section 3. The Senate of the United States shall be composed of two Senators from each State, [chosen by the Legislature thereof,][2] for six Years; and each Senator shall have one Vote.

Immediately after they shall be assembled in Consequence of the first Election, they shall be divided as equally as may be into three Classes. The Seats of the Senators of the first Class shall be vacated at the Expiration of the second Year, of the Second Class at the Expiration of the fourth Year, and of the third Class at the Expiration of the sixth Year, so that one-third may be chosen every second year; [and if Vacancies happen by Resignation, or otherwise, during the Recess of the Legislature of any State, the Executive thereof may make temporary Appointments until the next Meeting of the Legislature, which shall then fill such Vacancies].[3]

No Person shall be a Senator who shall not have attained to the Age of thirty Years, and been nine Years a Citizen of the United States, and who shall not, when elected, be an Inhabitant of that State in which he shall be chosen.

The Vice-President of the United States shall be President of the Senate, but shall have no vote, unless they be equally divided.

The Senate shall chuse their other Officers, and also a President pro tempore, in the absence of the Vice-President, or when he shall exercise the Office of the President of the United States.

The Senate shall have the sole

Power to try all Impeachments. When sitting for that purpose, they shall be on Oath or Affirmation. When the President of the United States is tried, the Chief Justice shall preside. And no person shall be convicted without the Concurrence of two thirds of the Members present.

Judgment in Cases of Impeachment shall not extend further than to removal from Office, and disqualification to hold and enjoy any Office of honor, Trust, or Profit under the United States: but the Party convicted shall nevertheless be liable and subject to Indictment, Trial, Judgment, and Punishment, according to Law.

Section 4. The Times, Places and Manner of holding Elections for Senators and Representatives, shall be prescribed in each state by the Legislature thereof; but the Congress may at any time by Law make or alter such Regulations, except as to the Places of Chusing Senators.

The Congress shall assemble at least once in every Year, and such Meeting shall [be on the first Monday in December,]⁴ unless they shall by Law appoint a different Day.

Section 5. Each House shall be the Judge of the Elections, Returns and Qualifications of its own Members, and a Majority of each shall constitute a Quorum to do Business; but a smaller number may adjourn from day to day, and may be authorized to compel the Attendance of absent Members, in such Manner, and under such Penalties, as each House may provide.

Each House may determine the Rules of its Proceedings, punish its Members for disorderly Behavior, and, with the Concurrence of two thirds, expel a Member.

Each House shall keep a Journal of its Proceedings, and from time to time publish the same, excepting such Parts as may in their Judgment require Secrecy; and the Yeas and Nays of the Members of either House on any question shall, at the Desire of one fifth of those Present, be entered on the Journal.

Neither House, during the Session of Congress, shall, without the Consent of the other, adjourn for more than three days, nor to any other Place than that in which the two Houses shall be sitting.

Section 6. The Senators and Representatives shall receive a Compensation for their Services, to be ascertained by Law, and paid out of the Treasury of the United States. They shall in all Cases, except Treason, Felony, and Breach of the Peace, be privileged from Arrest during their Attendance at the Session of their respective Houses, and in going to and returning from the same; and for any Speech or Debate in either House, they shall not be questioned in any other Place.

No Senator or Representative shall, during the Time for which he was elected, be appointed to any civil Office under the Authority of the United States, which shall have been created, or the Emoluments whereof shall have been increased, during such time; and no Person holding any Office under the United States shall be a Member of either House during his continuance in Office.

Section 7. All Bills for raising Revenue shall originate in the House of Representatives; but the Senate may propose or concur with Amendments as on other bills.

Every Bill which shall have passed the House of Representatives and the Senate, shall, before it become a Law, be presented to the President of the United States; If he approve he shall sign it, but if not he shall return it, with his Objections, to that House in which it shall have originated, who shall enter the Objections at large on their Journal, and proceed to reconsider it. If after such Reconsideration two thirds of that House shall agree to pass the bill, it shall be sent, together with the objections, to the other House, by which it shall likewise be reconsidered, and if approved by two thirds of that House, it shall become a Law. But in all such Cases the Votes of both Houses shall be determined by Yeas and Nays, and the Names of the Persons voting for and against the Bill shall be entered on the Journal of each House respectively. If any Bill shall not be returned by the President within ten Days (Sundays excepted) after it shall have been presented to him, the Same shall be a Law, in like Manner as if he had signed it, unless the Congress by their Adjournment prevent its Return, in which Case it shall not be a Law.

Every Order, Resolution, or Vote to which the Concurrence of the Senate and House of Representa-

tives may be necessary (except on a question of Adjournment) shall be presented to the President of the United States; and before the Same shall take Effect, shall be approved by him, or being disapproved by him, shall be repassed by two thirds of the Senate and House of Representatives, according to the Rules and Limitations prescribed in the Case of a Bill.

Section 8. The Congress shall have Power To lay and collect Taxes, Duties, Imposts and Excises, to pay the Debts and provide for the common Defence and general Welfare of the United States; but all Duties, Imposts and Excises shall be uniform throughout the United States;

To borrow money on the credit of the United States;

To regulate Commerce with foreign Nations, and among the several States, and with the Indian Tribes;

To establish an uniform Rule of Naturalization, and uniform Laws on the subject of Bankruptcies throughout the United States;

To coin Money, regulate the Value thereof, and of foreign Coin, and fix the Standard of Weights and Measures;

To provide for the Punishment of counterfeiting the Securities and current Coin of the United States;

To establish Post Offices and post Roads;

To promote the Progress of Science and useful Arts, by securing for limited Times to Authors and Inventors the exclusive Right to their respective Writings and Discoveries;

To constitute Tribunals inferior to the Supreme Court;

To define and punish Piracies and Felonies committed on the high Seas, and offenses against the Law of Nations;

To declare War, grant Letters of Marque and Reprisal, and make Rules concerning Captures on Land and Water;

To raise and support Armies, but no Appropriation of Money to that Use shall be for a longer Term than two Years;

To provide and maintain a Navy;

To make Rules for the Government and Regulation of the land and naval forces;

To provide for calling forth the Militia to execute the Laws of the Union, suppress Insurrections and repel Invasions;

To provide for organizing, arming, and disciplining the Militia, and for governing such Part of them as may be employed in the Service of the United States, reserving to the States respectively, the Appointment of the Officers, and the Authority of training the Militia according to the discipline prescribed by Congress;

To exercise exclusive Legislation in all Cases whatsoever, over such District (not exceeding ten Miles square) as may, by Cession of particular States, and the acceptance of Congress, become the Seat of the Government of the United States, and to exercise like Authority over all Places purchased by the Consent of the Legislature of the State in which the Same shall be, for the

Erection of Forts, Magazines, Arsenals, dock-Yards, and other needful Buildings;—And

To make all Laws which shall be necessary and proper for carrying into Execution the foregoing Powers, and all other Powers vested by this Constitution in the Government of the United States, or in any Department or Officer thereof.

Section 9. The Migration or Importation of such Persons as any of the States now existing shall think proper to admit shall not be prohibited by the Congress prior to the Year one thousand eight hundred and eight, but a tax or duty may be imposed on such Importation, not exceeding ten dollars for each Person.

The privilege of the Writ of Habeas Corpus shall not be suspended, unless when in Cases of Rebellion or Invasion the public Safety may require it.

No Bill of Attainder or ex post facto Law shall be passed.

[No capitation, or other direct, Tax shall be laid unless in Proportion to the Census or Enumeration herein before directed to be taken.][5]

No Tax or Duty shall be laid on Articles exported from any State.

No Preference shall be given by any Regulation of Revenue to the Ports of one State over those of another: nor shall Vessels bound to, or from, one State, be obliged to enter, clear, or pay Duties in another.

No Money shall be drawn from the Treasury, but in Consequence of Appropriations made by Law; and a regular Statement and Account of the Receipts and Expenditures of all public Money shall be published from time to time.

No Title of Nobility shall be granted by the United States: And no Person holding any Office of Profit or Trust under them, shall, without the Consent of the Congress, accept of any present, Emolument, Office, or Title, of any kind whatever, from any King, Prince, or foreign State.

Section 10. No State shall enter into any Treaty, Alliance, or Confederation; grant Letters of Marque and Reprisal; coin Money; emit Bills of Credit; make any Thing but gold and silver Coin a Tender in Payment of Debts; pass any Bill of Attainder, ex post facto Law, or Law impairing the Obligation of Contracts, or grant any Title of Nobility.

No State shall, without the Consent of the Congress, lay any Imposts or Duties on Imports or Exports, except what may be absolutely necessary for executing its inspection Laws: and the net Produce of all Duties and Imposts, laid by any State or Imports or Exports, shall be for the use of the Treasury of the United States; and all such Laws shall be subject to the Revision and Control of the Congress.

No State shall, without the Consent of Congress, lay any duty of Tonnage, keep Troops, or Ships of War in time of Peace, enter into any Agreement or Compact with another State, or with a foreign Power, or engage in War, unless actually invaded, or in such imminent Danger as will not admit of delay.

Article II

Section 1. The executive Power shall be vested in a President of the United States of America. He shall hold his Office during the Term of four years, and, together with the Vice-President, chosen for the same Term, be elected, as follows:

Each State shall appoint, in such Manner as the Legislature thereof may direct, a Number of Electors, equal to the whole Number of Senators and Representatives to which the State may be entitled in the Congress: but no Senator or Representative, or Person holding an Office of Trust or Profit under the United States, shall be appointed an Elector.

[The Electors shall meet in their respective States, and vote by Ballot for two persons, of whom one at least shall not be an Inhabitant of the same State with themselves. And they shall make a List of all the Persons voted for, and of the Number of Votes for each; which List they shall sign and certify, and transmit sealed to the Seat of the Government of the United States, directed to the President of the Senate. The President of the Senate shall, in the Presence of the Senate and House of Representatives, open all the Certificates, and the Votes shall then be counted. The Person having the greatest Number of Votes shall be the President, if such Number be a Majority of the whole Number of Electors appointed; and if there be more than one who have such Majority, and have an equal Number of Votes, then the House of Representatives shall immediately chuse by Ballot one of them for President; and if no Person have a Majority, then from the five highest on the List the said House shall in like Manner chuse the President. But in chusing the President, the Votes shall be taken by States, the Representation from each State having one Vote; a quorum for this Purpose shall consist of a Member or Members from two-thirds of the States, and a Majority of all the States shall be necessary to a Choice. In every Case, after the Choice of the President, the Person having the greatest Number of Votes of the Electors shall be the Vice-President. But if there should remain two or more who have equal votes, the Senate shall chuse from them by Ballot the Vice-President.]⁶

The Congress may determine the Time of chusing the Electors, and the Day on which they shall give their Votes; which Day shall be the same throughout the United States.

No person except a natural-born Citizen, or a Citizen of the United States, at the time of the Adoption of this Constitution, shall be eligible to the Office of President; neither shall any Person be eligible to the Office who shall not have attained to the Age of thirty-five years, and been fourteen Years a Resident within the United States.

[In Case of the Removal of the President from Office, or of his Death, Resignation, or Inability to discharge the Powers and Duties of the said Office, the same shall devolve on the Vice-President, and the Congress may by Law provide for the Case of Removal, Death, Resignation, or Inability, both of the President and Vice-President, declaring what Officer shall then act as President, and such Officer shall act accordingly, until the disability be removed, or a President shall be elected.]⁷

The President shall, at stated Times, receive for his Services a Compensation, which shall neither be increased nor diminished during the Period for which he shall have been elected, and he shall not receive within that Period any other Emolument from the United States, or any of them.

Before he enter on the execution of his Office, he shall take the following Oath or Affirmation:—"I do solemnly swear (or affirm) that I will faithfully execute the Office of President of the United States, and will, to the best of my Ability, preserve, protect, and defend the Constitution of the United States."

Section 2. The President shall be Commander in Chief of the Army and Navy of the United States, and of the Militia of the several States, when called into the actual Service of the United States; he may require the Opinion, in writing, of the principal Officer in each of the executive Departments, upon any subject relating to the Duties of their respective Offices, and he shall have Power to Grant Reprieves and Pardons for Offenses against the United States, except in Cases of Impeachment.

He shall have Power, by and with the Advice and Consent of the Senate, to make Treaties, provided two thirds of the Senators present concur; and he shall nominate, and by and with the Advice and Consent of the Senate, shall appoint Ambassadors, other public Ministers and Consuls, Judges of the supreme Court, and all other Officers of the United States, whose Appointments are not herein otherwise provided for, and which shall be established by Law: but the Congress may by Law vest the Appointment of such inferior Officers, as they think proper, in the President alone, in the Courts of Law, or in the Heads of Departments.

The President shall have Power to fill up all Vacancies that may happen during the Recess of the Senate, by granting Commissions which shall expire at the End of their next Session.

Section 3. He shall from time to time give to the Congress Information of the State of the Union, and recommend to their Consideration such Measures as he shall judge necessary and expedient; he may, on extraordinary occasions, convene both Houses, or either of them, and in Case of Disagreement between them, with respect to the Time of Adjournment, he may adjourn them to such Time as he shall think proper; he shall receive Ambassadors and other public Ministers; he shall take Care that the Laws be faithfully executed, and shall Commission all the Officers of the United States.

Section 4. The President, Vice-President and all civil Officers of the United States, shall be removed from Office on Impeach-

ment for, and Conviction of, Treason, Bribery, or other high Crimes and Misdemeanors.

Article III

Section 1. The judicial Power of the United States, shall be vested in one supreme Court, and in such inferior Courts as the Congress may from time to time ordain and establish. The Judges, both of the supreme and inferior Courts, shall hold their Offices during good Behaviour, and shall, at stated Times, receive for their Services, a Compensation, which shall not be diminished during their Continuance in Office.

Section 2. The judicial Power shall extend to all Cases, in Law and Equity, arising under this Constitution, the Laws of the United States, and treaties made, or which shall be made, under their Authority;—to all Cases affecting ambassadors, other public ministers and consuls;—to all cases of admiralty and maritime Jurisdiction;—to Controversies to which the United States shall be a Party;—to Controversies between two or more States;—[between a State and Citizens of another State;][8]—between Citizens of different States,—between Citizens of the same State claiming Lands under Grants of different States, and between a State, or the Citizens thereof, and foreign States, Citizens or Subjects.

In all Cases affecting Ambassadors, other public Ministers and Consuls, and those in which a State shall be Party, the supreme Court shall have original Jurisdiction. In all the other Cases before mentioned, the supreme Court shall have appellate Jurisdiction, both as to Law and Fact, with such Exceptions, and under such Regulations as the Congress shall make.

The trial of all Crimes, except in Cases of Impeachment, shall be by Jury; and such Trial shall be held in the State where the said Crimes shall have been committed; but when not committed within any State, the Trial shall be at such Place or Places as the Congress may by Law have directed.

Section 3. Treason against the United States, shall consist only in levying War against them, or in adhering to their Enemies, giving them Aid and Comfort. No Person shall be convicted of Treason unless on the Testimony of two Witnesses to the same overt Act, or on Confession in open Court.

The Congress shall have power to declare the Punishment of Treason, but no Attainder of Treason shall work Corruption of Blood, or Forfeiture except during the Life of the Person attainted.

Article IV

Section 1. Full Faith and Credit shall be given in each State to the public Acts, Records, and judicial Proceedings of every other State. And the Congress may by general Laws prescribe the Manner in which such Acts, Records and Proceedings shall be proved, and the Effect thereof.

Section 2. The Citizens of each State shall be entitled to all Privileges and Immunities of Citizens in the several States.

A Person charged in any State with Treason, Felony, or other Crime, who shall flee from Justice, and be found in another State, shall on demand of the executive Authority of the State from which he fled, be delivered up, to be removed to the State having Jurisdiction of the crime.

[No Person held to Service or Labour in one State, under the Laws thereof, escaping into another, shall, in Consequence of any Law or Regulation therein, be discharged from such Service or Labour, but shall be delivered up on Claim of the Party to whom such Service or Labour may be due.][9]

Section 3. New States may be admitted by the Congress into this Union; but no new State shall be formed or erected within the Jurisdiction of any other State; nor any State be formed by the Junction of two or more States, or parts of States, without the Consent of the Legislatures of the States concerned as well as of the Congress.

The Congress shall have Power to dispose of and make all needful Rules and Regulations respecting the Territory or other Property belonging to the United States; and nothing in this Constitution shall be so construed as to Prejudice any Claims of the United States, or of any particular State.

Section 4. The United States shall guarantee to every State in this Union a Republican Form of Government, and shall protect each of them against Invasion; and on Application of the Legislature, or of the Executive (when the Legislature cannot be convened) against domestic Violence.

Article V

The Congress, whenever two-thirds of both Houses shall deem it necessary, shall propose Amendments to this Constitution, or, on the Application of the Legislatures of two-thirds of the several States, shall call a Convention for proposing Amendments, which, in either Case, shall be valid to all Intents and Purposes, as part of this Constitution, when ratified by the Legislatures of three-fourths of the several States, or by Conventions in three-fourths thereof, as the one or the other Mode of Ratification may be proposed by the Congress; Provided that no Amendment which may be made prior to the Year One thousand eight hundred and eight shall in any Manner affect the first and fourth Clauses in the Ninth Section of the first Article; and that no State, without its Consent, shall be deprived of its equal Suffrage in the Senate.

Article VI

All Debts contracted and Engagements entered into, before the Adoption of this Constitution, shall be as valid against the United States under this Constitution, as under the Confederation.

This Constitution, and the Laws of the United States which shall be made in Pursuance thereof; and all Treaties made, or which shall be made, under the Authority of the United States, shall be the supreme Law of the Land; and the Judges in every State shall be bound thereby, any Thing in the Constitution or Laws of any State to the Contrary notwithstanding.

The Senators and Representatives before mentioned, and the Members of the several State Legislatures, and all executive and judicial Officers, both of the United States and of the several States, shall be bound by Oath or Affirmation to support this Constitution; but no religious Test shall ever be required as a qualification to any Office or public Trust under the United States.

Article VII

The Ratification of the Conventions of nine States shall be sufficient for the Establishment of this Constitution between the States so ratifying the same.

Done in Convention by the Unanimous Consent of the States present the Seventeenth Day of September in the Year of our Lord one thousand seven hundred and Eighty seven, and of the Independence of the United States of America the Twelfth. In Witness whereof We have hereunto subscribed our Names.

Articles in Addition to, and Amendment of, the Constitution of the Untied States of America, Proposed by Congress, and Ratified by the Legislatures of the Several States, Pursuant to the Fifth Article of the Original Constitution.

Amendment I[10]

Congress shall make no law respecting an establishment of religion, or prohibiting the free exercise thereof; or abridging the freedom of speech, or of the press; or the right of the people peaceably to assemble, and to petition the Government for a redress of grievances.

Amendment II

A well regulated Militia, being necessary to the security of a free State, the right of the people to keep and bear Arms shall not be infringed.

Amendment III

No Soldier shall, in time of peace, be quartered in any house, without the consent of the Owner, nor in time of war, but in a manner to be prescribed by law.

Amendment IV

The right of the people to be secure in their persons, houses, papers, and effects, against unreasonable searches and seizures, shall not be violated, and no Warrants shall issue, but upon probable cause, supported by Oath or affirmation, and particularly describing the place to be searched, and the persons or things to be seized.

Amendment V

No person shall be held to answer for a capital or otherwise infamous crime, unless on a presentment or indictment of a Grand Jury, except in cases arising in the land or naval forces, or in the Militia, when in actual service in time of War or public danger; nor shall any person be subject for the same offence to be twice put in jeopardy of life or limb; nor shall be compelled in any criminal case to be a witness against himself, nor be deprived of life, liberty, or property, without due process of law; nor shall private property be taken for public use, without just compensation.

Amendment VI

In all criminal prosecutions, the accused shall enjoy the right to a speedy and public trial, by an impartial jury of the State and district wherein the crime shall have been committed, which district shall have been previously ascertained by law, and to be informed of the nature and cause of the accusation; to be confronted with the witnesses against him; to have compulsory process for obtaining witnesses in his favor, and to have the Assistance of Counsel for his defence.

Amendment VII

In suits at common law, where the value in controversy shall exceed twenty dollars, the right of trial by jury shall be preserved, and no fact tried by a jury, shall be otherwise reexamined in any Court of the United States, than according to the rules of the common law.

Amendment VIII

Excessive bail shall not be required, nor excessive fines imposed, nor cruel and unusual punishments inflicted.

Amendment IX

The enumeration in the Constitution, of certain rights, shall not be construed to deny or disparage others retained by the people.

Amendment X

The powers not delegated to the United States by the Constitution, nor prohibited by it to the States, are reserved to the States respectively, or to the people.

Amendment XI (1798)[11]

The Judicial power of the United States shall not be construed to extend to any suit in law or equity, commenced or prosecuted against one of the United States by Citizens of another State, or by Citizens or Subjects of any Foreign State.

Amendment XII (1804)

The Electors shall meet in their respective States and vote by ballot for President and Vice-President, one of whom, at least, shall not be an inhabitant of the same State with themselves; they shall name in their ballots the person voted for as President, and in distinct ballots the person voted for as Vice-President, and they shall make distinct lists of all persons voted for as President, and of all persons voted for as Vice-President, and of the number of votes for each, which lists they shall sign and certify, and transmit sealed to the seat of the government of the United States, directed to the President of the Senate;—The President of the Senate shall, in the presence of the Senate and House of Representatives, open all the certificates and the votes shall then be counted;—The person having the greatest number of votes for President, shall be the President, if such number be a majority of the whole number of Electors appointed; and if no person have such majority, then from the persons having the highest numbers not exceeding three on the list of those voted for as President, the House of Representatives shall choose immediately, by ballot, the President. But in choosing the President, the votes shall be taken by states, the representation from each state having one vote; a quorum for this purpose shall consist of a member or members from two-thirds of the states, and a majority of all the states shall be necessary to a choice. [And if the House of Representatives shall not choose a President whenever the right of choice shall devolve upon them, before the fourth day of March next following, then the Vice-President shall act as President, as in the case of the death or other constitutional disability of the President.][12]—The person having the greatest number of votes as Vice-President, shall be the Vice-President, if such number be a majority of the whole number of Electors appointed, and if no person have a majority, then from the two highest numbers on the list, the Senate shall choose the Vice-President; a quorum for the purpose shall consist of two-thirds of the whole number of Senators, and a majority of the whole number shall be necessary to a choice. But no person constitutionally ineligible to the office of President shall be eligible to that of Vice-President of the United States.

Amendment XIII (1865)

Section 1. Neither slavery nor involuntary servitude, except as a punishment for crime whereof the party shall have been duly convicted, shall exist within the United States, or any place subject to their jurisdiction.

Section 2. Congress shall have power to enforce this article by appropriate legislation.

Amendment XIV (1868)

Section 1. All persons born or naturalized in the United States, and subject to the jurisdiction thereof, are citizens of the United States and of the State wherein they reside. No State shall make or enforce any law which shall abridge the privileges or immunities of citizens of the United States; nor shall any State deprive any person of life, liberty, or property, without due process of law; nor deny to any person within its jurisdiction the equal protection of the laws.

Section 2. Representatives shall be apportioned among the several States according to their respective numbers, counting the whole number of persons in each State, excluding Indians not taxed. But when the right to vote at any election for the choice of electors for President and Vice-President of the United States, Representatives in Congress, the Executive and Judicial officers of a State, or the members of the Legislature thereof, is denied to any of the male inhabitants of such State, being twenty-one years of age, and citizens of the United States, or in any way abridged, except for participation in rebellion, or other crime, the basis of representation therein shall be reduced in the proportion which the number of such male citizens shall bear to the whole number of male citizens twenty-one years of age in such State.

Section 3. No person shall be a Senator or Representative in Congress, or elector of President and Vice-President, or hold any office, civil or military, under the United States, or under any State, who, having previously taken an oath, as a member of Congress, or as an officer of the United States, or as a member of any State legislature, or as an executive or judicial officer of any State, to support the Constitution of the United States, shall have engaged in insurrection or rebellion against the same, or given aid or comfort to the enemies thereof. But Congress may by a vote of two-thirds of each House, remove such disability.

Section 4. The validity of the public debt of the United States, authorized by law, including debts incurred for payment of pensions and bounties for services in suppressing insurrection or rebellion, shall not be questioned.

But neither the United States nor any State shall assume or pay any debt or obligation incurred in aid of insurrection or rebellion against the United States, or any claim for the loss or emancipation of any slave; but all such debts, obligations, and claims shall be held illegal and void.

Section 5. The Congress shall have the power to enforce, by appropriate legislation, the provisions of this article.

Amendment XV (1870)

Section 1. The right of citizens of the United States to vote shall not be denied or abridged by the United States or by any State on account of race, color, or previous condition of servitude—

Section 2. The Congress shall have power to enforce this article by appropriate legislation.

Amendment XVI (1913)

The Congress shall have power to lay and collect taxes on incomes, from whatever source derived, without apportionment among the several States, and without regard to any census or enumeration.

Amendment XVII (1913)

The Senate of the United States shall be composed of two Senators from each State, elected by the people thereof, for six years; and each Senator shall have one vote. The electors in each State shall have the qualifications requisite for electors of the most numerous branch of the State legislatures.

When vacancies happen in the representation of any State in the Senate, the executive authority of such State shall issue writs of election to fill such vacancies: Provided, That the legislature of any State may empower the executive thereof to make temporary appointments until the people fill the vacancies by election as the legislature may direct.

This amendment shall not be so construed as to affect the election or term of any Senator chosen before it becomes valid as part of the Constitution.

Amendment XVIII (1919)[13]

Section 1. After one year from the ratification of this article the manufacture, sale, or transportation of intoxicating liquors within, the importation thereof into, or the exportation thereof from the United States and all territory subject to the jurisdiction thereof for beverage purposes is hereby prohibited.

Section 2. The Congress and the several States shall have concurrent power to enforce this article by appropriate legislation.

Section 3. This article shall be inoperative unless it shall have been ratified as an amendment to the Constitution by the legislatures of the several States, as provided in the Constitution, within seven years from the date of the submission hereof to the States by the Congress.

Amendment XIX (1920)

The right of citizens of the United States to vote shall not be denied or abridged by the United States or by any State on account of sex.

Congress shall have power to enforce this article by appropriate legislation.

Amendment XX (1933)

Section 1. The terms of the President and Vice-President shall end at noon on the 20th day of January, and the terms of Senators and Representatives at noon on the 3d day of January, of the years in which such terms would have ended if this article had not been ratified; and the terms of their successors shall then begin.

Section 2. The Congress shall assemble at least once in every year, and such meeting shall begin at noon on the 3d day of January, unless they shall by law appoint a different day.

Section 3. If, at the time fixed for the beginning of the term of the President, the President elect shall have died, the Vice-President elect shall become President. If a President shall not have been chosen before the time fixed for the beginning of his term, or if the President elect shall have failed to qualify, then the Vice-President elect shall act as President until a President shall have qualified; and the Congress may by law provide for the case wherein neither a President elect nor a Vice-President elect shall have qualified, declaring who shall then act as President, or the manner in which one who is to act shall be selected, and such person shall act accordingly until a President or Vice-President shall have qualified.

Section 4. The Congress may by law provide for the case of the death of any of the persons from whom the House of Representatives may choose a President whenever the right of choice shall have devolved upon them, and for the case of the death of any of the persons from whom the Senate may choose a Vice-President whenever the right of choice shall have devolved upon them.

Section 5. Sections 1 and 2 shall take effect on the 15th day of October following the ratification of this article.

Section 6. This article shall be inoperative unless it shall have been ratified as an amendment to the Constitution by the legislatures of three-fourths of'the several States within seven years from the date of its submission.

Amendment XXI (1933)

Section 1. The eighteenth article of amendment to the Constitution of the United States is hereby repealed.

Section 2. The transportation or importation into any State, Territory, or possession of the United States for delivery or use therein of intoxicating liquors, in violation of the laws thereof, is hereby prohibited.

Section 3. This article shall be inoperative unless it shall have been ratified as an amendment to the Constitution by conventions in the several States, as provided in the Constitution, within seven years from the date of the submission hereof to the States by the Congress.

Amendment XXII (1951)

No person shall be elected to the office of the President more than twice, and no person who has held the office of President, or acted as President, for more than two years of a term to which some other person was elected President shall be elected to the office of the President more than once.

But this Article shall not apply to any person holding the office of President when this Article was proposed by the Congress, and shall not prevent any person who may be holding the office of President, or acting as President, during the term within which this Article becomes operative from holding the office of President or acting as President during the remainder of such term.

Amendment XXIII (1961)

Section 1. The District constituting the seat of Government of the United States shall appoint in such manner as the Congress may direct:

A number of electors of President and Vice-President equal to the whole number of Senators and Representatives in Congress to which the District would be entitled if it were a State, but in no event more than the least populous State; they shall be in addition to those appointed by the States, but they shall be considered, for the purposes of the election of President and Vice-President, to be electors appointed by the State; and they shall meet in the District and perform such duties as provide

by the twelfth article of amendment.

Section 2. The Congress shall have power to enforce this article by appropriate legislation.

Amendment XXIV (1964)

Section 1. The right of citizens of the United States to vote in any primary or other election for President or Vice-President, for electors for President or Vice-President, or for Senator or Representative in Congress, shall not be denied or abridged by the United States or any State by reason of failure to pay any poll tax or other tax.

Section 2. The Congress shall have power to enforce this article by appropriate legislation.

Amendment XXV (1967)

Section 1. In case of the removal of the President from office or of his death or resignation, the Vice-President shall become President.

Section 2. Whenever there is a vacancy in the office of the Vice-President, the President shall nominate a Vice-President who shall take office upon confirmation by a majority vote of both Houses of Congress.

Section 3. Whenever the President transmits to the President pro tempore of the Senate and the Speaker of the House of Representatives his written declaration that he is unable to discharge the powers and duties of his office, and until he transmits to them a written declaration to the contrary, such powers and duties shall be discharged by the Vice-President as Acting President.

Section 4. Whether the Vice-President and a majority of either the principal officers of the executive department or of such other body as Congress may by law provide, transmit to the President pro tempore of the Senate and the Speaker of the House of Representatives their written declaration that the President is unable to discharge the powers and duties of his office, the Vice-President shall immediately assume the powers and duties of the office as Acting President.

Thereafter, when the President transmits to the President pro tempore of the Senate and the Speaker of the House of Representatives his written declaration that no inability exists, he shall resume the powers and duties of his office unless the Vice-President and a majority of either the principal officers of the executive department or of such other body as Congress may by law provide, transmit within four days to the President pro tempore of the Senate and the Speaker of the House of Representatives their written declaration that the President is unable to discharge the powers and duties of his office. Thereupon Congress shall decide the issue, assembling within forty-eight hours for that purpose if not in session. If the Congress, within twenty-one days after receipt of the latter written declaration, or, if Congress is not in session, within twenty-one days after Congress is required to assemble, determines by two-thirds vote of both Houses that the President is unable to discharge the powers and duties of his office, the Vice-President shall continue to discharge the same as Acting President; otherwise, the President shall resume the powers and duties of his office.

Amendment XXVI (1971)

Section 1. The right of citizens of the United States, who are eighteen years of age or older, to vote shall not be denied or abridged by the United States or by any State on account of age.

Section 2. The Congress shall have power to enforce this article by appropriate legislation.

[1] Modified by the Fourteenth and Sixteenth amendments.

[2] Superseded by the Seventeenth Amendment.

[3] Modified by the Seventeenth Amendment.

[4] Superseded by the Twentieth Amendment.

[5] Modified by the Sixteenth Amendment.

[6] Superseded by the Twelfth Amendment.

[7] Modified by the Twenty-fifth Amendment.

[8] Modified by the Eleventh Amendment.

[9] Superseded by the Thirteenth Amendment.

[10] The first ten amendments were passed by Congress September 25, 1789. They were ratified by three-fourths of the states December 15, 1791.

[11] Date of ratification.

[12] Superseded by the Twentieth Amendment.

[13] Repealed by the Twenty-first Amendment.

Admission of States

(See p. 66 for order in which the original thirteen entered the Union.)

Order of Admission	State	Date of Admission
14	Vermont	March 4, 1791
15	Kentucky	June 1, 1792
16	Tennessee	June 1, 1796
17	Ohio	March 1, 1803
18	Louisiana	April 30, 1812
19	Indiana	December 11, 1816
20	Mississippi	December 10, 1817
21	Illinois	December 3, 1818
22	Alabama	December 14, 1819
23	Maine	March 15, 1820
24	Missouri	August 10, 1821
25	Arkansas	June 15, 1836
26	Michigan	January 26, 1837
27	Florida	March 3, 1845
28	Texas	December 29, 1845
29	Iowa	December 28, 1846
30	Wisconsin	May 29, 1848
31	California	September 9, 1850

32	Minnesota	May 11, 1858
33	Oregon	February 14, 1859
34	Kansas	January 29, 1861
35	West Virginia	June 20, 1863
36	Nevada	October 31, 1864
37	Nebraska	March 1, 1867
38	Colorado	August 1, 1876
39	North Dakota	November 2, 1889
40	South Dakota	November 2, 1889
41	Montana	November 8, 1889
42	Washington	November 11, 1889
43	Idaho	July 3, 1890
44	Wyoming	July 10, 1890
45	Utah	January 4, 1896
46	Oklahoma	November 16, 1907
47	New Mexico	January 6, 1912
48	Arizona	February 14, 1912
49	Alaska	January 3, 1959
50	Hawaii	August 21, 1959

Presidents & Vice-Presidents

Term	President	Vice-President
1789-1793	George Washington	John Adams
1793-1797	George Washington	John Adams
1797-1801	John Adams	Thomas Jefferson
1801-1805	Thomas Jefferson	Aaron Burr
1805-1809	Thomas Jefferson	George Clinton
1809-1813	James Madison	George Clinton (d. 1812)
1813-1817	James Madison	Elbridge Gerry (d. 1814)
1817-1821	James Monroe	Daniel D. Tompkins
1821-1825	James Monroe	Daniel D. Tompkins
1825-1829	John Quincy Adams	John C. Calhoun
1829-1833	Andrew Jackson	John C. Calhoun (resigned 1832)
1833-1837	Andrew Jackson	Martin Van Buren
1837-1841	Martin Van Buren	Richard M. Johnson
1841-1845	William H. Harrison (d. 1841)	John Tyler
	John Tyler	
1845-1849	James K. Polk	George M. Dallas
1849-1853	Zachary Taylor (d. 1850)	Milliard Fillmore
	Milliard Fillmore	
1853-1857	Franklin Pierce	William R. D. King (d. 1853)
1857-1861	James Buchanan	John C. Breckinridge
1861-1865	Abraham Lincoln	Hannibal Hamlin

1865-1869	Abraham Lincoln (d. 1865) Andrew Johnson	Andrew Johnson
1869-1873	Ulysses S. Grant	Schuyler Colfax
1873-1877	Ulysses S. Grant	Henry Wilson (d. 1875)
1877-1881	Rutherford B. Hayes	William A. Wheeler
1881-1885	James A. Garfield (d. 1881) Chester A. Arthur	Chester A. Arthur
1885-1889	Grover Cleveland	Thomas A. Hendricks (d. 1885)
1889-1893	Benjamin Harrison	Levi P. Morton
1893-1897	Grover Cleveland	Adlai E. Stevenson
1897-1901	William McKinley	Garret A. Hobart (d. 1899)
1901-1905	William McKinley (d. 1901) Theodore Roosevelt	Theodore Roosevelt
1905-1909	Theodore Roosevelt	Charles W. Fairbanks
1909-1913	William H. Taft	James S. Sherman (d. 1912)
1913-1917	Woodrow Wilson	Thomas R. Marshall
1917-1921	Woodrow Wilson	Thomas R. Marshall
1921-1925	Warren G. Harding (d. 1923) Calvin Coolidge	Calvin Coolidge
1925-1929	Calvin Coolidge	Charles G. Dawes
1929-1933	Herbert C. Hoover	Charles Curtis
1933-1937	Franklin D. Roosevelt	John N. Garner
1937-1941	Franklin D. Roosevelt	John N. Garner
1941-1945	Franklin D. Roosevelt	Henry A. Wallace
1945-1949	Franklin D. Roosevelt (d. 1945) Harry S Truman	Harry S Truman
1949-1953	Harry S Truman	Alben W. Barkley
1953-1957	Dwight D. Eisenhower	Richard M. Nixon
1957-1961	Dwight D. Eisenhower	Richard M. Nixon
1961-1965	John F. Kennedy (d. 1963) Lyndon B. Johnson	Lyndon B. Johnson
1965-1969	Lyndon B. Johnson	Hubert H. Humphrey
1969-1973	Richard M. Nixon	Spiro T. Agnew
1973-1977	Richard M. Nixon (resigned 1974) Gerald R. Ford	Spiro T. Agnew (resigned 1973) Gerald R. Ford (appointed 1973)
1977-	James E. Carter, Jr.	Walter Mondale

Presidential Elections*

Election	Candidates	Parties	Popular Vote	Electoral Vote
1789	GEORGE WASHINGTON	No party designations		69
	John Adams			34
	Minor Candidates			35
1792	GEORGE WASHINGTON	No party designations		132
	John Adams			77
	George Clinton			50
	Minor Candidates			5
1796	JOHN ADAMS	Federalist		71
	Thomas Jefferson	Democratic-Republican		68
	Thomas Pinckney	Federalist		59
	Aaron Burr	Democratic-Republican		30
	Minor Candidates			48
1800	THOMAS JEFFERSON	Democratic-Republican		73
	Aaron Burr	Democratic-Republican		73
	John Adams	Federalist		65
	Charles C. Pinckney	Federalist		64
	John Jay	Federalist		1

*Candidates receiving less than 1% of the popular vote are omitted. Before the 12th Amendment (1804) the Electoral College voted for two presidential candidates, and the runner-up became Vice President. Basic figures are taken from *Historical Statistics of the United States, 1789-1945*, pp. 288-290.

Election	Candidates	Parties	Popular Vote	Electoral Vote
1804	THOMAS JEFFERSON	Democratic-Republican		162
	Charles C. Pinckney	Federalist		14
1808	JAMES MADISON	Democratic-Republican		122
	Charles C. Pinckney	Federalist		47
	George Clinton	Democratic-Republican		6
1812	JAMES MADISON	Democratic-Republican		128
	DeWitt Clinton	Federalist		89
1816	JAMES MONROE	Democratic-Republican		183
	Rufus King	Federalist		34
1820	JAMES MONROE	Democratic-Republican		231
	John Q. Adams	Independent Republican		1
1824	JOHN Q. ADAMS (Min.)*	Democratic-Republican	108,740	84
	Andrew Jackson	Democratic-Republican	153,544	99
	William H. Crawford	Democratic-Republican	46,618	41
	Henry Clay	Democratic-Republican	47,136	37
1828	ANDREW JACKSON	Democratic	647,286	178
	John Q. Adams	National Republican	508,064	83
1832	ANDREW JACKSON	Democratic	687,502	219
	Henry Clay	National Republican	530,189	49
	William Wirt	Anti-Masonic	33,108	7
	John Floyd	National Republican		11
1836	MARTIN VAN BUREN	Democratic	762,678	170
	William H. Harrison	Whig		73
	Hugh L. White	Whig	736,656	26
	Daniel Webster	Whig		14
	W. P. Mangum	Whig		11
1840	WILLIAM H. HARRISON	Whig	1,275,016	234
	Martin Van Buren	Democratic	1,129,102	60
1844	JAMES K. POLK (Min.)*	Democratic	1,337,243	170
	Henry Clay	Whig	1,299,062	105
	James G. Birney	Liberty	62,300	
1848	ZACHARY TAYLOR (Min.)*	Whig	1,360,099	163
	Lewis Cass	Democratic	1,220,544	127
	Martin Van Buren	Free Soil	291,263	
1852	FRANKLIN PIERCE	Democratic	1,601,274	254
	Winfield Scott	Whig	1,386,580	42
	John P. Hale	Free Soil	155,825	
1856	JAMES BUCHANAN (Min.)*	Democratic	1,838,169	174
	John C. Frémont	Republican	1,341,264	114
	Millard Fillmore	American	874,534	8
1860	ABRAHAM LINCOLN (Min.)*	Republican	1,866,452	180
	Stephen A. Douglas	Democratic	1,375,157	12
	John C. Breckinridge	Democratic	847,953	72
	John Bell	Constitutional Union	590,631	39
1864	ABRAHAM LINCOLN	Union	2,213,665	212
	George B. McClellan	Democratic	1,802,237	21
1868	ULYSSES S. GRANT	Republican	3,012,833	214
	Horatio Seymour	Democratic	2,703,249	80
1872	ULYSSES S. GRANT	Republican	3,597,132	286
	Horace Greeley	Democratic and Liberal Republican	2,834,125	66

*"Min." indicates minority President—one receiving less than 50% of all popular votes.

Election	Candidates	Parties	Popular Vote	Electoral Vote
1876	RUTHERFORD B. HAYES (Min.)*	Republican	4,036,298	185
	Samuel J. Tilden	Democratic	4,300,590	184
1880	JAMES A. GARFIELD (Min.)*	Republican	4,454,416	214
	Winfield S. Hancock	Democratic	4,444,952	155
	James B. Weaver	Greenback-Labor	308,578	
1884	GROVER CLEVELAND (Min.)*	Democratic	4,874,986	219
	James G. Blaine	Republican	4,851,981	182
	Benjamin F. Butler	Greenback-Labor	175,370	
	John P. St. John	Prohibition	150,369	
1888	BENJAMIN HARRISON (Min.)*	Republican	5,439,853	233
	Grover Cleveland	Democratic	5,540,309	168
	Clinton B. Fisk	Prohibition	249,506	
	Anson J. Streeter	Union Labor	146,935	
1892	GROVER CLEVELAND (Min.)*	Democratic	5,556,918	277
	Benjamin Harrison	Republican	5,176,108	145
	James B. Weaver	People's	1,041,028	22
	John Bidwell	Prohibition	264,133	
1896	WILLIAM McKINLEY	Republican	7,104,779	271
	William J. Bryan	Democratic	6,502,925	176
1900	WILLIAM McKINLEY	Republican	7,292,530	292
	William J. Bryan	Democratic; Populist	6,358,133	155
	John C. Woolley	Prohibition	208,914	
1904	THEODORE ROOSEVELT	Republican	7,628,834	336
	Alton B. Parker	Democratic	5,084,401	140
	Eugene V. Debs	Socialist	402,460	
	Silas C. Swallow	Prohibition	258,536	
1908	WILLIAM H. TAFT	Republican	7,678,908	321
	William J. Bryan	Democratic	6,409,104	162
	Eugene V. Debs	Socialist	420,793	
	Eugene W. Chafin	Prohibition	253,840	
1912	WOODROW WILSON (Min.)*	Democratic	6,286,820	435
	Theodore Roosevelt	Progressive	4,126,020	88
	William H. Taft	Republican	3,483,922	8
	Eugene V. Debs	Socialist	900,672	
	Eugene W. Chafin	Prohibition	206,275	
1916	WOODROW WILSON (Min.)*	Democratic	9,129,606	277
	Charles E. Hughes	Republican	8,538,221	254
	A. L. Benson	Socialist	585,113	
	J. F. Hanly	Prohibition	220,506	
1920	WARREN G. HARDING	Republican	16,152,200	404
	James M. Cox	Democratic	9,147,353	127
	Eugene V. Debs	Socialist	919,799	
	P. P. Christensen	Farmer-Labor	265,411	
1924	CALVIN COOLIDGE	Republican	15,725,016	382
	John W. Davis	Democratic	8,386,503	136
	Robert M. LaFollette	Progressive	4,822,856	13
1928	HERBERT C. HOOVER	Republican	21,391,381	444
	Alfred E. Smith	Democratic	15,016,443	87
1932	FRANKLIN D. ROOSEVELT	Democratic	22,821,857	472
	Herbert C. Hoover	Republican	15,761,841	59
	Norman Thomas	Socialist	881,951	

*"Min." indicates minority President—one receiving less than 50% of all popular votes.

Election	Candidates	Parties	Popular Vote	Electoral Vote
1936	FRANKLIN D. ROOSEVELT	Democratic	27,751,597	523
	Alfred M. Landon	Republican	16,679,583	8
	William Lemke	Union, etc.	882,479	
1940	FRANKLIN D. ROOSEVELT	Democratic	27,244,160	449
	Wendell L. Wilkie	Republican	22,305,198	82
1944	FRANKLIN D. ROOSEVELT	Democratic	25,602,504	432
	Thomas F. Dewey	Republican	22,006,285	99
1948	HARRY S TRUMAN (Min.)*	Democratic	24,105,695	303
	Thomas E. Dewey	Republican	21,969,170	189
	J. Strom Thurmond	States' Rights Democratic	1,169,021	39
	Henry A. Wallace	Progressive	1,156,103	
1952	DWIGHT D. EISENHOWER	Republican	33,778,963	442
	Adlai E. Stevenson	Democratic	27,314,992	89
1956	DWIGHT D. EISENHOWER	Republican	35,590,472	457
	Adlai E. Stevenson	Democratic	26,022,752	73
1960	JOHN F. KENNEDY (Min.)*	Democratic	34,221,531	303
	Richard M. Nixon	Republican	34,107,474	219
1964	LYNDON B. JOHNSON	Democratic	43,126,233	486
	Barry M. Goldwater	Republican	27,174,989	52
1968	RICHARD M. NIXON (Min.)*	Republican	31,783,783	301
	Hubert H. Humphrey	Democratic	31,271,839	191
	George C. Wallace	American Independent	9,899,557	46
1972	RICHARD M. NIXON	Republican	47,168,963	520
	George S. McGovern	Democratic	29,169,615	17
1976	JAMES E. CARTER, JR.	Democratic	40,827,292	297
	Gerald R. Ford	Republican	39,146,157	240

*"Min." indicates minority President—one receiving less than 50% of all popular votes.

Justices of the Supreme Court

Name (Chief Justices in Italics)	Service (Terms)	(Years)
John Jay (N.Y.)	1789-1795	6
John Rutledge (S.C.)	1789-1791	2
William Cushing (Mass.)	1789-1810	21
James Wilson (Pa.)	1789-1798	9
John Blair (Va.)	1789-1796	7
James Iredell (N.C.)	1790-1799	9
Thomas Johnson (Md.)	1792-1793	½
William Paterson (N.J.)	1793-1806	13
John Rutledge (S.C.)*	1795-1795	
Samuel Chase (Md.)	1796-1811	15
Oliver Ellsworth (Conn.)	1796-1800	4
Bushrod Washington (Va.)	1798-1829	31
Alfred Moore (N.C.)	1800-1804	4
John Marshall (Va.)	1801-1835	34
William Johnson (S.C.)	1804-1834	30
Brock Livingston (N.Y.)	1806-1823	17
Thomas Todd (Ky.)	1807-1826	19
Joseph Story (Mass.)	1811-1845	34
Gabriel Duval (Md.)	1811-1835	24
Smith Thompson (N.Y.)	1823-1843	20

Name (Chief Justices in Italics)	Service (Terms)	(Years)
Robert Trimble (Ky.)	1826-1828	2
John McLean (Ohio)	1829-1861	32
Henry Baldwin (Pa.)	1830-1844	14
James M. Wayne (Ga.)	1835-1867	32
Roger B. Taney (Md.)	1836-1864	28
Philip P. Barbour (Va.)	1836-1841	5
John Catron (Tenn.)	1837-1865	28
John McKinley (Ala.)	1837-1852	15
Peter V. Daniel (Va.)	1841-1860	19
Samuel Nelson (N.Y.)	1845-1872	27
Levi Woodbury (N.H.)	1845-1851	6
Robert C. Grier (Pa.)	1846-1870	24
Benjamin R. Curtis (Mass.)	1851-1857	6
John A. Campbell (Ala.)	1853-1861	8
Nathan Clifford (Maine)	1858-1881	23
Noah H. Swayne (Ohio)	1862-1861	19
Samuel F. Miller (Iowa)	1862-1890	28
David Davis (Ill.)	1862-1877	15
Stephen J. Field (Calif.)	1863-1897	34
Salmon P. Chase (Ohio)	1864-1873	9
William Strong (Pa.)	1870-1880	10
Joseph P. Bradley (N.J.)	1870-1892	22
Ward Hunt (N.Y.)	1872-1882	10
Morrison R. Waite (Ohio)	1874-1888	14
John M. Harlan (Ky.)	1877-1911	34
William B. Woods (Ga.)	1880-1887	7
Stanley Matthews (Ohio)	1881-1889	8
Horace Gray (Mass.)	1881-1902	21
Samuel Blatchford (N.Y.)	1882-1893	11
Lucius Q. Lamar (Miss.)	1888-1893	5
Melville W. Fuller (Ill.)	1888-1910	22
David J. Brewer (Kans.)	1889-1910	21
Henry B. Brown (Mich.)	1890-1906	16
George Shiras, Jr. (Pa.)	1892-1903	11
Howell E. Jackson (Tenn.)	1893-1895	2
Edward D. White (La.)	1894-1910	16
Rufus W. Peckham (N.Y.)	1895-1909	14
Joseph McKenna (Calif.)	1898-1925	27
Oliver W. Holmes (Mass.)	1902-1932	30
William R. Day (Ohio)	1903-1922	19
William H. Moody (Mass.)	1906-1910	4
Horace H. Lurton (Tenn.)	1910-1914	4
Edward D. White (La.)	1910-1921	11
Charles E. Hughes (N.Y.)	1910-1916	6
Willis Van Devanter (Wyo.)	1911-1937	26
Joseph R. Lamar (Ga.)	1911-1916	5
Mahlon Pitney (N.J.)	1912-1922	10
James C. McReynolds (Tenn.)	1914-1941	27
Louis D. Brandeis (Mass.)	1916-1939	23
John H. Clarke (Ohio)	1916-1922	6
William H. Taft (Conn.)	1921-1930	9
George Sutherland (Utah)	1922-1938	16

Name	Service	
(Chief Justices in Italics)	(Terms)	(Years)
Pierce Butler (Minn.)	1923-1939	16
Edward T. Sanford (Tenn.)	1923-1930	7
Harlan F. Stone (N.Y.)	1925-1941	16
Charles E. Hughes (N.Y.)	1930-1941	11
Owen J. Roberts (Pa.)	1930-1945	15
Benjamin N. Cardozo (N.Y.)	1932-1938	6
Hugo L. Black (Ala.)	1937-1971	34
Stanley F. Reed (Ky.)	1938-1957	19
Felix Frankfurter (Mass.)	1939-1962	23
William O. Douglas (Conn.)	1939-1975	36
Frank Murphy (Mich.)	1940-1949	9
Harlan F. Stone (N.Y.)	1941-1946	5
James F. Byrnes (S.C.)	1941-1942	1
Robert H. Jackson (N.Y.)	1941-1954	13
Wiley B. Rutledge (Iowa)	1943-1949	6
Harold H. Burton (Ohio)	1945-1958	13
Fred M. Vinson (Ky.)	1946-1953	7
Tom C. Clark (Tex.)	1949-1967	18
Sherman Minton (Ind.)	1949-1956	7
Earl Warren (Calif.)	1953-1969	16
John M. Harlan (N.Y.)	1955-1971	16
William J. Brennan (N.J.)	1956-	
Charles E. Whittaker (Mo.)	1957-1962	5
Potter Stewart (Ohio)	1958-	
Byron R. White (Colo.)	1962-	
Arthur J. Goldberg (Ill.)	1962-1965	3
Abe Fortas (Tenn.)	1965-1969	4
Thurgood Marshall (Md.)	1967-	
Warren E. Burger (Minn.)	1969-	
Harry A. Blackmun (Minn.)	1970-	
Lewis F. Powell, Jr. (Va.)	1971-	
William H. Rehnquist (Ariz.)	1971-	
John Paul Stevens (Ill.)	1975-	

Index

Index